T0361250

KALININGRAD: THE EUROPEAN AMBER REGION

This book may also be identified as a publication of the Copenhagen Peace
Research Institute and the Åland Island's Peace Institute

Kaliningrad: The European Amber Region

Edited by
PERTTI JOENNIEMI
JAN PRAWITZ

Routledge
Taylor & Francis Group

LONDON AND NEW YORK

First published 1998 by Ashgate Publishing

Reissued 2018 by Routledge
2 Park Square, Milton Park, Abingdon, Oxon OX14 4RN
711 Third Avenue, New York, NY 10017, USA

Routledge is an imprint of the Taylor & Francis Group, an informa business

Publisher's Note
The publisher has gone to great lengths to ensure the quality of this reprint but points out that some imperfections in the original copies may be apparent.

Disclaimer
The publisher has made every effort to trace copyright holders and welcomes correspondence from those they have been unable to contact.

A Library of Congress record exists under LC control number: 98007937

ISBN 13: 978-1-138-32416-9 (hbk)
ISBN 13: 978-0-429-44762-4 (ebk)

Contents

Acronyms

AWACS	Airborne Warning and Control System
BALTBAT	Baltic Peacekeeping Battalion
BALTNET	Baltic Air Surveillance and Control Network
BALTOP	Sea rescue exercises in the Baltic sea region
BALTRON	Baltic Minesweeper Squadron
BEAR	Barents Euro-Arctic Region
CBM	Confidence Building Measure
CBSS	Council of Baltic Sea States
CFE	Treaty on Conventional Forces in Europe
CIS	Commonwealth of Independent States
COPRI	Copenhagen Peace Research Institute
CPC	Conflict Prevention Centre
CSBM	Confidence and Security Building Measures
CSCE	Council on Security and Cooperation in Europe
EBRD	European Bank for Reconstruction and Development
EU	European Union
FEZ	Free Economic Zone
GATT	General Agreement on Tariffs and Trade
GDR	German Democratic Republic
IGC	Intergovernmental Conference, EU
IISS	International Institute for Strategic Studies, London
IMF	International Monetary Union
INF	Agreement on eliminating all intermediate and short-range land based missiles.
JCG	Joint Consultative Group of the CFE
KOOR	Kalingrad Special Defence Region/Area
MD	Military District
NATO	North Atlantic Treaty Organization
NPT	Non-Proliferation Treaty
OSCE	Organization for Security and Co-operation in Europe
PfP	Partnership for Peace
PHARE	Polish-Hungarian assistance to the economy, applies to the Central European states
ROO	Rules of Origin
SFOR	Stabilization Force (NATO force in Bosnia)

SIPRI	Stockholm International Peace Research Institute
START	Agreement on reduction of strategic nuclear weapons
TACIS	Technical assistance for the Commonwealth of Independent States, applies to the former Soviet Union
TLE	Treaty Limited Equipment
Tochka	Surface-to-surface missile
UNCLOS	United Nations Convention on the Law of the Sea
UNIDO	United Nations Industrial Development Organization
WEU	Western European Union
WTO	World Trade Organization

Contributors

Lyndelle D. Fairlie, Associate Professor, Department of Political Science, College of Arts and Letters, San Diego State University, California, USA.

Gennady M. Fyodorov, Rector of Kaliningrad State University, Russia.

Algirdas Gricius, Associate Professor, Institute of International Relations and Political Science, University of Vilnius, Lithuania.

Pertti Joenniemi, Project Director, Copenhagen Peace Research Institute, Denmark.

Helena Kropinova, Senior Researcher, Institute for Environment, Kaliningrad State University, Russia.

Zdzislaw Lachowski, Senior Research Fellow, Stockholm International Peace Research Institute, Sweden.

Peer H. Lange, Senior Research Fellow, Stiftung Wissenschaft und Politik, Forschungsinstitut für Internationale Politik und Sicherheit, Ebenhausen, Germany.

Ingmar Oldberg, Senior Researcher, National Defence Research Establishment, Stockholm, Sweden.

Klaus Carsten Pedersen, Director, The Danish Foreign Policy Society, Copenhagen, Denmark.

Jan Prawitz, Visiting Researcher, Institute of International Affairs, Stockholm, Sweden.

Anatoly Trynkov, Head of Department, Russia's Institute for Strategic Studies, Moscow, Russia.

Christian Wellman, Deputy Director, Schleswig-Holstein Institute for Peace Research, Kiel, Germany.

Preface

Kaliningrad, located in the south-eastern corner of the Eastern Baltic Seaboard, denotes an unusual degree of remoteness, marginality and dependency.

The region's geographic detachment from mainland Russia and its wedged position between Lithuania and Poland have produced a number of rather traditional debates. These pertain to the *oblast*'s military saliency, and more generally to Russia's sovereignty and its territorial integrity, but also to some less conventional themes such as regionalism and the devolvement of power within Russia. These latter issues include the relationship between Moscow as the centre and Kaliningrad as a periphery, i.e. issues relating to the question how Russia should be organized and what it basically is in the post-Cold War situation.

In the context of Kaliningrad, the old and traditional often seems to stand in stark contrast with the new and incoming. There is much in the region that culturally, politically or economically remains firmly hooked into the past while at the same time – due to its location – it is more exposed to European trends than Russia in general. This position turns Kaliningrad unavoidably into a key factor denoting Russia's approach towards the rest of Europe, and – what is perhaps equally interesting – a site reflecting the European Union's treatment of Russia.

There is no doubt that issues concerning Kaliningrad's ambiguous history, its special status, problems of transit by land or sea, the peculiarities of the region's economy and its sensitive role with respect to Russia's integrity still inform much of the discourse. However, there are also new themes present in the discussion. Linking in to the various European networks is obviously one of these. It is understood, in this context, that the core issue is one of counteracting peripherality – the success of which is being determined by access to various networks rather than by anything related to the region's geographic location. Kaliningrad's locale is thus not viewed as a fatal syndrome implying danger, backwardness and isolation. Its position as the westernmost part of Russia can also, to an increasing degree, provide a viable platform for cultural contacts, economic interaction and political cooperation. It is being recognized that regions such as Kaliningrad can, at least in principle, become competitive within the new European political and economic order.

Thus it may remain peripheral in some ways and yet occupy a far more central position in others.

Moreover, it seems important to remember that visions of margins and cores, centres and peripheries are created on different grounds. Social spatialisation is a result of both discursive and non-discursive elements, practices and processes. This implies that Kaliningrad is not just out there as a fact of life waiting to be described and analyzed in an objective fashion. It is, on the contrary, quite dependent on how it is approached, discussed and placed in perspective.

This book reflects a concern for Kaliningrad. Too little is known about the region, developments in the recent years have not been sufficiently covered and it is rarely integrated, in terms of analysis, with the way post-Cold War Europe is viewed more generally. The effort is hence one of remedying at least some of these shortcomings, provide information on a broad spectrum of themes, to broaden the perspectives and to insert Kaliningrad more firmly on the current European agenda.

This concern has been shared by Olof Palme's International Centre, which – together with the Åland Island's Peace Institute – funded this project. We express our gratitude for this to both institutions. The Copenhagen Peace Research Institute has, for its part, provided strong support in the editorial work of the book, carried out by Tor Nonnegaard-Petersen, Jesper Sigurdsson, and Mads Vöge, which we also gratefully note.

Copenhagen and Stockholm, January 1998

Pertti Joenniemi   Jan Prawitz

1 Kaliningrad: Problems and Prospects

INGMAR OLDBERG

Starting-points

When the Baltic states and Belarus became independent in 1991, the Kaliningrad region (*oblast* in Russian) suddenly became an exclave separated from the rest of Russia. Since then its future has been a common topic of discussion in the states around the Baltic Sea and many questions have been posed: Will it be a forward military bastion of Russia, a "second Cuba", menacing its neighbours, or will it be a free trade area, a "Baltic Hong Kong" contributing to peace and prosperity? Since Kaliningrad is the westernmost part of Russia, it could become a problem to many states on the Baltic Sea, if Russia would start to rearm or if internal problems in the area are not controlled. But its location could also be a blessing, if local ambitions to develop market economy and attract investments from nearby Western states would succeed (Huldt 1996: 6).

Another vital question is whether Kaliningrad can become a bone of contention between Russia, Germany, Poland and Lithuania. Its situation reminds us of former East Prussia, which in 1918 was separated from Germany by a Polish "corridor". In 1939 this became a major pretext for Hitler to unleash the Second World War (Müller-Hermann 1995: 7f). Today's Kaliningrad has been called a "Jerusalem on the Baltic", an almost insolvable problem (Oldberg 1995: 335).

Kaliningrad can also be seen as a test case for more general questions. Its development may give an indication on whether Russia as a whole will stake on armament and confrontation with the West or peace and cooperation, and whether Russia moves toward centralisation or decentralization/disintegration.

This chapter will try to help cast some light on these questions and analyze the arguments for and against the alternatives. In so doing it gives a short survey of the history of the region, an outline of its current military, political, and economic problems and an introduction to its international context.

From Königsberg to Kaliningrad

The history of today's Kaliningrad region and the whole former region of East Prussia is a drama of five peoples, who all to various extents have used history to buttress territorial claims. The first historically recorded inhabitants were the Prussians, the third major Baltic people beside the Latvians and the Lithuanians. They went down in history by lending their name to the area and the German state of Prussia, much like the Tatar Bulgars gave their name to Slavic Bulgaria. In the 13th century the heathen Prussians were conquered and christened by the Teutonic Order, which carried out a crusade on papal commission. The Prussians were then gradually assimilated by German colonizers and their language died out by the 17th century.

The Teutonic Order founded towns and built castles, among them Königsberg (1255) in honour of the crusading Bohemian king Otokar II, and laid the ground for 700 years of German domination.

However, the Germans' further expansion was resisted by the Lithuanian Grand Duchy, which had its heyday in the 14th century. After Lithuania and Poland were united by royal marriage (1386), the Order was defeated at Grunwald (1410). Its power then declined and many Polish Mazovians and Lithuanians moved into the region. In 1525 the last Grand Master of the Order, Albrecht of Hohenzollern, made Prussia a secular, Lutheran duchy, formally under the Polish (Catholic) crown. In 1544 a university was founded in Königsberg, the oldest in all territories that later became parts of the Soviet Union.

In the 17th century Prussia was gradually taken over by the German state of Brandenburg and shook off Swedish and Polish influence.[1] The *Kurfürst* of Brandenburg here crowned himself King of Prussia in 1701. When Poland was divided in 1772 and Prussia acquired lands west of the Vistula, East Prussia (as it was called henceforth) was no longer separated from the rest of the state and it played an important role in the German resistance to Napoleon and later.

After Germany's defeat in the First World War and the recreation of Poland, East Prussia again became an exclave and it remained part of Germany only as a result of a plebiscite. Its northernmost part of Memel

(Klaipeda) was seized by the resurrected Lithuanian state in 1923 but ceded to Hitler in early 1939.

At the end of the Second World War the Russians definitely entered the stage. Tsarist Russia had occupied East Prussia in 1758-62, partly also in 1915, but the Soviet Union did it more thoroughly after its troops conquered the German stronghold of Königsberg in April 1945. At conferences with his Western allies during and after the war, Stalin demanded Königsberg and the surrounding area on the grounds that the USSR needed compensation for its war losses, wanted an ice-free port on the Baltic Sea, and on the claim that the area originally was Slavic. But he promised to respect Polish independence and ceded the southern two thirds of East Prussia to Poland. Even though the area had never been Slavic, Königsberg is not totally ice-free, and Stalin was not going to respect Polish sovereignty, the Western allies at the Potsdam peace conference in July-August 1945 agreed to Stalin's claim.[2] The Memel region was soon handed over to Soviet Lithuania by Stalin (Petersen 1992: 1ff; Wörster 1995: 156ff; Gnauck 1992: 49ff; Romanov 1995: 42). Thus East Prussia was divided into three parts.

The division of East Prussia also served the Soviet interest in weakening Germany, involving Poland on the Soviet side, and keeping the Balts in check.

The Soviet conquest of Königsberg had far-reaching consequences in the region itself. Firstly, the composition of the population was completely changed. Out of the more than one million German inhabitants, the majority of those who survived the fierce battles fled to Germany, many died from hunger, illness or violence, and the rest were deported to Germany in the late 1940s (Wörster 1995: 160f). Instead of the Germans, mainly Russians but also Belarussians, Ukrainians and others–often people who had lost their homes in the war–were offered a place there. Most of them settled in the towns and all were russified. Nowadays about two thirds of the population are born in the region, but the total figures have not yet reached pre-war levels, which probably is unique in Europe[3] (Gnauck 1992: 52f; Zverev 1996: 8f; Zverev & Fedorov 1995: 100ff).

Secondly, the region was quickly sovietized by the imposition of Communist dictatorship and planning economy. In 1946 it became an *oblast* of the Russian Socialist Federal Soviet Republic (RSFSR), and all towns got Russian names. Königsberg was renamed after the deceased Soviet President Mikhail Kalinin. No attempts were made to follow the Polish example in Gdansk and restore the old town of Königsberg, which had been severely damaged by Allied bombing and fierce fighting. Instead plain buildings in the typical Soviet "baracko" style were built. Typically, the remnants of the medieval castle in the city centre were blown up in 1969, and in its place a huge House of the Soviets, generally called the "Monster", was erected but never quite finished.

Finally, the Kaliningrad region became one of the most militarized areas in Europe. After the war it was totally sealed off from Poland and the west, and even Soviet citizens had limited access. The armed forces and the military industry became the biggest employers in the region, and the civilian structure was tailored to military needs, which greatly distorted the economy and hampered its development[4] (Hoff & Timmermann 1993: 40; Wellmann 1996: 164f).

The changing military importance of Kaliningrad

As already mentioned the Soviet Union took the Kaliningrad region by force and Stalin's primary motive for claiming it obviously was of a military nature. In the postwar period the region was then developed into a base for strategic reserves behind the Soviet and Warsaw Pact forces in Central Europe in accordance with an offensive strategy, directed mainly against NATO forces in West Germany and the Baltic straits. The headquarters of the Soviet Baltic fleet was moved from Leningrad to Kaliningrad in 1956, and the deep sea port of Baltiysk (formerly Pillau) became a major naval base. The region, which was part of the Baltic Military District, also harboured strong army units, mainly the 11th Guards Army, air and air defence forces, and border troops[5] (Petersen 1992: 29ff; Nordberg 1994: 85ff).

Soviet President Gorbachev's detente policy since the end of the 1980s, which was continued by Russian President Yeltsin, meant that the Soviet armed forces were shifted to defence and were reduced in accordance with the CFE Treaty of Paris of 1990. When the Baltic states were free, the Soviet (Russian) Baltic fleet lost 80 per cent of its bases, and half its ships and all submarines had to move. Compared with ten years ago, the naval personnel was reduced by half, the number of ships by two thirds, and the air force by 60 per cent. Baltiysk received Western naval visits, and the Baltic fleet in 1994 started to participate in naval exercises with NATO in the Baltic (Yegorov 1995: 128).

True, the collapse of the Warsaw Pact and the withdrawal of Soviet (Russian) troops from the GDR (often by ferry from Mukran to Klaipeda) and in 1992-1994 from the Baltic states, led to the stationing of troops and weapons in the Kaliningrad region, where the forces thus temporarily increased. However, since 1993 the numbers of units and soldiers have gradually sunk. So has weapons strength in most respects, and the figures are now far below the CFE limits.[6]

Another reason for the reduction of forces in Kaliningrad was the economic crisis in Russia. This also had other effects. As elsewhere in Russia, sharp cuts in military spending, especially since 1992, led to a reduction of army and naval exercises and air force training. Sometimes electricity was switched off due to unpaid bills. The officers received less (or sometimes no) salaries, social benefits and pensions than before, and the housing situation was desperate. There was a lack of draftees leaving the army units only half-manned, which meant more work for officers and NCOs. All this contributed to discontent, low morale, corruption and violence, and many officers left for other jobs[7] (*Krasnaia Zvezda*, 29 June & 16 September 1995).

However, Kaliningrad retained some military significance for Russia. The retreat from Central Europe and the Baltic states meant that Kaliningrad became its only naval base on the Baltic Sea besides St Petersburg deep in the Gulf of Finland, and it remained a forward base for air and air defence forces in peacetime, even if it was vulnerable to attack in wartime (Huldt 1996: 4; Nordberg 1994: 86f).

Under the impression of growing Russian nationalism and self-assertiveness the Russian military also underlined their interest in the region. In 1994 it became a special defence district under the commander of the Baltic fleet directly subordinated to the Defence Minister. According to the Commander of the Russian naval forces, its tasks now are to defend the region and Russia's territorial integrity, its civilian shipping and economic zone in the Baltic, with support from the rest of Russia (Gromov 1995: 10ff). Despite all problems an exercise with 11,000 men was conducted in 1994. The Baltic naval infantry participated in the war in Chechnya like that of other fleets (*Krasnaia Zvezda*, 19 March 1994 & 19 May 1995; *Segodnia*, 6 May 1994).

The naval commander Yegorov moved the target for disarmament in the region from 25,000 men to 40,000-45,000 men, which seems to mean that roughly the present numbers will be maintained. In negotiations with NATO, Russia threatened to increase its forces in Kaliningrad toward the allowed limit, unless the subceilings on Russia's flanks were not raised (Yegorov 1995: 130; *Krasnaia Zvezda*, 19 April 1994).

All this worried the neighbouring Baltic States and Poland, even though the total Russian threat had diminished. They had only recently liberated themselves from Russia and got rid of Russian troops. The Baltic states had to build up their own armed forces from scratch, and were still weaker than the garrison in Kaliningrad, not to speak of the forces in Russia which back them up. Especially Lithuania felt threatened, situated as it is next to Kaliningrad and Belarus, a state which since 1994 became more and more integrated with Russia militarily and economically. Therefore the Baltic states, separately and jointly, insisted that the Kaliningrad region should be demilitarized, totally or partly.

Even if it is bigger, also Poland worried about Kaliningrad, because its military forces in accordance with the Warsaw Pact military doctrine were deployed in the West. It has decided to redeploy some forces toward the Kaliningrad border. Both the Baltic states and Poland use the Russian troops in Kaliningrad as an argument for being admitted into NATO.

Concerning the attitudes of other states, officially Germany has declared that it is not worried by the Russian troops in Kaliningrad and it has not demanded demilitarization. Germany has in fact reduced its naval forces in the Baltic considerably.

The Russian leadership dismissed all Western concern about its forces in Kaliningrad as unfounded. Then deputy prime minister Shakhrai in 1994 emphasized that demilitarization would limit Russian sovereignty and recommended to expand the naval base. Other officials declared that it is rather Kaliningrad that is threatened. They warned that if the Baltic states and Poland should join NATO, Russia would stop reducing and instead reinforce its military positions there. Some military have even hinted at placing tactical nuclear weapons in the region[8] (Kwizinskij 1994: 52f; Gromov 1995: 12f; Vardomskii et al 1995: 33ff; *Segodnia*, 23 June 1995). This of course fomented distrust among the neighbours still further.

The transit problem

Kaliningrad's exclave position is a problem both for Russia and its neighbours, especially Lithuania, since the most important railways and roads to Russia pass through that country, moreover through its largest cities. Several incidents occurred with Russian military transports, which

Lithuania considered to be its greatest military threat after the Russian occupation troops had left in August 1993. Russian aircraft were forbidden to cross Lithuanian airspace without permission, but continued to do so since Lithuania could not stop them and the alternative route over the Baltic Sea was much longer (Negotiations 1992: 148f; *Krasnaia Zvezda*, 18 May 1994).

In order to facilitate the withdrawal of Russian forces from Central Europe and the other Baltic states, Lithuania allowed railway transports from Klaipeda to Kaliningrad and then onwards to Russia, while it was very restrictive against military transports from Russia to Kaliningrad (*Nezavisimaya Gazeta*, 6 March 1993). According to an agreement of 1993, which formally only covered troops from Germany up to 1995 and never was ratified by the Lithuanian parliament, Russia had to ask permission for every transport, submit to inspections and pay fees. The troops are not allowed to leave the wagons or carry weapons, the trains were not permitted to make unauthorized stops. In October 1994 Lithuania's Labour government – under pressure from the conservative opposition of ex-President Landsbergis – laid down new rules intended to limit the traffic and sharpen control even more[9] (Soglashenie 1993; *Baltic Observer*, 13 October 1994).

Russia of course wanted as free a passage as possible by rail and road and rejected the Lithuanian rules. Exploiting Lithuania's remaining dependence on export to Russia as a means of pressure, Russia did not ratify an already signed agreement on most-favoured-nation status and threatened to reduce its civilian transit traffic to Klaipeda (*Izvestiia*, 16 July 1994; *Baltic Independent*, 17 June & 15 July 1994; *Segodnia*, 20 July 1994). In January 1995 a compromise was reached, by which Russia ratified the MFN agreement and Lithuania prolonged the 1993 agreement (*Izvestiia*, 21 January 1995; *Baltic Independent*, 27 January 1995). This was later extended year by year.

However, Russia's discomfort from Lithuanian restrictions on military transit should not be exaggerated. In 1994 only one per cent of all goods was military, and only a fraction of this was personnel and weapons (Zverev 1996: 17). Most military goods to Kaliningrad went by sea. A ferry-line was established between Baltiysk and ports in the Gulf of Finland, which were to be expanded (*Krasnaia Zvezda*, 19 March & 9 April 1994; *Nezavisimaya Gazeta*, 6 March 1994; *Izvestiia*, 28 October 1994). This of course meant a drain on scarce Russian resources, and for the Baltic states it added to the naval threat, since protection of shipping remains one of the tasks of the Russian Baltic fleet.

Thus civilian transit became the most important problem for Russia. In 1993 Lithuania introduced restrictions such as compulsory police escort at the transporter's expense and a high advance deposit in dollars, visa was required for CIS citizens (except Kaliningraders) and in 1994 railway tariffs were raised for transit to Kaliningrad, whereby Russian metal export to the West was steered over to the Lithuanian port Klaipeda (*Izvestiia*, 28 October 1994; *Segodnia*, 28 May & 6 July 1994; Zverev 1996: 17). Transit costs contributed to the economic slump in Kaliningrad (more on this below) and increased Russian hostility to Lithuania.[10]

Another solution for Russia, which could be used as a means to add pressure on Lithuania, was to get access to Kaliningrad through Poland, and discussions on this were held. Kaliningrad intensified contacts with Belarus, whose president Lukashenka wanted total integration with Russia, and the parties agreed on expanding Belarusian use of ports in Kaliningrad and building road and railway connections through Poland. In March 1996 President Yeltsin himself expressed the hope that Poland would allow Russia to build a motorway to Kaliningrad in order to give Belarus access to the sea.[11]

Poland approved of upgrading its road network and communications with Kaliningrad and Belarus, but like Lithuania it sharply rejected every idea of a "corridor" across the country, since that was perceived as a threat to its sovereignty, reviving memories of the interwar problems with German transit. A "corridor" to Kaliningrad would also jeopardize Poland's improved relations with Lithuania and increase competition for its own transit trade in Gdansk-Gdynia. There were also ecological concerns for areas in northeastern Poland (*Segodnia*, 20 July 1994, 28 February 1996; *Izvestiia*, 28 October 1994, 5 & 13 March 1996; *Nezavisimaya gazeta*, 13 February & 22 March & 10 April 1996).

Thus Kaliningrad's exclave position creates complicated problems for both Russia and its neighbours and no permanent solutions have been found. But the problem is at least becoming less military and more economic in character, and it may be eased as an effect of increasing cross-border trade.

Plans of a free economic zone and political autonomy

Gorbachev's policy of detente and democratization not only led to military changes in the Kaliningrad region but also to more economic and political autonomy. Inspired by Western experts, reform economists in Kaliningrad and elsewhere worked out plans of a free economic zone, called "Yantar" (FEZ Amber) with the aim of restructuring and developing the economy of the region. The idea was exploit its favourable geographical position close to Western Europe with ice-free ports at the Baltic and railways with both European and Russian widths. Foreign investments were to be attracted by favourable taxation and customs rates, free profit export, a good industrial and social infrastructure, and a cheap and well-trained work force. Self-sufficiency in energy and foodstuffs production was also to increase. Kaliningrad should become a centre for economic cooperation in the Baltic region, a test case for market reforms in Russia, and a springboard for Western firms looking for the vast Russian market. Increased autonomy would enable the region to apply for support from European banks and institutions.

The idea of a Free Economic Zone was promoted in Moscow by Yuri Matochkin, Kaliningrad's elected representative in the Russian Supreme Soviet, who in 1991 became head of the administration (Dörrenbächer 1994: 37ff; Hoff & Timmermann 1993: 42; Fedorov & Zverev 1995: 54ff). In 1993 Matochkin expressed the hope that Kaliningrad in ten years would become the Baltic Hong Kong. Local polls showed that the plans of a Free Economic Zone were supported by a majority of the population, especially among the youth[12] (*Svenska Dagbladet*, 12 June 1993; Dörrenbächer 1994: 45f).

In 1994 the Kaliningrad administration presented a law proposal to the Federal Assembly, according to which the regional governor should be a minister in the federal government. The region was to have a separate line in the federal budget just like Moscow and St Petersburg, and be enabled to introduce customs, taxes, and quotas (*Segodnia*, 28 May & 26 Nov 1994; *Nezavisimaya gazeta*, 2 June 1994).

Ambitions in Kaliningrad also went in the direction of acquiring more decision-making power. In 1993 both Governor Matochkin and the chairman of the regional Soviet Semenov, even though they supported opposite sides in the power struggle between President Yeltsin and the Supreme Soviet under its chairman Khasbulatov, agreed to propose a referendum on making the *oblast* an autonomous republic just like the ethnic ones in the Russian Federation. This meant that the region should have its own constitution and laws and representation in federal bodies. The Kaliningrad administration already had its own department for foreign relations and planned to have a similar committee in the local Duma. (Rapport från CFF & FOA 1994). It also strove to diminish the military influence, sometimes even talking about "demilitarization". However, the regional administration always emphasized that Kaliningrad was part of Russia and should remain so. Small groups in Kaliningrad like the Baltic Republican Party went still further and proposed the creation of an independent Baltic, West Russian republic[13] (Fedorov 1993: 9).

In Moscow, Gorbachev and after him Yeltsin supported these ambitions of the Kaliningrad administration to the extent that they coincided with the general policy of economic reforms and free trade with the West. In 1990 foreigners were allowed to visit the region, and border passages were soon opened. A tourist industry started by developing the hotels and printing information. Symbolically, Kaliningrad was the only Russian region which went over from Moscow time to the Baltic states' time zone.

In July 1990 Kaliningrad became one of Russia's six Zones of Free Entrepreneurship; in June 1991 the region was granted customs and taxation exemptions; and in September that year the Yantar zone was officially established with the expressed aim to raise living standards, promote foreign trade and investments. Matochkin was appointed head of the administration by Yeltsin and subjected to him. Central investments in agriculture and infrastructure were promised in several decrees. In December 1992, locally produced goods were exempted from export tariffs and imported goods from customs and turnover tax for ten years, if they stayed in the region. The region was promised to have a say on land use, to register foreign firms and (according to a decree of 1995) sign deals with them (Dörrenbächer 1994: 37ff; Sundquist 1994: 1f; Matotschkin 1994: 26f; Zverev 1996: 13; *Rossiiskie Vesti*, 20 May 1995). In a special issue of the Foreign Ministry monthly "International Affairs" (1995: 6f), the chairman of the Federation Council Vladimir Shumeiko, who happened to represent Kaliningrad, thought that autonomy in Kaliningrad in the form of a FEZ or a special political entity could be put on the agenda. He hoped the region could become a centre for international congresses and fairs, and a territory of visa-free tourism.

During his election campaign in June 1996 President Yeltsin visited Kaliningrad and promised 100 per cent support, including expansion of the ports in Kaliningrad and Baltiysk (*Kaliningradskaia Pravda* & *Svobodnaia Zona*, 25 June 1996).

Indeed, the Free Economic Zone had some measure of success. More foreign firms registered, and more foreign investment and trade went to Kaliningrad than to Russia in general[14] (Vardomskii et al 1995: 17; *Nezavisimaya gazeta*, 22 May 1996). The region was allowed to keep a growing share of the taxes and payments[15] (*Kaliningradskaia Pravda*, 29 August 1996; *Segodnia*, 25 August 1994).

Also the military seemed to accept the idea of a Free Economic Zone. As mentioned above, the military forces and garrisons were reduced, and important defence industries, e.g. the main shipyard, converted to civil production[16] (Hoff & Timmermann 1993: 40; Rapport från CFF & FOA 1994: 12). For instance, the civilian administration in the naval town Baltiysk was upgraded, part of the port was opened to foreign trade, and the military left the Vistula spit across the Baltiysk sound. With the consent of the navy and Kaliningrad, Baltiysk signed an agreement leasing the spit to a German firm, which was to build holiday resorts there (*Rossiiskie Vesti*, 31 May & 1 December 1995; Kondrashov 1995).

The neighbouring countries of Kaliningrad, which worried about the military presence there, of course liked the drive for economic liberalization and political autonomy. Free trade agreements were signed (more on this below).

Obstacles to FEZ and autonomy

The bold plans and efforts to create a Free Economic Zone and political autonomy were, however, faced with formidable problems. To start with, the heavy legacy of fifty years of planned economy and militarization could not be wished away. The infrastructure was more a disadvantage than an advantage, since it was lopsided and worn down, and the environmental problems were enormous, which all required vast investments to be remedied.[17] This was true for example for the port of Kaliningrad. Besides, the sea channel to Kaliningrad is only seven meters deep and so narrow that it generally only permits one-way traffic. Thence the plans to open Baltiysk for foreign trade and to build a new port for container traffic at

Svetlyi halfway between Kaliningrad and Baltiysk (Müller-Hermann 1994: 17).

Moreover, instead of being a springboard to Russia, Kaliningrad's exclave position proved a great liability. It had problems reaching producers and customers in Russia, and its products proved uncompetitive on the international market (Fedorov & Zverev 1995: 127). Most of its production at the beginning of the 1990s went out of the region, and 90 per cent of the raw materials were taken from outside. For example, 80 per cent of electricity came from the nuclear power station of Ignalina until 1994, when Lithuania cut it short because of unpaid bills, and Kaliningrad had no refinery even for its own oil. Instead electricity, gas, and refined oil had to be taken from Russia (Swerew 1996: 11f; Fedorov & Zverev 1995: 24; Dörrenbächer 1994: 67ff).

As Lithuania and Belarus erected customs barriers and transport tariffs rose, the costs in Kaliningrad rose above those in Russia, and subsidies from the Russian budget did not fully compensate for them. As already mentioned, Kaliningrad suffered from the conflict between Russia and Lithuania over trade and military transit rights.

Kaliningrad was also hit especially hard by the ongoing economic crisis and transition to the market in Russia. The price rises on oil hit ocean fishing, on which Kaliningrad's fish industry, its biggest industrial branch, in Soviet times a third in size after Vladivostok and Murmansk, rested, and catches went down dramatically. Most of it was sold abroad, which angered foreign fishermen and deprived the home industry of fish, at the same time as imported fish products flooded the home market. The meagre quotas that Russia was allotted in the Baltic Sea were not exhausted and some were sold, because the fishing fleet was not adapted to that sea, its ships were ageing and in need of repair[18] (Zverev 1996: 10; Vardomskii et al 1995: 11ff).

In spite of the development plans, the economy of the *oblast* continued to deteriorate and industrial production to fall – more than the Russian average. Even the amber monopoly firm went bankrupt. Wages were lower and prices higher than in Russia proper. This was partly offset by duty-free import of Polish and Lithuanian consumer goods, which however hit the local producers.

Despite promises of federal support, investments in the Kaliningrad *oblast* actually sank (by 50 per cent 1994-1995), and hence planned water purification plants and new electricity producing stations to substitute imports were not built.[19] The *oblast* budget for 1994 (which was taken in October that year!) was underbalanced by 40 per cent and resulted in a call for help to the President, government and parliament (*Segodnia*, 6 July & 27 Oct 1994; *Izvestiia*, 18 November 1994; Vardomskii 1995: 9ff). In 1996 Matochkin complained that almost all Russian capital had been concentrated to Moscow, where all major banks were. The staff of federal agencies in Kaliningrad was bigger than that of the regional administration, which had to pay 50 per cent of its budget to maintain it (*Rossiiskaia gazeta*, 27 January 1996).

Furthermore, even if foreign trade grew and joint ventures were numerous, imports greatly dominated over exports and the actual amount of foreign investment in the region was pitiful, e.g. compared with that in Poland.[20] One explanation for this was that economic legislation remained contradictory and fluid, and concrete rules of implementation were lacking, which created incertitude. There were no solid investment guarantees. Imports were not exempted from customs if goods were sent on to the rest of Russia. For example, in March 1995 Yeltsin suddenly by a decree abolished the customs exemptions, which should have lasted for ten years, and this led to annulment of contracts and a sharp fall in foreign trade (Dörrenbächer 1994: 44ff; Vardomskii et al 1995: 15; Matochkin 1996: 4f; *Rossiiskaia gazeta* 20 & 27 January 1996). One rationale for scrapping the customs exemptions in March 1995 was that all regions of Russia should have equal terms. Other regions of Russia in the Far North and Far East complained that they too were isolated most of the year and needed special favours (Vardomskii et al 1995: 16f, 48).

Another great hurdle was the fact that foreign firms could buy property but not land under it. Business was also hampered by visa requirements, transport and communication problems and the rule of prepayment. As a result of all this, most joint ventures only existed on paper, most of them went into trade and services, often importing western consumer and luxury goods, and exporting raw materials. There was also illegal export of drugs, weapons, and refugees[21] (*Nezavisimaya gazeta*, 26 October 1994).

In view of these problems, the Baltic states became more attractive to foreign investors than Kaliningrad, since they provided more stable, favourable conditions and started to show real growth. St Petersburg became a serious alternative for foreign investors, who wanted to establish themselves in the Russian market and avoid extra transport problems. Foreign trade went over from Kaliningrad to the Baltic and Russian ports in the Gulf of Finland (Vardomskii 1995: 20ff; *European* 1995: 70f).

As elsewhere in Russia, the continuing economic crisis in Kaliningrad led to falling living standards and misery for many people, especially state employees, pensioners, students etc, thus also to discontent and growing criminality (Fedorov & Zverev 1995: 100, 115). This together with growing Russian nationalism in all Russia had the political consequence of undermining support for market reforms and Western contacts. A poll in Kaliningrad in 1993 showed waning support for the Free Economic Zone and a 70 per cent disapproval of foreign land ownership. Vladimir Nikitin, leader of a national patriotic society, who in June 1993 was elected deputy chairman of the *oblast's* duma, argued that Russian, not foreign entrepreneurs, should be favoured. The bad economic situation and the need of subsidies from the centre spoke against any decoupling of the region from Russia. In fact, Kaliningrad was the region least suitable for being a free zone, claimed Nikitin (Dörrenbächer 1994: 42ff).

In the Duma elections of December 1993, Zhirinovskii's Liberal Democratic Party (LDPR) became the biggest party and in Kaliningrad it got more than the average Russian vote. Two years later the Communists came out ahead of the LDPR both in Russia and Kaliningrad, whereas the reform parties lost[22] (Vardomskii 1995: 49; *Rossiiskaia gazeta*, 6 January 1996).

Under the influence of the nationalist trend, Yeltsin started to tighten the reins of the centre over the provinces. In the new Constitution adopted by referendum at the same time as the 1993 elections, the personal powers of the President were enlarged, the sovereignty of the ethnic republics was restricted, and regions (*oblast*) like Kaliningrad were not granted a similar status with their own constitutions. Moscow in 1993 disavowed a trade agreement, which Kaliningrad had signed with Lithuania, and retained control over border and visa questions (Rapport från CFF & FOA 1994: 5; *Izvestiia*, 18 November 1994). Not surprisingly the Kaliningrad law proposal "On Raising the Status of the Kaliningrad *Oblast*" during 1994 changed names to "On Strengthening the Sovereignty of the Russian Federation on the Territory of the Kaliningrad *Oblast*" (*Nezavisimaya gazeta*, 2 June 1994; *Segodnia*, 2 June & 26 November 1994).

Also security concerns and the military remained an obstacle to free trade and Western engagement in the region. Due to their own economic distress, the military demanded help from the administration for building houses for officers, retraining them for civilian professions, etc (*Krasnaia Zvezda*, 28 April 1994). The military authorities still imposed restrictions on civilian activities and international trade, e.g. in the Baltiysk straits. The press in Moscow criticized the agreement on building holiday resorts on the Vistula spit for selling out security interests. The deal was soon disavowed by Matochkin and the Germans withdrew (*Kaliningradskaia Pravda*, 39 August 1995; *Rossiiskie Vesti*, 31 May & 22 August 1995; *Rossiiskaia Gazeta*, 31 January 1996). The administration tried to belittle the military influence in Kaliningrad and claimed that market and armour in fact were compatible[23] (Zverev 1996: 25 f).

Deputy Prime Minister Shakhrai, who had headed a party defending regional interests, in 1994 wrote two articles attacking "local separatism" and "creeping (Western) expansion" in Kaliningrad – at the same time as he noted how insignificant Western investment really was. He feared that economic advantages for its population would turn out to be strategic losses for Russia. He recommended "mechanisms of state regulation" in this and similar regions, or more specifically a federal law, in which the state should take all responsibility for their development. Free trade zones should be confined to small areas like ports, which one could afford to improve, and strict customs control be maintained, wrote Shakhrai (*Nezavisimaya gazeta*, 26 July & 26 October 1994). During his reelection campaign in 1996, President Yeltsin made a point of visiting Baltiysk and emphasized that the region belongs to Russia (*Kaliningradskaia Pravda*, 25 June 1996).

In January 1996 a federal law on Kaliningrad and a power division agreement were finally signed. According to these Kaliningrad became a "Special", not "Free" Economic Zone, and federal oversight was emphasized, leaving no room for independent foreign relations. The federation reserved control over the military industry, mineral resources, energy production, transport, and mass media (!). Foreigners could not purchase land, but lease it for periods yet to be settled. The law was for three years and rules of implementation were still missing. Matochkin concluded that "the zone is only being formed". In July some duty-free import quotas were introduced.

On the other hand, the Kaliningrad *oblast* got back some favours. It became a "Free Customs Zone" for products imported to it from other states, products imported from other states and then reexported (transshipment), and products manufactured in the zone and then exported or sent to Russia. Products were considered produced in the zone if their value increased by 30 per cent (electronic products 15 per cent), which favoured processing of imported goods. No special licensing of entrepreneurial activity was needed[24] (*Rossiiskaia gazeta*, 27 & 31 January 1996; Matochkin 96: 6f; *Königsberger Express* 1996: 9).

Thus Kaliningrad has swung from moves toward a free zone and autonomy to more central control and emphasis on Russia's military and state interests, and then seemingly reached some kind of balance. The future will tell whether the favours suffice to compensate Kaliningrad for its exclave problems. A hopeful sign was that a big South Korean firm in July 1996 signed an agreement with Russian partners on investing one billion dollars on a car assembly factory in Kaliningrad, which was to produce 50-55,000 cars a year (*Segodnia*, 31 July 1966).

Whether Kaliningrad will succeed to a large extent also hinges on the overall economic development in Russia, which since 1995 seems to have stabilized a little. In the autumn of 1996 monthly inflation was reduced almost to nil, western credits were forthcoming, and salaries were on the rise[25] (*Kaliningradskaia Pravda*, 29 August 1996). However, no breakthrough with growing production etc. has been made as in neighbouring ex-Communist states.

Also the political situation seemed to calm down in 1996 when Yeltsin was reelected President, thus averting the threat of a Communist comeback, but his illness of that period and the prospect of new elections again dimmed the future or the reforms in Russia including Kaliningrad. In Kaliningrad, Matochkin, Yeltsin's protegé and the main free zone protagonist, lost the governor elections in October 1996, but his successor, Leonid Gorbenko, director of the Kaliningrad fishing port, though supported by the Communists, also paid allegiance to the Free Economic Zone ideas and emphasized regional self-reliance.

The German connection

The future of the Kaliningrad exclave, especially if it stakes on free trade, also depends on the neighbouring states' attitudes and interests. The above-mentioned Russian fear of growing foreign influence was mainly pointed against Germany and Germans. It probably was most profound among elderly people in the region, who had participated in the Second World War and were not born there. This anxiety probably lay behind the refusal to allow a German consulate in Kaliningrad. Shakhray in 1994 claimed that Germany is methodically fortifying its economic, cultural and social positions in the region.

Most indignation was shown by ultranationalists like the "liberal democrats". Their representative in the first federal Duma warned that a Free Economic Zone could lead to a German takeover and make Kaliningrad a "small Alaska", whereas the Russians would be asked to leave. Paradoxically, Zhirinovskii in his contacts with German radical nationalists had earlier proposed a Russian-German alliance, within which Germany could get the *Königsberg* region back (*Kaliningradskaia Pravda*, 5 April 1994; Hoff & Timmermann 1993: 39; *Osteuropa-Archiv* 7: 379). Even sound Russian researchers at the Moscow Carnegie Foundation still seem to fear a takeover by Germany, claiming that it has a "conceptual leadership" concerning the regions future (Vardomskii 1995: 24ff).

Also people in Poland and Lithuania were concerned about growing German presence and influence in Kaliningrad. Polish leaders have spoken out against a reemergence of East Prussia and even resisted plans of building highways through Poland to Germany (Zverev 1996: 19; *Osteuropa-Archiv* 1993: 365ff). Similarly, Lithuania had reason to dislike a German return to Kaliningrad, since the next step could be claims on the old Memel area.

What then is the basis for the Russian misgivings? The main underlying reason is of course the fact that Kaliningrad was German for 700 years and Germany now is the strongest economic power in Europe. Furthermore, Germany quickly became Kaliningrad's second largest trading partner and investor (Zverev 1996: 20f; *Iantarnyi Ostrov Rossii* 1995). The overwhelming majority of tourists also came from Germany (75,000 in 1992). Most of them were former East Prussians, whose organisations were and still implicitly are revanchist. Right-wing parties in Germany also claimed the region back.

German economists and politicians were among the first to espouse ideas on the future of Kaliningrad, in which Germany was assigned a greater or smaller role. The best-known projects came from the *Die Zeit* editor countess Marion von Dönhoff, who was born in the area and among its first foreign visitors. She first proposed a Russian-German-Polish condominium, then autonomy, cooperation with the Baltic states à la Benelux and membership in the European Union[26] (Gnauck 1992: 57; *Baltic Independent*, 9 October 1992; Dönhoff 1993: 46ff).

Another factor behind the Russian fears was the Volga Germans. At the end of the 1980s they started to move to Kaliningrad from Kazakhstan and Central Asia, because they felt threatened by ethnic conflicts there and were losing hope of getting back their autonomous republic, from which they had been deported by Stalin. A chairman of a German cultural society in Kaliningrad wanted 200,000 Volga Germans to move in, and according to a poll among them in 1991, 80 per cent among them were interested[27] (Misiunas & Taagepera 1993: 344f; Gnauck 1992: 53). The present numbers are uncertain, ranging from the official figure of 4,600 to estimates up to 20,000, and most of the Volga Germans live in the countryside. They were admitted by local authorities, because they had a reputation of being hard-working and were expected to attract help from Germany (*Izvestiia*, 18 November 1994; Rapport från CFF & FOA 1994; Vardomskii 1995: 27; Petersen 1994: 4f).

In Germany, the migration of Volga Germans to Kaliningrad was supported primarily by right wing xenophobic groups, partly because this served to keep the Volga Germans from emigrating to Germany. According to German law, all German descendants are entitled to citizenship in the Federal Republic, even if their forefathers have lived in other states for centuries. Only in 1989-1992 half a million Volga Germans came. Another calculation was that if the Volga Germans became dominant in the region and if it became autonomous or independent, it could in time be affiliated with Germany.

On the other hand, there are many more reasons to doubt that Germany and Germans are able and willing to come back and take over Kaliningrad. To start with, the first initiatives were taken by the Russians in the region. As a result of detente and glasnost in the late 1980s, the intelligentsia in the region started to take an interest in the region's German past. Old buildings were restored, and the memory of the great philosopher Immanuel Kant was cherished. Proposals were made to name the city *Kantgrad* or restore the old name. The first efforts of the administration to attract foreign business and tourists were mainly directed to Germany.

Further, the authorities were in a position to stop German penetration and seek other friends, when they wanted to do so. Local authorities often refused the Volga Germans settlement and building permits, and federal aid to Russian migrants from ex-Soviet lands did not encompass Kaliningrad. Many Volga Germans were soon dissatisfied with the conditions and people's attitude towards them, so they preferred to move on to Germany and advise their kin remaining in Central Asia to go directly to join all the others in rich Germany (Petersen 1994: 1-7; Lieven 1993: 211f; Misiunas & Taagepera 1993: 345).

Besides, the Volga Germans who moved to Kaliningrad were actually very few in comparison with the Russians and will not become dominant by any stretch of imagination. The number of migrants from the Caucasus has actually grown more than that of Volga Germans[28] (*Izvestiia*, 18 November 1994). Finally, it is doubtful whether the Volga Germans really can be considered Germans, since they have mixed with other peoples through the centuries and rarely speak German.

More importantly, there is hardly any ground to believe that the German government has claims on Kaliningrad, and Russian officials both in the Foreign Ministry and Kaliningrad recognize this (Anisimov 1995: 28f; Songal 1995: 64f). Since the 1940s Germany has been a stable and peaceful democracy, which is totally integrated into the European Union. It makes more efforts than most Western states to maintain friendship with Russia. Claims on Kaliningrad would also greatly disturb its good relations with Poland, Lithuania and other neighbours. Indeed, Germany has recognized its post-war borders in several international treaties, e.g. in connection with the reunification in 1990.

The German government thus accepts that Kaliningrad belongs to Russia and is very cautious with political statements about its future. Instead it restricts itself to cultural and economic support and prefers to channel this through international organisations like the EU and their aid programmes together with Poland and other neighbours or to delegate it to German provinces (*Länder*) and private firms and organisations, which are also anxious about sticking to the official line (Bingen 1993: 45ff; Zverev 1996: 21; Müller-Hermann 1994: passim).

It should also be noted that taking over Kaliningrad would be a burden also for the strong German economy, which now is grappling with the problem of raising the whole former GDR to West German levels, and add almost a million Russian to its ethnic minorities. Concerning the Volga Germans, the German government officially supports the idea of restoring their republic on the Volga and neither supports nor rejects their settlement in Kaliningrad. In the autumn of 1994 the German ambassador to Moscow went so far as to say that Germany did not support such settlement, because Kaliningrad is not an area with a compact German population like Omsk for example. *Land Brandenburg* gives aid to both German and Slavic peasants in Kaliningrad (Petersen 1994: 5).

Finally it can be added that the extreme nationalist and revanchist groups in Germany that do raise claims are small and insignificant. The former East Prussians are old and dying out, and their organisations concentrate on human aid and erection of historical monuments, taking pains not to worry the Russian authorities. Even the *Bund der Vertriebenen* accepts that Kaliningrad remains a part of Russia (Koschyk 1994: 137ff). Only their claims to get property back or compensation can cause problems. In short, Russia has precious little to fear from Germany as far as Kaliningrad is concerned.

Which are the Polish interests?

Kaliningrad's future is also affected by the ambitions of Poland, its largest immediate neighbour. Since the Soviet Union fell apart and Kaliningrad's borders were opened, Polish influence there has grown considerably due to the dynamic economic development in Poland. Poland soon became its most important trading partner, mainly in imports, with the greatest number of investors, although the amount of capital was not as high[29] (Fedorov & Zverev 1995: 130; *Iantarnyi ostrov Rossii* 1995: 180).

In May 1992 Presidents Yeltsin and Walesa signed an agreement on cooperation between Kaliningrad and the northeastern regions of Poland, which resulted in a common council with regular meetings. Kaliningrad was also favoured by an agreement on visa-free travel between Russia and Poland. Poland was the first country to open a consulate in Kaliningrad, which in turn got a representative in the Russian consulate in Gdansk. The communications and border passages were built out (Dörrenbächeer 1994: 92ff; Zverev 1996: 19f; Boryschkowski 1994: 85ff).

As already said, Poland supported the ambitions of the Kaliningrad administration to create a Free Economic Zone, but it seemed less interested in internationalising the region, which probably can be explained by Poland's tragic experiences from Danzig between the world wars. Poland also disliked the influx of Volga Germans and wanted Russia to demilitarize the region.

What then of territorial claims? Poland did demand the area at the end of the war, and even today there exist extreme nationalist groups and parties (like Moczulski's KNP), which openly demand "Królewiec" as Kaliningrad is called in Polish on historic, juridical, and military grounds as well as a means to counter Lithuanian claims (below).One writer in 1992 argued that the region is economically connected with northeastern Poland and should be a compensation for Poland's territorial and human losses in the war. It could be populated by Poles from all the former USSR

(*Osteuropa Archiv* 1993: 364ff; Vardomskii 1995: 45f; Wörster 1995: 162).

Others proposed an East European community excluding Russia and a division of Kaliningrad between Poland, Lithuania, as well as Belarus and Ukraine which need ports on the Baltic.

However, such views actually have extremely few proponents in today's Poland. Official representatives of different governments have instead unequivocally recognized Russia's territorial integrity and raised no claims on Kaliningrad. The border has been demarcated and accepted in international treaties (Sakson 1993: 39; Sakson 1994: 101ff).

There are strong reasons for such a standpoint. Janusz Onyszkiewicz, ex-Defence Minister and Deputy Chairman of the Sejm's Defence Committee, has compared Russia with Great Britain, which has held onto Gibraltar and the Falklands despite great distances. In his view Russia was entitled to keep Kaliningrad as a reward for its victory in the war and the area should now serve to integrate Russia into Europe (Sakson 1993: 33ff; Oldberg 1995: 353).

Moreover, claiming Kaliningrad would strain Poland's relations with its neighbours and disturb its plans to be admitted into NATO and the EU, which is its main foreign policy objective. The principle of maintaining the postwar borders would be disrupted. Radical nationalists in Germany would be justified in claiming formerly German parts in Western Poland. Lithuania could take action against its Polish minority, and Russia could exploit all these conflicts. And if Poland in the end were to take over Kaliningrad, this would be a heavier burden on its economy and create worse minority problems than in the German case. A division of Kaliningrad between Poland and Lithuania might reduce these problems but could also lead to disagreement over the shares. Thus Poland has more to gain from peaceful cooperation and detente with Kaliningrad as part of Russia.

Lithuanian claims and interests

Kaliningrad's future is finally bound to be influenced also by its second close neighbour Lithuania and its intentions. In fact, Lithuanians have made more claims on the region than the other neighbours. In an opinion poll of 1991, almost half the respondents agreed that certain neighbouring territories should belong to Lithuania (Palezkis 1994: 119). Extreme nationalists in Lithuania and exile groups in the USA openly claimed "Lithuania Minor", as the northern and eastern part of today's Kaliningrad is called, or the whole region.

Other conservative politicians pleaded for the idea of making Kaliningrad a fourth Baltic republic (Paleckis 1993: 27ff; Vardomskii 1995: 46ff). When President, Vytautas Landsbergis called not only for the demilitarization of Kaliningrad but also its "decolonization", whatever that means. In early 1994, as a leader of the conservative opposition, he wanted the government to support its decoupling from Russia, which half its population allegedly desired. On another occasion he said that the least that was in Lithuania's interest was to make Kaliningrad an independent state (*Baltic Observer*, 3 March 1994; Zverev 1996: 16).

In October 1994 President Brazauskas in a speech at the United Nations said that he remained "hopeful" about the region and the Lithuanian minority there and suggested talks about it in the framework of the EU so-called Stability Pact (*Baltic Independent*, 7 October 1994; Palezkis 1994: 120ff; Zverev 1996: 16). The border between Lithuania and Kaliningrad has not been demarcated and there is a conflict over its exact position mainly on the Kuronian spit, and over the delimitation of the sea outside it.[30]

There were many arguments for the claims. Historical-ethnic claims were based on references to the Prussians, the extinct Baltic people who first inhabited the area, and the importance of "Karaliaucius" (*Königsberg* in Lithuanian) in the 19th century, when Lithuanian culture was suppressed in Tsarist Russia and found a refuge there. It was also mentioned that Lithuanians still live in the region[31] (Gnauck 1992: 49ff). A legal argument cited by leader of the Centrist party was that the Potsdam agreement only gave Russia the region for fifty years and that the Russian title to it had not been confirmed by international documents. There are rumours that Stalin at the end of the war offered Königsberg to the Lithuanian Communist party leader Snieckus (Zverev 1996: 16ff; Misiunas & Taagepera 1993: 336f; Palezkis 1994: 117). As economic arguments one could refer to the fact that Kaliningrad was most integrated with and dependent on Lithuania in Soviet times before the border was drawn. In 1957-1965, when Khrushchev divided the Soviet Union into regional economic councils (*sovnarkhozy*), Kaliningrad's economy fell into the Lithuanian unit and was directed from Vilnius.

The main reason for the demands and claims probably was the above-mentioned fact that Lithuanians after gaining independence felt threatened by the Russian military presence in Kaliningrad, which for some time remained high, and the then frequent military transports across the country.

However, all Lithuanian governments recognized Russia's territorial integrity just like Russia recognized Lithuania's.[32] The opposition leader Landsbergis pointed out that questioning the present status of Kaliningrad or demanding demilitarization was not tantamount to territorial claims (Zverev 1996: 16). Concerning the extreme nationalists, one can observe that they were very few, at least renounced violent solutions and saw the question as very long-term.

In actual fact the arguments behind the claims had little basis. As for history, Lithuania had been a Grand Duchy stretching as far as to the Black Sea but it had never really covered East Prussia, and it only had overlordship over East Prussia for some decades, when Lithuania was united with Poland and increasingly subordinated to it until its divisions in the late 18th century. Concerning the Lithuanian minority, it comprised of a tiny 2.1 per cent (18,000) in 1989, most of whom had moved there after the war, and since then it has shrunk to 0.4 (Misiunas & Taagepera 1993: 348; Fedorov & Zverev 1995: 102). As mentioned above, the inclusion of Kaliningrad into Russia has been legally recognized in several international agreements.

Moreover, the reasons for Lithuania not to raise a claim to Kaliningrad are even more compelling than for Germany and Poland. Claims have already spurred some extremists in Russia to make counterclaims on Klaipeda and can inspire Poland to do the same *vis-à-vis* the Vilnius region, which earlier belonged to Poland, and the Russian and Polish minorities in Lithuania could be activated.[33] Claims would also spoil any chances for Lithuania to join NATO and the EU, which are seen as the best ways of finding security against a Russian reconquest.

On top of all that Lithuania would probably find it very hard to "digest" the region. Since Russians and other Slavs make up 95 per cent of Kaliningrad's population of above 900,000 inhabitants, incorporating them would give Lithuania, which is 80 per cent Lithuanian, a serious minority problem similar to those in Estonia and Latvia. As importantly, the region would be an enormous burden on the Lithuanian economy, which is much smaller and weaker than the Polish one and remains dependent on trade with Russia.

Instead of raising claims, official Lithuania supported the demilitarization of Kaliningrad and its ambitions to get more autonomy inside Russia. It greeted multilateral Western involvement in the region, for example under the aegis of the EU. When the military transits decreased and the threat perception dissipated, public opinion support for raising claims also waned (Palezkis 1994: 119). If a means of pressure on Russia is needed, the transit question still exists.

Lithuania granted inhabitants in the Kaliningrad region – but no other Russian and CIS citizens – visa-free travel, and in 1994 a Lithuanian consulate was opened in Kaliningrad. Lithuania also stood to gain from resuming the old economic ties with Kaliningrad. After the compromise over military transit and MNF status for Lithuania, Lithuanian export quickly rose from the fifth to the first place 1994-1995 in Kaliningrad's trade statistics. Lithuania offered to sell electricity to Kaliningrad in the hope of getting Russian gas in return (Fedorov & Zverev 1995: 130; *Rossiiskaia gazeta*, 27 January 1996; *Nezavisimaya gazeta*, 22 May 1996). Thus in spite of the transit problems and Lithuanian equivocation about the status of Kaliningrad, which made relations with Lithuania the most difficult, also these tended to normalize.

Uncertain prospects

Kaliningrad undoubtedly was the greatest problem in the Baltic Sea region that the Soviet Union bequeathed to Russia. It was overmilitarized and as an exclave extremely dependent on transit to Russia for its economic survival. This inspired fears among the neighbours, which only just had got rid of Russian troops and become fully independent. Some groups in these states, especially Lithuania, also raised claims to Kaliningrad or wanted it to become a state of its own.

However, as Kaliningrad opened its borders, the military presence gradually diminished, and temporary compromises were reached on the military transit questions, its relations with the neighbours also improved and became more economic in nature.

The governments in Lithuania, Poland, and Germany recognized Kaliningrad as an integral part of Russia for strong reasons. The legal basis for claims was lacking. Raising claims would spoil their relations with Russia and each other and reduce the chances of Poland and Lithuania to be admitted into NATO. If any state nevertheless were to take over

Kaliningrad, its Russian population and immense economic-social problems would be great or intolerable burdens. Also a division of the region would give rise to enough conflicts and costs. Thus it is up to Russia and Kaliningrad itself what the future of the region will be.

In line with democratization and transition to market economy in Russia, Kaliningrad was proclaimed a Free Economic Zone and got more power over regional affairs. This was welcomed in the neighbouring states and foreign trade increased.

But the economic preconditions were bad and the promised favours uncertain, so foreign investment did not fulfil the expectations and the economic crisis deepened. Growing Russian nationalism and fear of Western influence made Moscow circumscribe the economic and political decision-making powers of Kaliningrad so that the Economic Free Zone practically ceased to exist, and more emphasis was put on its military significance. The Russian military intervention in Chechnya was another sign of this tendency.

However, Moscow could not fulfil its promises of support to Kaliningrad either, and the crisis deepened there. In January 1996 the region got back some of its favours as a Free Customs Zone.

For the future several alternatives can be conceived the Kaliningrad region, depending on the development in Moscow.

If a centralized and nationalist Russia like the present one would overcome the economic crisis, Kaliningrad could get more support and its military role be maintained and even reinforced. This could undercut free trade in the region and increase tension with the neighbours. They would then be more anxious to join NATO, which would in turn make Russia strengthen its positions in Kaliningrad further.

If a nationalist and centralist Russia could not overcome the economic crisis, which seems more likely, at the same time as the economic development in the West would proceed, worsened conditions in Kaliningrad might induce its population to turn its hopes from Moscow to the West again. Tension between Moscow and Kaliningrad would grow. The neighbours would react in the same way as above and might also be affected by the growth of crime, illegal trade with weapons, drugs, refugees, and environmental problems in Kaliningrad.

If Russia would become more democratic and decentralized, Kaliningrad could continue in the direction of demilitarization and free economic zone. This could inspire the neighbouring states to increase trade and investment more confidently than so far and make agreements with the

EU possible.[34] This alternative would probably lead to economic development in the region and make it a model for all Russia.

Kaliningrad as a city is already one of the Russian cities most exposed to foreign trade. Due to its relatively small size in comparison with for example St Petersburg, foreign trade and aid can have a real impact like in Estonia. The problem is to create legal preconditions and win the confidence of Western investors without creating suspicions in Moscow. In order to avoid these, Western aid should take place under the aegis of European and international organisations as it has already done.

The last alternative resembles the original ideas for a Free Economic Zone and clearly is the preferable one. That does not mean that it is the most likely one. The future of Kaliningrad is open and subject to the wills and expectations of many actors.

Notes

1 Sweden held Pillau and other ports in the vicinity from 1626 to 1635.
2 However, they did not (like e.g. Sweden) accept the Soviet incorporation of the Baltic states (where there are more ice-free ports).
3 In 1947 there were 290,000 inhabitants, of whom 15,000 in Kaliningrad, in 1959 611,000, in 1989 871,000, in 1995 926,000, of whom in Kaliningrad 419,000. In 1994 80 per cent registered as Russians, 7.3 per cent as Belarussians, 6 per cent as Ukrainians. For the current composition and recent changes, see table in Fedorov's chapter in this book.
4 According to Swerew (1995: 10f), the military industry employed 15.9 per cent of the industrial workforce in 1985. See also Wellman's chapter in this volume.
5 According to a local source quoted by Wellmann 1996: 167, there were also nuclear weapons in the area in 1993, but military sources now deny the presence of any nuclear and chemical weapons (Vardomskii et al. 1995: 39).
6 The exact number of troops is a moot question due to remaining secrecy, and estimates depend greatly on vested interests. Lithuanians tend to give the highest figures, the Kaliningrad administration the lowest. (Vardomskii et al 1995: 38 claim 200,000!) According to the Military Balance 1994-95: 117 and 1996-1997: 114 the army forces (excluding naval, air, interior (police) and border forces) have dwindled from 103,000 in 1993 to 24,000 in 1996 (*Military Balance 1994-1995, 1996-1997*). Swedish officials already in 1994 mentioned a total figure of about 60,000 men (*SvD*, 20 May 1994). The number of combat aircraft fell from 155 in 1990 to 28 in 1996 but the number of tanks and attack helicopters actually rose somewhat (*Military Balance 1996-1997:* 114). For

analyses of the present forces, see Pedersen's, Gricius', and Lachowski's chapters in this volume.

7　See also Trynkov's chapter in this volume.

8　On the Russian view, see Trynkov's chapter in this book.

9　For more on the transit problems, see Gricius', Lachowski's, Lange's, and Fairlie's chapters in this book.

10　As one response to the transit problems, nationalist groups like Zhirinovskii's LDPR and security people in Kaliningrad disputed Lithuania's takeover of Memel, which was seen as an ideal corridor to Belarus. A Russian foreign ministry expert suggested to drop claims to Klaipeda in exchange for free transport to Kaliningrad, but at the same time conceded that Russia could not claim Klaipeda since it was not the only heir to the USSR (KP, 25 June 1996).

11　For more on Belarus and the "Polish corridor", see Fairlie's and Lachowski's chapters in this book.

12　Dörrenbächer mentions a total of 76 per cent and 64 per cent in polls in 1992 and 1993.

13　This idea was supported by 8 per cent, the autonomous republic by 18 per cent in 1993.

14　See also other chapters in this volume.

15　From 45 per cent 1992 to 70 per cent 1995.

16　More on this in Wellman's chapter.

17　More on this in Fedorov's chapter. On environmental problems, see Kropinova's chapter.

18　In 1994-1995 fish export made Namibia Kaliningrad's third export country. (Fedorov & Zverev 1995: 123 ff)

19　Only 17 per cent of federal investment programmes were financed in 1995 (KP, 14 Aug 1996).

20　10 million USD was invested in 1994 (Vardomskii et al 1995: 17 f), at the end of 1995 the accumulated sum of foreign investment in joint ventures amounted to merely 27 million USD (Investitsii 1996). All Russia received 1 billion USD in 1995, Poland six according to Matochkin in RG, 27 Jan 1996.)

21　According to former deputy prime minister Shakhrai, smuggling increased by 1993 per cent in January-September 1994 !

22　Interestingly, General Lebed's Congress of Russian Communities came out third in the Kaliningrad region in 1995, and Lebed came second ahead of Ziuganov in the naval town Baltiisk in the first round of the Presidential elections in June 1996.(*Vestnik Baltiiska* 1996: 26).

23　More on this in Fairlie's chapter.

24　For more on the law, see Fedorov's and Gricius' chapters.

25　For example, real wages in the first half of 1996 increased by 8 per cent in

Russia, by 16.6 per cent in Kaliningrad.

26 Dönhoff's article was printed without commentary in the Russian foreign policy journal.

27 The total number of Germans in the USSR in 1989 was about 2 million.

28 Officially, the percentage of Armenians grew from 0.2 1989 to 0.9 1994, Germans from 0.2 to 0.7 (See table in Fedorov's chapter).

29 As for invested capital in joint ventures by May 1996 Belarus, Sweden, and France came out ahead of Poland. ('Investitsii' 1996) For more on the Polish relations, see Lachowski's chapter.

30 Concerning the sea border, Lithuania wanted to draw the base line at right angles to the coast, whereas Russia wanted the Kuronian spit as the base.

31 In the northern districts of the region almost half the population spoke Lithuanian in 1911, and 61,000 did so in 1931 (Misiunas & Taagepera 1993: 336 f, Palezkis 1994: 117).

32 Even if Stalin is said to have offered *Königsberg* to Lithuania in 1945, its leader allegedly did not accept.

33 See footnote 10. Also Vardomskii (1995: 46) claims there are no legal acts about the transfer of Klaipeda to Lithuania.

34 Concerning the EU and long-term economic developments, see Fairlie's chapter.

References

Anisimov, Alexander (1995), "The region in the context of international relations", *International Affairs* (Moscow), no. 6, pp. 26-32.

Bingen, Dieter (1993), "Das deutsche Resümee", in *Zukunft des Gebiets Kaliningrad (Königsberg): Ergebnisse einer internationalen Studiengruppe.* Sonderveröffentlichung. Köln: Bundesinstitut für ostwissenschaftliche und internationale Studien, pp. 45-54.

Boryschkowski, Jozef (1994), "Das Kaliningrader Gebiet und Polen", in Ernst Müller-Hermann (ed.), (1994), *Königsberg/Kaliningrad unter europäischen Perspektiven.* Bremen: Verlag H. M. Hauschild, pp. 85-100.

Department of Sea and River Ports (Kaliningrad), (1995), "A European Crossroads, Icefree Port and Transportation Hub", *International Affairs* (Moscow), no. 6, pp. 67-71.

Dönhoff, Marion von (1993), "Kaliningrad region and its future", *International Affairs* (Moscow), no. 8, pp. 46-49.

Dörrenbächer, Heike (1994), "Die Sonderwirtschaftszone Jantar von Kaliningrad (Königsberg)", *Arbeitspapiere zur internationalen Politik, No 81.* Bonn: Forschungsinstitut der Deutschen Gesellschaft für auswärtige Politik.

Fedorov, Gennady (1993), "Das Kaliningrader Resümee", in *Zukunft des Gebiets Kaliningrad (Königsberg): Ergebnisse einer internationalen Studiengruppe*. Sonderveröffentlichung. Köln: Bundesinstitut für ostwissenschaftliche und internationale Studien, pp. 5-14.

Fedorov, Gennady M. and Yurii M. Zverev (1995), *Kaliningradskie alternativy*. Kaliningrad: Kaliningradskii Gosudarstvennyi Universitet.

Forum Kaliningrad (1996), *Slutrapport*. Karlskrona: Baltic Institute.

Gnauck, Gerhard (1992), "Kaliningrad" in Sven Gustavsson and Ingvar Svanberg (eds.), *Gamla folk och nya stater*. Stockholm: Gidlunds bokförlag, pp 49-57.

Gromov, Felix N. (1995), "Znachenie Kaliningradskogo osobogo raiona dlia oboronosposobnosti Rossiiskoj Federatsii", *Voennaia Mysl*, no. 4, pp. 9-13.

Grönick, Ritva *et al.* (eds.), (1995), *Vilnius/Kaliningrad: Ideas on Cooperative Security in the Baltic Sea Region*. Helsinki: Nordic Forum for Security.

Hoff, Magdalene and Heinz Timmermann (1993), "Kaliningrad: Russia's future gateway to Europe?". *RFE/RL Research Report* 36 (2), pp. 37-43.

Huldt, Bo (1996), *Kaliningrad as a strategic hub: after the Cold War?* Paper presented for the conference "Forum Kaliningrad 96" in Karlskrona, 27-28 February 1996.

Iantarnyi Ostrov Rossii (1995). Kaliningrad: Kaliningradskii Oblastnoi Komitet Gosstatistiki.

Investititsii v Kaliningradskuiu Oblast iz-za Rubezha (1996). Material from Komitet Porazvitiiu SEZ Iantar. Kalininigrad: Administratsiia Kaliningradskoi Oblasti.

Kondrashov, Aleksandr (1995), "Baltiyskaia Aliaska?", *Argumenty i Fakty*, no. 44. pp. 16-17.

Koschyk, Hartmut (1994), "Kaliningrad/Königsberg: Risiken und Chancen einer Entwicklung", in Ernst Müller-Hermann (ed.), *Königsberg/Kaliningrad unter europäischen Perspektiven*. Bremen: Verlag H. M. Hauschild, pp. 137-144.

Kwizinskii, Anatol (1994), "Kaliningrad: Ein Prüfstein für die Zukunft des neuen Europa?" in Ernst Müller-Hermann (ed.), *Königsberg/Kaliningrad unter europäischen Perspektiven*. Bremen: Verlag H. M. Hauschild, pp. 41-54.

Lieven, Anatol (1993), *The Baltic Revolution: Estonia, Latvia, and Lithuania and the Path to Independence*. New Haven and London: Yale University Press.

Matochkin, Yuri (1996), "Kaliningrad Today", in Forum Kaliningrad (1996), *Slutrapport*. Karlskrona: Baltic Institute, pp. 9-15.

Matotchkin, Yuri (1994), "Kaliningrad und Europa", in Ernst Müller-Hermann (ed.), (1994), *Königsberg/Kaliningrad unter europäischen Perspektiven*. Bremen: Verlag H. M. Hauschild, pp. 25-30.

Misiunas, Romuald J. and Rein Taagepera (1993), *The Baltic States: The Years of Dependence*. Berkeley and Los Angeles: University of California Press.

Müller-Hermann, Ernst (ed.), (1994), *Königsberg/Kaliningrad unter europäischen Perspektiven*. Bremen: Verlag H. M. Hauschild.

Negotiations with The Russian Federation concerning the Withdrawal of Russian Military Forces from the Territory of the Republic of Lithuania. Chronology and Selection of Documents. Vilnius: Republic of Lithuania: Office of Public Affairs and Supreme Counsel.

Nordberg, Erkki (1994), *The Baltic Republics. A Strategic Survey*. Helsinki: National Defence College.

Oldberg, Ingmar (1995), "Kaliningrad-områdets framtid: Kasern, handelsplats eller stridsäpple?", *Internasjonal politikk* vol. 53, no. 3, pp. 335-356.

Osteuropa-Archiv (1993), "Polens Interesse an Kaliningrad", *Osteuropa-Archiv*, no. 7, pp. 364-379.

Palezkis, Justas (1993), "Das litauische Resümee", in *Zukunft des Gebiets Kaliningrad (Königsberg): Ergebnisse einer internationalen Studiengruppe*. Sonderveröffentlichung. Köln: Bundesinstitut für ostwissenschaftliche und internationale Studien, pp. 22-34.

Palezkis, Justas (1994), "Fast unser Land oder Nachbarland", in Ernst Müller-Hermann (ed.), (1994), *Königsberg/Kaliningrad unter europäischen Perspektiven*. Bremen: Verlag H. M. Hauschild, pp. 115-127.

Petersen, Phillip A. (1994), "Kaliningrad: Transition from the Garrison State", paper for NATO Advisor Christopher Donnelly, 2 December.

Petersen, Phillip A. and Crane C. Petersen (1992), *The Security Implications of and Alternative Futures for the Kaliningrad Region*. Washington: Potomac Foundation, VA.

Rapport från CFF and FOA studieresa till Kaliningrad 5-8 April 1994. Stockholm: Centralförbundet Folk och Försvar, pp. 1-19.

Romanov, Valentin (1995), "Kaliningrad as an integral part of Russia", *International Affairs* 6 (Moscow): 42-49.

Sakson, Andrzej (1993), "Resümee" in *Zukunft des Gebiets Kaliningrad (Königsberg): Ergebnisse einer internationalen Studiengruppe*. Sonderveröffentlichung. Köln: Bundesinstitut für ostwissenschaftliche und internationale Studien, pp. 33-44.

Sakson, Andrzej (1994), "Das Problem des Gebiets Kaliningrad/Königsberg in der polnischen Politik", in Ernst Müller-Hermann (ed.), (1994), *Königsberg/Kaliningrad unter europäischen Perspektiven*. Bremen: Verlag H. M. Hauschild, pp. 101-113.

Shumeiko, Vladimir (1995), "Kaliningrad Region: A Russian Outpost", *International Affairs* (Moscow), no. 6: 3-7.

Soglashenie mezhdu pravitelstvom Litovskoi Respublikoi i Pravitelstvom Rossiiskoj Federatsii o tranzitnykh perevozkakh (1993).Vilnius.

Songal, Alexander (1995), "Searching for more effective cooperation mechanisms", *International Affairs* (Moscow), 6: 62-66.

Sundquist, Eva (1994), "Kaliningrad: Budding Economic Zone?", *Östekonomiskt meddelande*. Stockholm: Institute of East European Economics, 27 June, pp. 1-2.

The Military Balance (1994-1995). London: International Institute of Strategic Studies.

The Military Balance (1996-1997). London: International Institute of Strategic Studies.

Vardomskii, Leonid *et al.* (1995), "Kaliningradskaja oblast Rossiiskoj Federatsii: Problemy i perspektivy", in *Kaliningradskaya oblast – Segodnya, zavtra*. Moskva: Nauchnye doklady Moskovskogo tsentra Karnegi.

Wellmann, Christian (1996), "Russia's Kaliningrad exclave at the Crossroads", *Cooperation and Conflict* (Stockholm), 31(2): 161-183.

Wörster, Peter (1995), "The Northern Part of East Prussia", pp. 156-177 in Forsberg, Tuomas (ed.), *Contested Territories, Border Disputes at the Edge of the Former Soviet Empire*. Aldershot: Edward Elgar.

Yegorov, Vladimir G. (1995), "Cooperative security in Northern Europe", pp. 127-133 in Grönick, Ritva et al (eds.), (1995), *Vilnius/Kaliningrad. Ideas on Cooperative Security in the Baltic Sea Region*. Helsinki: Nordic Forum for Security, pp. 127-133.

Zukunft des Gebiets Kaliningrad (Königsberg): Ergebnisse einer internationalen Studiengruppe (1993). Sonderveröffentlichung. Köln: Bundesinstitut für ostwissenschaftliche und internationale Studien.

Zverev, Jurij M. (1996), *Russlands Gebiet Kaliningrad im neuen geopolitischen koordinatenfeld*. Köln: Berichte des Bundesinstituts für ostwissenschaftliche und internationale Studien (BiOst), no. 6.

2 The Social and Economic Development of Kaliningrad

GENNADY M. FYODOROV

Dynamics of the regions development

The Kaliningrad region is a small exclave of the Russian Federation. The first years after the second World War were marked by a process of economic reconstruction and creation of new branches, i.e. ocean fishery, engineering and light industry.

The rates of industrial growth were rather high until the mid of 1960s as indicated by table 2.1.

Table 2.1 The levels of production growth (drop) in industry and agriculture in the Kaliningrad Region for the period of 1947-1995

	1950 (%) 1947 *	1955 (%) 1950 *	1960 (%) 1955 *	1965 (%) 1960 *	1970 (%) 1965 *	1975 (%) 1970 *	1980 (%) 1975 *	1985 (%) 1980 *	1990 (%) 1980 *	1995 (%) 1990 *
Industry	410	230	210	160	137	136	106	120	108	39
Agriculture	...	...	...	133	120	114	91	128	112	50

* - comparing to

References:
The Kaliningrad Region in the eighth five-year plan (1972). Kaliningrad.
The Kaliningrad Region in the eleventh five-year plan (1986). Kaliningrad.
Yantarny Ostrov Rossii. Kaliningrad.
The Kaliningrad Regional statistics committee (1996).

Later they levelled down to the average rates of Russia as a whole.

Table 2.2 **The rates of production growth/drop in industry and agriculture in the Russian Federation for the period of 1946-1995**

	1950 (%) 1946 *	1955 (%) 1950 *	1960 (%) 1955 *	1965 (%) 1960 *	1970 (%) 1965 *	1975 (%) 1970 *	1980 (%) 1975 *	1985 (%) 1980 *	1990 (%) 1985 *	1995 (%) 1990 *
Industry	211	179	158	145	153	136	127	130	117	50
Agriculture	...	130	133	109	125	98	103	149	149	67

* - comparing to

References:
Natsionalnaia Ekonomia RSFSR v 1960 godu (1961). Moscow.
Natsionalnaia Ekonomia RSFSR v 1989 godu (1990). Moscow.
Yantarni Ostrov Rossii (1996). Kaliningrad.

As in other regions the growth of industry began to slow down in the second half of the 1970s due to the fact that the sources of growth (i.e. building of new enterprises and employment growth) were exhausted and the scientific-technical reinforcement of production was rather slow. In 1989 industrial and agricultural potential of the region reached 0.6 per cent of the total production in Russia. That is, by the beginning of 1990s the Kaliningrad region was viewed as one of the average industrial-agricultural regions of the Russian Federation. The branches of specialisation were as follows:

* Fishery
* Machinery
* Paper and pulp industry
* Amber and oil production
* Agriculture, oriented on meat and milk production
* Sea transport
* Health-resort complex
* Ocean researches and maritime education

After the disintegration of the Soviet Union in 1991 the Kaliningrad region became Russia's exclave. Some 400 km of foreign territories (Lithuania, Belarus and Latvia) separated the Kaliningrad region from the mainland. It became more difficult to preserve the links between industrial enterprises, raw and energy suppliers as well as passenger routes. Moreover, faced with the transition to the market economy, the regional economy is now pressured by the complexity of the new conditions and the required specialisation. Production dropped considerably as illustrated by figures 2.1 and 2.2.

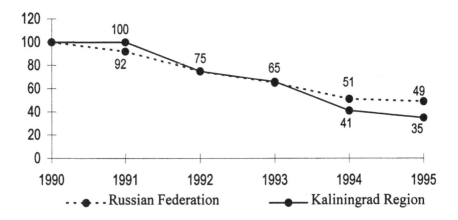

Figure 2.1   The growth of industrial production

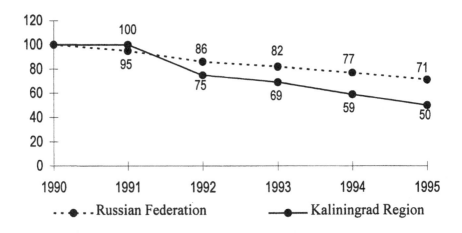

Figure 2.2   The growth of agricultural production

For the period of 1990-1995, production sharply declined and the rates of recession became higher, as compared with the rates in the Russian Federation as a whole. According to official statistics, industrial production fell by 61 per cent, agricultural production by 50 per cent compared to 51 per cent and 29 per cent respectively in Russia as a whole.

Changes in the structure of industry as a result of the new geopolitical situation

At present the structures of industry do not comply with the new economic conditions of the region's geopolitical situation. Due to a sharp rise in prices for fuel and lack of state subsidies, the fishing industry with its remote fishery areas became mainly unprofitable. Fishery production declined by 63 per cent in 1990-1995.

Distant sources of raw materials and semi-products as well as broken industrial ties with suppliers make it difficult to develop the machinery. These problems are further pumped by the conversion of the military-oriented production. In 1995 machinery production comprised only 24 per cent as compared with 1990.

In 1989 61 per cent of industrial personnel and 61 per cent of the volume of production output belonged to the fishery and machinery. By 1995 their employment share decreased by 56 per cent, and the volume of production was cut by 26 per cent.

A considerable fall occurred in the production of cellulose, which was based on the usage of timber, delivered from Russia's Northern regions. Hence the production of pulp and paper can be profitable only in the case of being export-oriented. In 1994 60 per cent of exported cellulose was produced in the region, but the pulp production was cut by 3.5 times in 1990-1994. In 1995 the output of cellulose doubled as compared with 1994, and almost the whole amount of the produced cellulose went abroad. Nowadays the role of this branch in industrial structure is more important than in 1989.

The branch structure of the region's industry differs a lot from its structure in 1989.

Table 2.3   Development of the branch structure of the region's industry, 1989-1995 in per cent

Branch	Number of employees 1989	1995	Production volume 1989	1995
Fishery	19.8	26.2	33.3	17.2
Meat & Milk	3.2	5.0	7.7	12.9
Other branches of food industry	3.1	5.5	3.8	9.9
Machinery	41.9	29.9	27.9	8.7
Paper & Pulp	7.4	9.7	7.2	13.9
Forestry & Timber Production	5.3	4.5	3.7	3.1
Power Supply	2.7	4.6	1.3	15.6
Fuel	0.5	1.3	1.2	8.7
Coke-Chemicals	0.4	0.9	0.8	1.0
Building Materials	3.9	3.5	2.6	2.3
Light Industry	7.7	4.1	4.9	1.3
Flour-Grinding, Crops & Fodder	0.8	0.9	3.2	3.9
Others	4.1	3.9	2.5	1.5
Total	100.8	100.0	100.1	100.0

References:
Yantarni Ostrov Rossii (1996). p. 153. Kaliningrad.
Fyodorov, Gennady, M., Zverev Yury, M. *Kaliningradskie Alternativy* (1995). p.p. 119-120. Kaliningrad.

The share of energy supply and fuel industry grew due to the price change. The food industry (except fishery) decreased less than similar processes in industry on the average. Now it's role has become quite important. On the other hand, the role of building and light industry has been diminished.

In fact, the industrial character of the region is on the verge of vanishing. And, as is evidenced by the dynamics of the regional branch structure (i.e. agriculture, transport, construction, etc.), these are also experiencing a crucial period. Investments enabling modernisation and structural reorganisation of the region, as required by the new economic and geopolitical conditions, are of outmost importance.

In 1990-1995 more than 20 schemes and programmes were put forward in order to remedy the situation prevailing in the region. Many of them are not applicable, as they might result in the loss of RF sovereignty over this territory with all ensuing consequences for the population. This applies to ideas on establishing a "Euroregion Kaliningrad/Königsberg", a condominium under the auspices of the European Community or Germany, or turning Kaliningrad into an independent Baltic republic. This goes for the creation of an autonomous German republic on the territory of the region with a consequential trans-settlement of the major part of Russian Germans into the region as well. Such "projects" provoke separatism and arouse anxiety in the RF political circles and the regional population, which is primarily Russian (Table 2.4).

Table 2.4   National structure of the population of the Kaliningrad Region

Nationalities	1979	1989
Russians	78.3	78.5
Belarussians	9.0	8.5
Ukranians	6.8	7.2
Armenians	0.1	0.2
Germans	0.1	0.2
Lithuanians	2.4	2.1
Poles	0.5	0.5
Tatars	0.4	0.4
Mordvas	0.5	0.4
Jews	0.5	0.4
Chuvashes	0.3	0.3
Azerbaidzhanians	0.1	0.2
Others *	1.0	1.1

*: Moldovians, Gipsies, Latvians, Georgians, Uzbeks, Kazakhs, etc.)
Source: *Yantarni Ostrov Rossii* (1996) p.51. Kaliningrad.

Suggestions on the military development of the region as a Russian Baltic outpost serve as a counterpoise to them.

Proposals of a social-economic nature perceive the Kaliningrad region as an integral part of the Russian Federation, and one that plays an important role in the economy of the country. The sources of development are hence also depicted differently (federal budget, non-state internal and foreign capital) in branch priorities as to schemes of management and the ways of co-operation with foreign countries.

Ideas of the region's self-financing and preservation of the present branch structure of the economy with some slight changes failed to be implemented due to the insufficient financial resources necessary for the reconstruction and the restructuring of the economy. (*Kaliningradskaia Pravda*, 10 November 1990). Efforts to attract federal budget resources and Russian investors to the region failed as well. The government issued a number of documents, presupposing financial support for the region[1], but their implementation was incomplete. However, they had a positive impact on the social-economic situation in the region.

For some time the dominant idea influencing the regional development (which is still of first importance), was that of establishing a Free Economic Zone (FEZ) on the whole territory of the region, as set down by the Supreme Soviet of the Russian Soviet Federal Socialist Republic in June 1991 in the decree passed by the Chairman of the RF Supreme Counsel and later approved by the RF authorities in December 1993.[2] FEZ "Yantar" presupposes an active involvement of the foreign capital freed from taxation, customs and other duties (Matochkin 1990).

For a short period of time the volume of the region's external trade increased rapidly and the spectrum of trade became wider (Tables 2.5, 2.6). There was a considerable growth in the export of goods produced in the region as well as transport services offered by the Kaliningrad trade and fishing vessels to foreign companies. The region's ports began to handle cargoes of third countries for re-export. This included, for example, fertilizers from Belarus.

However, the exemptions were granted only partially. Therefore, the volume of export per capita, stimulated within the frames of FEZ, comprised only 500 $ in 1995 against 520 $ in RF on the average. Yet the region's share in Russia's export is constantly growing. In 1992 it comprised 0.2 per cent, in 1993 – 0.3 per cent and in 1995 – 0.6 per cent. It should also be noted that the structure of the region's export differs from that of the Russian Federation, where oil and gas prevail. Kaliningrad's export primarily consists of semi-products (cellulose, frozen fish, etc.) and some 17 per cent is dedicated to export of oil. This is to say that although FEZ failed to unfold due to a lack of sufficient foreign investments, absence of legislation and unclear administrative procedures, it had a positive effect on the development of the export branches of the region's economy.

Table 2.5   The structure of the Region's export (in million US dollars)

	1992	1995
Fish	30.0	37.3
Oil	2.0	78.4
Pulp	11.0	66.2
Paper & Cardboard	0.4	21.0
Coke	0.5	4.0
Fertilizers	-	48.0
Amber ware	0.4	1.5
Furs	0.1	2.2
Metals	-	22.0
Vessels	-	20.0
Drinks	0.6	10.7
Services	1.5	58.8
Others	44.5	88.9
Summary	91.0	459.0

Source: *Yantarni Ostrov Rossii* (1996) p.178. Kaliningrad.

The support offered by the government to the region was mainly in line with the expectations, and in particular the beliefs underlying the federal programme of the regional development of the years 1994-1995. It was expected that the federal budget sources would amount to some 26 per cent of the total volumes required either by way of direct investments or in the form of taxation preferences and taxation credit allotted to the region, this boosting the influx of private capital as well. However, so far the volume of investments has been marginal. Their economic and social role is quite modest and the federal programme still remains to be implemented.

More broadly, since the end of the 1980s the region has experienced and has been forced to cope with a complicated economic situation and yet the financial and legislative support from Moscow has remained rather scant.

Table 2.6   Distribution of the Region's external trade (in million US dollars)

Country	Export		Import	
	1992	1995	1992	1995
The Baltic Countries:				
Lithuania	-	15.9	1.0	102.7
Poland	14.0	9.0	16.0	91.0
Germany	15.0	25.0	9.0	48.0
Estonia	-	15.3	-	1.0
Latvia	-	5.7	-	11.2
Norway	0.1	3.4	-	14.7
Finland	7.0	2.0	-	10.4
Denmark	0.2	4.0	-	7.2
Sweden	11.0	1.0	-	5.9
Total	47.3	81.3	26.0	292.1
Switzerland	-	97.0	-	1.5
Netherlands	-	17.4	-	23.4
Great Britain	-	7.1	1.0	29.3
USA	0.4	1.0	1.0	31.3
Italy	7.0	16.0	-	12.0
Namibia	1.0	20.5	-	-
Austria	-	11.5	-	6.4
Belgium	-	1.9	-	10.8
Japan	-	0.8	-	8.6
Hungary	-	6.2	-	2.1
France	0.1	2.0	-	4.6
Others and not divided among countries	35.2	196.3	26.0	137.9
Summary	91.0	459.0	54.0	560.0

Source: *Yantarni Ostrov Rossii* (1996) p.180. Kaliningrad.

In 1995 the economic situation in the region further worsened and the recession in production was higher than in the country as a whole. Industrial production declined by 14 per cent and agricultural production by 15 per cent. The volume of construction work in housing decreased by 32 per cent and industry by 29 per cent. A fall could also be discerned in the volume of cargo transportation. The income level of the whole population dropped by 26 per cent and 36 per cent of the inhabitants received a salary below a subsidiary level. The total amount of unemployed people reached 43.600 people (i.e. 10 per cent of the labour force) by the end of 1995, and out of these 25.000 people had an official status of unemployed. The official level of unemployment was 5.8 per cent, i.e. twice as high as the rate in the Russian Federation on the average. The level of crime went up by 3 per cent, and offences against persons increased by 6 per cent (*Yantarny Krai*, 3 February 1996).

It appears that until now, the Regional Administration has failed to take stock of the favourable geopolitical position of the region in order to solve the main problems of regional development. Neither the idea of FEZ, nor the proper federal funding have been implemented. Moreover, the region receives very scant subsidies compared to many other regions in Russia.

The law on a Special Economic Zone in the Kaliningrad region replaced former decrees and enactments. The purpose has been to support economic activities in the region. It was adopted by the State Duma in November, 1995, and recognised by the Federal Council and signed by the President in January, 1996 (*Yantarny Krai*, 2 February 1996).

Significance of the law "on the special economic zone in the Kaliningrad region"

The Special Economic Zone (SEZ) embraces the territory of the Kaliningrad region as a whole, with the exceptions of the military establishments and oil exploration on shelves. It mainly provides a customs tax free zone. In other words, all goods imported into the region (from other Russian regions and from abroad) are tax-free, and this goes for all goods produced in the region and exported from the region as well.

Other preferences in the context of the SEZ require additional decision-making by the state bodies of power. This applies to the preferential terms of investments and business activity, which are determined by the law. Thus, tax preferences for Russian and foreign business and investors are now under consideration, although the terms of preferences and their amount have not yet been defined. They are required to be "in accordance with the taxation codes of the Russian Federation and the codes of the Kaliningrad region".

However, the Russian taxation code does not specify special zones, and the SEZ can only account for the preferences, common for all regions.

Similarly, according to the law, such preferences can be granted to banks in case they contribute to the implementation of the Federal programme of the SEZ development. Again, these preferences are set by the Administration pending co-ordination with the Federal Government and Russia's Central Bank.

The Federal programme itself is stipulated by the law mentioned above. As a priority task, the state is obliged to provide financing for its implementation, although this programme has firstly to be adopted by the Government of the Russian Federation.

As to the implementation of the law, the most disputable question has been the question of the SEZ management. Suggestions have been launched to create a management committee on federal level. The possibility of an independent SEZ administration has also been considered. However, according to the law, the SEZ management is to be carried out by regional bodies. The administration of the Kaliningrad region performs the tasks of the SEZ administration, thus providing for some intensification of regional self-management in the sphere of economic decision-making. The regional administration must co-ordinate the influx of Russian and overseas investments and stimulate business activities. It is entitled to sign agreements with investors and businesses on the implementation of investment projects and on the lease of regional land property, including real estate. The region has the right to sign agreements with administrative-territorial formations of other countries on economic, scientific-technical, cultural and sport co-operation, but these agreements come into effect only after they have been recognised by the Ministry of Foreign Affairs of the Russian Federation.

The region has been granted the right to set limitations for customs free terms (i.e. to impose quotes on import) in order to create favourable conditions for the local manufacturers. However, these measures must be co-ordinated with the Government. Experience shows that the process of co-ordination may be rather time-consuming, as evidenced by the failure of the attempt made by the regional Administration in February 1996 to reduce Western importation of some food products and building materials into the region. An enactment was adopted by the Administration, but not co-ordinated with the Government, and hence it failed to enter force. This is why the process of its recognition dragged out.

Despite some inconsistencies and uncertainties, the law on the SEZ in the Kaliningrad region plays an important role in stimulating regional development. Investors have become more attracted to the region. New investment projects (for example, financing provided by the South Korean partners for automobile assembly at the previously almost bankrupt ship building factory "Yantar"), as well as foreign programmes of scientific-technical support have emerged. The prices for consumer goods in the region have gone down and are lower than in other regions of the country.

The fact that the SEZ law was adopted on the federal level entails formal recognition of the idea that a Free (special) Economic Zone is needed. Such a recognition remained uncertain during the process of implementing the SEZ law (Presidential Decrees, State Resolutions), which strived for analogous conditions of economic activity. These conditions were never properly established and hence the idea of a Free Economic Zone "Yantar" lost its validity. The process created unstable conditions of management and deprived investors and businessmen of trust in the whole project.

The launching of the SEZ project has mitigated suspicions about any separatism, which used to exist among some specialists and people. However, such beliefs still prevail to some degree and therefore special articles were added to the law, aimed at preventing any separatism.

The law on the SEZ underlines the importance of Kaliningrad's social-economic development for the Russian Federation, and does so in order to tune down any fears about the region's separation from the Russian Federation. It is stated that the international agreements of the Russian federation concerning questions of the Kaliningrad region must contain documents certifying the status of the Kaliningrad region as an integral part of the Russian Federation. Similar documents must be a part of agreements between the Kaliningrad region and the administrative-territorial formations of the foreign countries. The SEZ law also implies that "foreign physical and juridical persons, international organisations (associations), including Russian and foreign physical and juridical persons, are granted the right for land tenure on the SEZ territory only in accordance with the lease agreements, which do not grant the right for permanent ownership".

The law on the SEZ is only a small constituent element of the whole RF economic legislation, as the regional economy comprises a part of economy of the whole country. Therefore, the social-economic situation in the region is primarily dependent on those processes that pertain to the

Russian national economy at large. However, the economic situation and the ways of dealing with problems of transition towards a market economy are different in each region.

As for the Kaliningrad region, two general conclusions emerge. Firstly, the market transformations are more intensive here than in most other Russian regions. According to experts estimations this is in line with trends pertaining to regions such as Moscow, St.-Petersburg, Nizhny Novgorod, i.e. Kaliningrad belongs to a category of rather developed regions. The SEZ law tends to confirm this. Secondly, in addition to the transition to the market, there is a problem of the exclave position of the Kaliningrad region, i.e. the region being geographically detached from the rest of Russia. The law on the SEZ aims at easing this problem and improving the chances of the region to get access to the all-Russian market, and also to enter the European as well as the world markets.

The economic restructuring is complicated by the lack of investments

However, there are also complications of a legislative nature. For example, the President forwarded to the State Duma amended documents concerning the specificity of the FEZ management. In the case of the SEZ, direct subordination to the government is required, but the regional administration is bypassed, which was not the case with the FEZ law.

For its part the regional administration made an attempt to regulate provisional import and import of some building materials by means of issuing a corresponding decree in February 1996 (*Kaliningradskaia Pravda*, 22 February 1996). This decree is not yet in force as it has still to be recognised by the Government.

In general it appears that the new law has failed to provide stability in regional terms of management. This is unfortunate as legislative stability is required to achieve an influx of investments, including foreign investments. Thus financing of projects in the sphere of regional development remains uncertain, and obviously a more detailed scientific strategy and improved tactical plans for the region's development are needed.

It appears that the aspiring for a Free Economic Zone did not spur the region's economic development. However, it brought about certain quantitative changes in the economic environment. About 1.000 joint and foreign ventures have been established (the total number of the managing subjects in all branches is 17,000, out of which 14,500 belong to the sphere of private and mixed property). Their share in the total volume and investments is between one and two per cent, but they are already responsible for some 40 per cent of the export-oriented products, manufactured in the region. Their activity helps to spread market relations and to update the working staff's qualifications, these serving as a basis for the further growth of investments and production, provided that there are favourable conditions for economic development.

Russian capital is interested in future investments into the region's economy. It is no coincidence that many affiliates of the Russian banks are located here. Investments will be encouraged by the preferential taxation terms, as well as by investments coming from federal budget sources.

In 1994 87 per cent of the resources to the Kaliningrad region had their origin in other regions of the Russian Federation, and the region's share of ready-made products exported to RF reached 97 per cent. This was the situation despite that raw materials and semi-product are mostly exported abroad. Therefore, the formation of the regional market should run parallel to a similar process of linking up with the all-Russian market, especially as the interest of the foreign partners in the region is mostly based on the idea that Kaliningrad potentially provides access to the wider Russian market.

Due to the region's isolation from mainland Russia, it is important to empower the regional bodies with additional possibilities to regulate the region's economy. This principle constitutes a corner stone of the Charter of the region and its Agreement with the federal bodies of power.

The region should have taxation preferences similar to off-shore zones and the right to regulate customs fees, as has been stipulated in the law on the Special Economic Zone (SEZ). Federal support is needed to create economic restructuring. On the one hand, the regional economy is detached from the all-Russian market and, on the other hand, there are conditions for its integration into the common European market.

Investment and investment policy

The core problem of the regional economy in Kaliningrad, common for the Russian economy as a whole, consists of investments or rather investments into production. For the last five years the general volume of capital investments from the foreign countries comprised only 10 million dollars. The preferences, contained in the law on a Special Economic Zone have not reversed the situation. National private capital, including regional capital, does not considerably contribute to the amount of regional investments, regardless of the fact, that there are 29 commercial banks and 54 affiliates located in the region. (*Ekonomika i zhizn* 1996).

In 1995 out of the total volume of capital investments (i.e. 862 billion roubles or 190 million dollars according to the official rate of the Central Bank of Russia), 30 per cent was received from the republic's budget and 7 per cent from the local budget; 20 per cent was provided by the centralised non-budget investment foundations, preferential state investment credits and by the foundation for the state support of priority branches. Only 43 per cent was allocated by the enterprises and the population (in 1990 their share comprised 65 per cent of the capital investments) (*Yantarny Ostrov Rossii* 1996). Less than a half of all financial resources went to the building of industry (including 24 per cent for industry, 3 per cent to agriculture and 17 per cent to transport), whereas in 1980s their amount comprised more than one third (*Yantarny Ostrov Rossii* 1996). In 1994 the regional share of the total volume of the country's capital investments made only 0.49 per cent (taking into account that its share in the total number of the population was 0.62 per cent), and in 1995 it amounted to 0.38 per cent.

How can these investment problems be solved? Firstly, we need to chart the social-economic situation as a whole, as well as the feasibility of the active economic policy implementation, ensuring the growth of production in the country.

A report prepared by the Expert Institute (*Rossia na Puti k 2000 godu, 1996*), focusing on various perspectives of the Russian economy, highlights the current strategies for development. It presupposes that a policy of macro-economic stabilisation (the drop of inflation by 1.5-2.0 per cent per month) is implemented in combination with the stimulation of private investments into production by means of state guarantees. The limiting of inflation is possibly due to the growth of consumer goods import and to the production of new competitive goods by Russian manufactures. Moreover, the market is now recovering from an internal shock. In order to stimulate private investments, state institutions have to be reinforced, formal procedures need to be simplified once companies start their activities, and an anti-corruption campaign has to be implemented. As for direct state investments and foreign credits received from the state (i.e. the World

Bank, the European Bank of Reconstruction and Development), they are to be earmarked for the private business system development. To a certain extent such investments may be realised on competitive basis.

It seems that at the beginning of 1996 an "optimistic" scenario will yield a production growth by 2-3 per cent yearly during a first stage, and the rate of growth will reach 10 per cent a year by 2000.

The state investments have not been and will not be distributed evenly amongst the Russian regions. The general stipulations of the RF regional policy (*Rossiskaia Gazeta*, 9 April 1996), worked out by the Government, covers the priority regions, the so-called "points of growth", capable of immediate response and of providing a serious contribution to solving the all-Russian social-economic problems. The Kaliningrad region can and must become one of these. The federal support for production and social infrastructure development to the region (i.e. transport, telecommunications, staff retraining systems, etc.) will serve as a means of attracting Russian and foreign private capital interested in developing export-oriented and import-replacing productions. Moreover, such production will be further stimulated by the establishment of the Special Economic Zone. The SEZ offers a framework for working out the Federal programme for restructuring the region's infrastructure and economy. A special committee headed by the Deputy Prime Minister A. Bolshakov has been formed to efficiently settle various problems pertaining to the region's activity.

The budget support offered to the region in 1993-1996, turned out to be one of the regional maintenance mechanisms. According to it, federal funds are granted to investors (banks) on a competitive basis, which in their turn submit for tender their own investment projects aimed at attracting internal financial resources. 52 per cent of the total credit sum received in 1995 has been dedicated to sponsoring 15 industrial projects, 22 per cent was granted for five energy projects and 17 per cent for four building projects. The remaining credit was allocated for financing six more projects, devoted to various branches of the regional economy. These include the "Bineks" corporation (expansion of the petrol stations system), the joint-stock company "Cepruss" (reconstruction of the paper and pulp production), the joint-stock company "Baltkran" (doubling crane production), the joint-stock company "Kaliningradmorneftegaz" (increase in oil exploration) and others.

The law on the cancellation of customs duties regarding exported goods, produced in the region, as well as on goods imported into the region, is of no less financial importance. The region gained approximately 600 billion roubles in February-August 1996 (i.e. more than 100 million dollars) as a result of this law. For example, the growth of prices for consumer goods has dropped, as compared with the average rate in Russia. Thus, if by the beginning of 1996 the average regional prices for consumer goods comprised 2,364,000 roubles or 97.3 per cent of the average level in Russia, by the end of August the prices went down and reached 209,000 roubles or 80.7 per cent of the average level in the country.

Priorities of the regions development

Thus, several factors determine potential positive changes in the region's development. They consist of an implementation of an optimistic scenario of economic development in the country; the purposeful regional policy pursued on the state level; implementation of the SEZ law in the Kaliningrad region; consecutive activity of the regional bodies of power, aimed at attracting investments into the region's economy as well as stimulation of private national and international investments. A forecast of the social-economic development of the region for the period of 1996-2000, based on the prerequisites mentioned above, has been presented by a group of scholars (Fyodorov et. al. 1996).

Three scenarios have been offered and put on probation, i.e. an optimistic, a pessimistic and a more probable variant.

The pessimistic scenario pays attention to the strengthening of the administrative-command methods of management, economic financing primarily at the expense of the state financial sources and the protection of domestic manufacturers by means of customs taxation.

Initially, such measures may have a positive impact on agriculture, provided that customers' demands for goods will increase, protected by customs duties and therefore becoming less expensive. Such measures may be temporarily successful in terms of preventing the downfall of industrial production. However, in the future industrial and agricultural growth will quite probably slow down.

The process of restructuring as well as the immediate improvement of the quality of goods will become rather problematic, if we choose this variant of the regional development. It will not only undermine external economic activity and affect adversely the influx of foreign investments. The exclave position of the region will create additional obstacles for exporting goods into other regions of Russia. As soon as the internal regional market is saturated, agricultural growth will decrease and the traditional structure of industry will hamper the process of development.

Contrary to what is outlined above, an optimistic scenario presupposes a rapid development of market relations and an implementation of the SEZ. This will generate growth in the industry with structural changes allowing to achieve the average rates of growth by the end of the 1990s (i.e. approximately 5 per cent). The process of stabilisation will ensure a rapid increase in agriculture reaching by the year 2005 practically the level of the pre-crisis production (1990). Internal market will restrict growth in production. The highest rates of production of some 10 per cent a year corresponding to those during the first half of 1960s (the period of reinforcement and restructuring of industry) could be achieved after the year 2000. The level of production in 1990 will be surpassed in the years 2007-2008 (Table 2.7).

Table 2.7 **Evaluation of industrial and agricultural dynamic growth in the Kaliningrad Region for the period of 1995-2010 1990=100**

	90	95	96	97	98	99	00	05	10
Industry	100	39							
Scenarios:									
Optimistic			39	41	44	48	53	83	133
Pessimistic			37	37	37	38	40	44	50
Most probable			37	37	38	39	42	68	109
Agriculture	100	50							
Scenarios:									
Optimistic			46	46	49	54	59	95	120
Pessimistic			46	49	52	56	57	63	70
Most probable			46	45	46	48	53	85	112

Sources: Fyodorov, Gennady M., Zverev, Yury M., Korneevets, Valentin S. *Economic and social development of the Kaliningrad Region and foreign post-socialistic countries of the Baltic region: comparative analysis* (1996). Kaliningrad: Kaliningrad University Press; "Russia on the way to 2000" (1996).

Voprosy Ekonomiki, N2.

Regarding the most probable scenario, it presupposes development of the market economy, too. However, as a result of an imperfect implementation of economic policy in the country as a whole and carrying out the SEZ conception in the Kaliningrad region in particular, the period of economic reforms may be more time-consuming than expected. Therefore, at the first stage of the project, the growth rates would remain less intense, compared to those of the optimistic scenario. Yet, it seems that by the year 2010 the production level of the year 1990 will be surpassed, and requirements for the products quality will become higher, which will serve as a good basis for the latter to compete on the world market (in 1990 in most of the cases the goods quality failed to comply with European standards).

A new structure of the national economy will be created, corresponding to the geopolitical needs of the region. The role of the transport and tourism complexes will grow. More attention will be paid to production of food and industrial products as well as to the building industry. The share of metal-consuming engineering, fishery and paper and pulp industry will decline.

International organisations speed up carrying out the projects of the regional development. Special help is offered by the UNIDO and EU (within the TACIS programme). There is an increased amount of work, carried out by the local scientists, developing a number of projects at the request of the regional administration. This may amount into a programme of the regional social-economic development and the creation of favourable conditions in order to get investments necessary for the region. Special attention is paid to the reconstruction of infrastructure, the creation of a telecommunication system, restructuring of industry, support of small business, the use of the scientific-technical potential and the upgrading of the educational system.

Numerous Russian and foreign researchers should pool their efforts to work out a basis required, allowing the taking into account foreign experience and our own realities. The strategic line of this joint work should consist of a further strengthening of the role of the regions in external relations of the country as well as the implementation of the Law on the Special Economic Zone in the Kaliningrad region with regard to the all-Russian and local interests and interests of the overseas partners.

Export-oriented production and first of all the pulp and paper industry have already increased their volume of production. During 1995 the region's export abroad increased 1.2 times. This export consists of cellulose, frozen fish, oil and coal, i.e. raw materials and semi-products. A more comprehensive usage of the scientific-technical and production potential of the region allows to count for production of export and import-replacing goods in the processing industry.

A mutually profitable economic co-operation among the states of the Baltic region, European Union and the neighbouring countries in particular is of equal importance. The prospects for the region to enter a common European transport system (this would provide the option of coordinating the activitites of the Kaliningrad, Polish and Lithuanian ports in the matter of accommodating Russian, Belarus and Kazakhstan cargoes) are good, thus contributing to the solving of the problems of the regional power supply and to form an international complex on the Baltic coast (Sopot–Svetlogorsk–Palanga). There are prerequisites for industrial co-operation (for example, in shipbuilding and ship repairs) and for strengthening ties in the agricultural sector, building and building industry. Approximately three thousand Lithuanian builders have already been hired to work in the Kaliningrad region in addition to several Polish companies working actively in Kaliningrad. The regional demands include various types of products, produced by the building industry of the neighbouring countries.

At present, programmes of border co-operation are worked out, discussed and partially implemented. However, they should become more comprehensive and specific.

The future reinforcement of the regional policy, pursued by the federal government, will inevitably draw attention to the feasibilities, provided by the geographical position of the region and the development of export-oriented productions, that utilise domestic scientific-technical potential and process Russian raw materials for export to the external market.

The three sea ports – Kaliningrad trade port, Kaliningrad and Pionersk fish ports, small sea ports in Svetly and Baltyisk, river ports for vessels "river-sea", located in Kaliningrad and in Sovetsk – contribute to the conditions for development of sea transport. A massive cargo transit route runs through the region from Russia to the West and from the West to Russia. The Russian Federation has a distinct need for such an option. In 1994 the Russian ports along the Baltic Sea dealt only with 21 million tons of cargo, whereas 47 million tons were handled by the ports of the Baltic states. For these services the Russian Federation paid more than 200 million dollars, a sum which could have been paid to the Russian ports, had they been provided with appropriate capacities and furnished with an up-to-date level of technology.

The capacity of Kaliningrad ports (including fish ports) comprise more than six million tons of cargo a year, but in 1995 only half of this was used. According to the state experts' estimation, the capacity can potentially reach 12 million tons (that is less than the amount outlined in a number of suggested proposals), although considerable measures are required for the ports' reconstruction, necessary in order to have transit via the territories of Lithuania, Belarus and Latvia (increased traffic capacity, regulation of transport fees). In each case Kaliningrad's development as a transport link is dependent on the formation of a common economic space in the Baltic region (including Russia) and the measures to end the discrimination of Russian cargoes. If this is not the case, estimations of the ports' expansion will be void of any economic ground.

In order to increase the efficiency of Russian sea ports in the Baltic Sea area, interaction between St.-Petersburg and Kaliningrad transport complexes is needed.

An upgrading of the port capacities in the Kaliningrad or in the Leningrad regions entails ecological problems. If the services of the Baltic ports for Russian cargoes are cheaper than construction and exploitation of new Russian ports in the Baltic region, then investments should be used for other purposes (first of all, for reconstruction of production). Therefore, new construction projects are often rejected for ecological reasons and due to their industrial nature, as opposed to the projects of recreation zone on the Baltic coast. However, the final decision has not yet been made.

In addition to the sea connection, Kaliningrad should be part of the common system of European motor-, railroads and air routes. Unfortunately, the Russian government is not actively participating in international projects of co-operation in the Baltic region (e.g., the VASAB-2010 Project), whilst this involvement could draw more attention to Russia's interests and feasibilities in creation of a common transport net in the Baltic area.

As for machinery, one should look into the problems of each of the enterprises, as soon as they do not present a unified complex and there are practically no production ties between them. On the whole, one should pay attention to the consumption of material, in most cases taking into account that this is unwarranted in view of the remoteness of the raw sources.

Prior to organisation of the substituting productions in the sphere of raw-supplying regions (which will require at least five years), export-oriented paper and pulp industry still has good prospects. Moreover, provided that questions concerning full raw material consumption and the quality of products are solved, the preservation of these branches is a valid option even in the long term perspective.

The prospects of development in the sphere of fuel and energy complex should also be reflected upon. In my view the creation of new capacities (building of a new heating station estimated to reach 540 MWt) as an alternative to the present energy import is not sufficiently grounded. Such projects turn out to be quite expensive and the means, required for their implementation, can be used more efficiently in other fields. Actually, it seems to be more pertinent to study the problem of a falling energy consumption.

An extensive use of the local natural resources (rock salt, etc.), except for amber, is feasible only at significant expenditures and requires additional economic grounds. A large project of rock salt output with delivery to other RF regions as well as aimed at export is under consideration. There are also local projects of oil and natural gas processing, although the small deposits are hardly worth the on-site oil-processing. Instead there are deliveries to large processing enterprises (despite the fact, that the projects, concerning processing of imported oil are economically supported). However, the creation of small new productions utilising local turf, brown coal and building materials are not ostracised.

Kaliningrad's recreational capacities, consisting of a 140 km long coast, may be attractive for the Russian population and for foreign tourists as well. However, the creation of the appropriate infrastructure is conceivable only with the help of the federal investments and requires private domestic and foreign investments, too. There are programmes for regional recreational complexes and attempts for implementation are already underway.

Schemes for a varied production of a number of goods (for the regional population and for export) can be achieved by means of a special programme, presupposing development and endorsement of the small business. This programme has already entered into force, but its realisation has to be speeded up. It enables a rational use of the natural and labour potential of the region, and allows the implementation of these scientific-technical projects, suggested by the regional scientific and project design institutions. Finding a solution to many of the problems of the regional agro-industrial complex is conceivable along these lines.

For foreign investors the prospects of the region may be especially attractive as there is free access to the Russian market. This goes particularly for the various processing industrial branches (engineering, consumer-goods production). The opportunity to import parts for assembling and materials under the preferential terms, their further processing, output of ready-made products and the export of these products manufactured on the Russian territory, without taxation in other RF regions, may attract foreign investors. However, we cannot exclude the rise in taxes on a number of goods imported to Russia from various Western countries. The preferences are expected to substitute additional transport expenditure on the import of goods to the Russian Federation, but also provide a higher profit, being produced at a place with high consumer demands. Moreover, the region possesses a qualified working staff and a developed system of staff training.

The key question, predetermining further development of the region under different conditions, pertains to formation of the population's mentality. In this respect the region is already among five more advanced Russian regions. Developing the system of education and training of staff facilitates this process further, as does the advancement of strengthening the region's financial basis.

Admittedly, the present situation in Kaliningrad can be perceived as being more severe than the political and economic situation in Russia in general. This is mainly due to the position of an exclave. In addition to this, Russia's relations with the Baltic countries (especially with Lithuania), Poland and Belarus are of prime significance. The development of the exclave's position is highly dependent on these relations, i.e. elimination of barriers and reduction of prices for the regional transport connection with the main part of the Russian Federation, as well as realisation of the Russian export-import operations via the territory of the region.

Russia's political and economic relations with the EU countries are no less important. Should Russia be viewed, along with the Baltic states, as a future member of the EU, then Russia's relations with the Baltic states would be more firm and beneficial for the Kaliningrad region. In order to achieve this, both sides – Russia and the EU countries – should pursue what is in their mutual interest. Moreover, Russia's economy has to be turned into a market economy and the policy must be that of democracy, pending reforms underway in Russia. A future Russian market capable of import and export of various goods on a larger scale from and to Europe is extremely valuable for the overseas partners. It would increase the prospects of the Russian Federation integrating with the European Union. However, the Russian authorities and businessmen have yet to realise the advantages of the common market, void of any competition. The development of the Kaliningrad region as a free zone within the Russian and the Baltic (i.e. common European) economic space will serve as a promoting factor.

Formation of the common economic space (including RF), pending solution of continuous political questions would allow a dismissal of many questions (less dependence on the neighbouring countries with the help of formation of their own energy basis, searching for alternative transport connection, evading Lithuania, etc.).

It appears that settlement of the various complicated questions pertaining to the region's development is feasible. This opens up perspectives for turning the tide and introducing steps of development.

Notes

1 *On the emergency measures of economic stabilisation in the Kaliningrad region* (25.05.1994). Enactment of the Government of the Russian Federation N531, and *On the social-economic development of the Kaliningrad region* (12.08.1992). Enactment of the Government of the Russian Federation N573.
2 *On the Kaliningrad Region* (07.12.1993). Decree of the President of the Russian Federation.

References

Amber Island of Russia. Statistical Collection (1996), Kaliningrad: Regional State Statistics Committee Press.

Fydorov, G.M. and Y.M. Zverev (1995), *Kaliningrad Alternatives.* Kaliningrad: Kaliningrad University Press.

Fydorov, G.M.; Y.M. Zverev and V.S. Korneevets (1996), *Economic and social development of the Kaliningrad Region and foreign post-socialistic countries in the Baltic area.* Kaliningrad: Kaliningrad University Press.

Matochkin, Y.S. and A.Y. Barinov *et al.* (1990), *Conception of the free business zone in the Kaliningrad region.* Kaliningrad: Central Economic Development Committee of The Kaliningrad Region.

National Economy of the R.S.F.S.R. in 1960 (1961), Statistical collection. Moscow: Finance and Statistics Press.

National Economy of the R.S.F.S.R. in 1989 (1991), Statistical collection. Moscow: Finance and Statistics Press.

"Number of commercial banks and branches in regions of Russia" (1996), *Ekonomika i Zhizn,* 11: 4.

"Russia Towards the Millennium" (1996), *Voprosy Economici,* 2: 4-50.

The Kaliningrad Region in the Eleventh Five-Year Plan (1972), Statistical Collection. Kaliningrad: Regional State Statistics Committee Press.

The Kaliningrad Region in the Eleventh Five-Year Plan (1986), Statistical Collection. Kaliningrad: Regional State Statistics Committee Press.

The Kaliningrad Regional Statistics Committee (1996), Updated Information. Kaliningrad: Regional State Statistics Committee Press.

3   Kaliningrad – Relevant Options

PEER H. LANGE

Modernization for the 21st century: the relevant denominator

Pondering about the Kaliningrad *oblast* should focus on future parameters rather than depart from present conditions. The *oblast*, still retaining essential aspects of its Stalinistic past, is bound to share the ongoing turbulent development towards an electronically determined future, i.e. encounter conditions that fundamentally differ in most aspects from our present time. This development is under way both in the West and Russia – though the speed and determination may differ.

This conquered land is Russia's window to Europe – as St. Petersburg functioned in view to the West two centuries ago. It is a location almost encapsulated by a neighbourhood turning western in a dynamic fashion. Westernizing implies openness to the outer world and the globe. Westernizing means competition, and a dynamic development boosted by liberal and pluralistic freedom. However, the entity of Kaliningrad might be regarded by its neighbours as an alien element in need of adaptation in order not to block the changes imposed by modernisation. Hence the *oblast* is bound to be caught up by the tensions caused by its relation to the "great soil" (Russia's homelands) on the one hand and the increasing western world that surrounds it on the other.

Apart from geopolitical conditions, the *oblast* is exposed to dramatic structural challenges in the context of ongoing processes of development. It is required

- to transform from highly militarized and diversified economic structures modelled along the lines of a centralized and plan-bound economy to a structure of its own, one that allows socio-economic integration with the environment;
- to adapt to the ongoing modernization of the adjacent societal structures in the Baltic Sea region;
- to participate as a prominent and pioneering (instead of a remote and forgotten) part of Russia in the technological and structural

57

modernization of this nation;
- to act as Russia's forerunner in responsible participation in European affairs.

The effects of globalization

Globalization is one of the most demanding challenges of our days. Accompanying the rise of the information age, based on rapid electronization of every part of our economic and social structures, globalization does not allow any political entity to stay apart from it without severe consequences. The Kaliningrad *oblast* is no exemption from this. Almost the whole neighbourhood – Belarus being the single exemption – is obviously drawn into this process. Globalization exposes the competitiveness as well as social and political standards of a given political entity to worldwide challenges.

Consequently, any self-isolation, in a Stalinistic manner, will cause shortages in the accumulation of knowledge with negative consequences for development. An insight of the Gorbachev-leadership, which raised the awareness of reform is needed.

Neither the agriculture in the *oblast*, nor its lumber industry meet the standards of the external environment. The fishing industry is better off but lacks the political preconditions (law, tax, investment) needed to participate successfully in the surrounding free market system. Productivity requires that the costs are kept low. One of the characteristics of the former Soviet societal model consisted of hidden unemployment, i.e. ineffective organisation of labour.

At present the capitalistic model suffers from overproduction. A growing amount of unemployed has to be paid for by a declining workforce. This implies socio-political hardships.

The Kaliningrad *oblast* has been less exposed to heavy-industrialisation than many other parts of Russia. In particular, it has not been burdened by a heavy armament industry and related strains of conversion.

Poland as well as the Baltic countries are opting for middle-sized or small enterprises – the traditional base of their economic structures. Herein lies, if a similar pattern is followed, a chance for the Kaliningrad area to transform itself into a model-*oblast* for Russia as a whole. It has to be taken into account that globalization leads to a diversification of low-cost/low social standard labour and highly paid trend-setting ingenuity/higher social standards. Employment is distributed accordingly (as indicated by the present German problems).

It hence appears that Kaliningrad has to define its position on such a ladder of qualitative productivity and choose a way of participating in the distribution of labour – with regard to other parts of Russia as well as to external surroundings. One has to depart from the conception that globalization pertains to information and knowledge. The intellectual abilities required during the information age do not only rest on academic knowledge but hinge rather on the degree of modern education. This in turn is dependent on a high frequency of contacts originating with a broad freedom of movement.

This is why the Kaliningrad *oblast*, being more exposed to the outer "near abroad" than other parts of Russia, needs specific regulations that provide for this basic condition of modernization in line with global standards. Moreover, globalization rests on technical openness. This in turn creates the need for specific regulations if the exclave is to be linked up with the surrounding network of technical relations, especially communications.

For this to occur, an abrupt distancing from any Soviet-style is needed (and is partly under way). This is a must if Kaliningrad is to comply with its dynamic environment.

There is no denying, however, that globalization also involves extensive dangers and various destabilizing trends such as drugs, diseases, criminality or ecological damage.

The countermeasures also have a global reach. Russia is part and parcel of these efforts, although the specifics of the exclave of Kaliningrad require special solutions and regulations. This fact too pertains to the ongoing federalization of Russia, designed to overcome the weaknesses of the former over-centralized state structure. In one of its aspects, globalization means global investment. In order to attract investment, promising preconditions have to be created. Instability is, in this respect, the most effective hindrance to investment. Russia is unable to attract investment because of prevailing instability.

This goes also for Kaliningrad and the situation will only change if sufficiently stable conditions are opted for. For this to materialize, a certain distancing to mainland Russia is required and the so far sleeping beauty of the "Free Economic Zone" has to be woken up. Certain legislative self-reliance is also needed. This in turn makes it mandatory also to be recognized by the outer world as a stable region. That might call for some kind of self-determination in economic, social and socio-political questions, perhaps strengthened by specific international legal obligations.

Needed: A safe-way of its own between Western overproduction and present Russian under-productivity

Russia is presently struggling with disastrous under-productivity, caused by the breakdown of the socialist market system, the obligatory but difficult restructuring of the economic system, the lack of investment in Russia itself, capital leaving the country and a lack of solid state financing (tax income). In this context Kaliningrad may remain a remote, uninteresting appendix to Russia as long as it stays fully dependent on the all-Russian administration and financial support. Russia's interest in this area seem to be limited to holding on to a war-trophy, and any future oriented perspectives are lacking. Dependence on Russia's inherent under-productivity hampers linking up with the changes under way in the neighbouring states.

Germany, in contrast, is suffering from over-productivity in ship and car building, production of steel and agriculture. As a consequence, *Rationalisierung* as the new *Leitmotiv* means leaner workforce, and meaner output. Furthermore, traditional industries do migrate to new *Standorte*. In principle, the former peoples democracies and occupied Soviet republics are facing similar problems on a more limited scale while restructuring their economies: the workforce needs to be reduced and the quality standards have to be improved. The Soviet societal and educational model was predominantly oriented at mass production. Such production tends to become part of the market by leaning on labour and keeping the living-standard down.

If the welfare and prosperity of Kaliningrad itself is to take the front seat, a specific role has to be assumed, more in the line with the changes of the nearby environment and detached from Russia's difficulties of production similar to those of the *alte Länder* (as to inject a new German term into a Russian constellation) and typical for the traditional capitalistic structures.

From industry to services

Estonia serves as a model for turning from heavy industries towards services, which were previously underestimated. Service-production gains in importance in the information age. It is equally vulnerable to over-productivity as is industrial production and it also depends on unhindered relations with the outside world.

The Kaliningrad *oblast* is located amidst nations eager to create new and intense relations. One important example is the order in the air heavily militarized during the Soviet rule. Things are fundamentally changing from Warsaw to Tallinn – leaving the air above this *oblast* in the shadow. This complicates the transit to Kaliningrad, as Russia declined to be involved in this process of modernization when invited by the US initially to join the "Regional Air Control Initiative". The district may thus remain a remote area even to air-traffic. This conflicts with any perspective of getting involved in the air traffic servicing system developing around Kaliningrad – leaving aside the even more important defense-related implications and the consequent need for confidence-building leaning on modern technology.

Königsberg was and Kaliningrad is again connected to the West-European system of railways. It used to be an area linking in to the Baltic states. The West-European railway system is in the midst of a dramatic modernization process and there is a promise in the air that it may again play a decisive role in terms of transport. Rails are preferable to roads as the problems experienced in the alpine region indicate. The whole Via Baltica and related projects, including the linkages to Kaliningrad, have to be considered anew with this in mind.This is no small matter as the railway system in Russia, a remnant of the Soviet period, is below any modern standards. Investments in turn hinge on the view that the system is believed to have a future. As long as the perspectives of the "Amber region" (the Free Economic Zone of Kaliningrad) remain diffuse and are intimately linked to those of the mainland, Russia's foreign investors are not keen to transfer capital.

Kaliningrad's harbour potential pertains to the value of the region as a transport centre. It could play an important role in the servicing of northern Polish Prussia and Belarus. It has the potential of mediating rail cargoes from the west to east – and have the same function in regard to sea-/air-/land traffic services. The preconditions for this to occur consists of the existence of stable political perspectives, including free trade. This has been understood in all the Baltic states at the present stage of national reorientation and new cooperative patterns are emerging in defining future roles for the various Baltic ports. Also Russia has the option in the case of Kaliningrad to pursue a similar line instead of applying less promising avenues.

Communication in the age of information differs fundamentally from the Soviet style centralisation with every phone call having to pass through Moscow. Estonia has already completed the construction of a nation-wide mobile phone network. This aspect of modernization is still to be implemented in the case of Kaliningrad. Some promising steps have already been taken – although it remains to be seen, whether the macrostructures designed allow for an effective regional inter-operability.

The dialectics of integration and separation – eroding centralized states

Whereas in the West a tendency towards integration seems to prevail, the opposite seems to be true for Eastern Europe. However, that is a misleading impression. Also in the West one finds tendencies of diversification – be it regionalization or a breaking off of previously integrated parts of nation states or parts of the population. The need for economic cooperation or integration prevails in a similar fashion in the East. Taken together, there are dialectic processes of integration and disintegration. The question is which one of these ties in with modernization and the creation of welfare in the electronic age.

These trends run parallel with the fading role of the nation-state in the context of globalization and the diminishing role of European nation-states as traditional power-players. Russia is unable to claim the position of a superpower and shows signs of discomfort with its diminished role. At the same time Russia faces the need to establish a given degree of federalism, a challenge encountered for the first time in her history.

Russia lacks the historical experience of having colonies or exclaves encapsulated within other states. The Kaliningrad *oblast*, Sevastopol and the Dnjestr Republic are new phenomena exposing Russia to the challenge of managing such separated territories while at the same time introducing a certain degree of federalism. Consequently, the problem posed by

Kaliningrad is also part of a general problem. That is to say that the area is a litmus test for Russia's ability to abandon the Soviet heritage of overcentralization and to provide space for local differentiation. In the case of Kaliningrad this implies differentiation in adapting to the modernization process of the environment.

The outcome would be, if such a line is pursued, that the most westward location of Russia turns into the most westernized one. Reluctance to comply with the challenges implies, in turn, a rejection of the global process of modernization.

Relevant scales of interests

Moscow decides the fate of the Kaliningrad exclave. Decisions about the *oblast* hinge on the general estimations of Russia's position and role. The options for the region depend on how Russia's interests will be defined.

Horizons and limits of national interest

The defining of national interests is hard if not impossible. Men define interests, not nations. Nations are embedded in evolutions that create preconditions and parameters for the fate of nation-states.

However, there are some characteristics that allow for a cautious description of what Russia's major interests could be. Firstly, Russia left behind the Soviet (Marxist) visions of human development that separated the Soviet Union from the western world. Russia is thus far more ready to accept mutual interdependence and the need for cooperation. Russia has also been able to abdicate the roles of an empire and superpower. However, due to national pride, it is tempted to perceive itself as a "big power". This largely unfounded view tends occasionally to give raise to attitudes resembling former pretensions.

At present, the ongoing discussion about the army reform clearly shows Russia's limitations. The limits that are there will bring about a basic restructuring of the societal and economic fundaments. Russian national interests will be increasingly defined by internal demands.

Up till now, Kaliningrad has been predominantly treated by Russian politicians as an external problem. Instead, besides the need to assess it as a specific problem of Russia's federal structure, it needs to be conceptualized as a problem of internal modernization.

Russia between North and South, West and East

NATO is still seen in Russian threat analysis as part of a potential threat stemming mainly from the United States. The West in general has been accused of cheating Russia in conventional arms control and of depriving her of strategic strongholds won by Stalin. In this sense, Kaliningrad stands, together with the Kurilles and Sevastopol, for some kind of last resort.

Sometimes the exclave is seen, along with the Kurilles, as a conquered territory not to be given up. A picture of new encirclement arises, fortified by fears pertaining to a growing "southern threat". This threat is defined – if specified at all – in terms of disturbing ethnic influences rather than a serious military threat, i.e. differently from American perceptions, that tend to centre on the acquisition of means of mass destruction by "southern" powers. The worst case scenario of an alleged "western threat", aired by the former Prime Minister Ryshkov, consisted of the view that Russia could be the next victim of another "desert storm" carried out by the Western powers. Military threat assessments single out an alleged "invasion capability" of NATO in the northwestern theatre of military action (the Baltic area) according to NATO's overall amphibious capability – neglecting the never-aggressive political decision-making process within NATO, the dispersion of those amphibious means, their lack of readiness and the insufficient strength of the western invasion-capable forces against a powerful state with the power that Russia still appears to have.

As long as the world is viewed along these lines, Kaliningrad will be treated as a fortress rather than a door-opener to the outer world. This can easily become a self-fulfilling prophecy with self-isolation provoking isolation.

Kaliningrad's neighbourhood: a region in flux

Kaliningrad is part and parcel of the Baltic Sea region. It is Europe's fastest changing region. It turned from a frozen sea-lane of dormant communication into a vividly developing scenery – and not merely in the sphere of economy. The political changes are even more impressive. On the Southern coastline, the structural changes in Germany and Poland need no special naming: industrial and social reconstruction in Germany, industrial and socio-political adaptation to the standards of Western integration in Poland. The improvement of the relations between these two countries is an even greater achievement.

On the northern coast, Sweden and Finland reconsidered their neutrality and turned to the integrating Europe. They will both contribute a renowned constructiveness to the future structures of a greater Europe. The Swedish social model stands challenged, as does the German famous "social market system". Both of these have to be adapted to the new conditions of the information age and both nations will try to preserve the essentials of their societal models. Europe's North will have a stronger say in all-European affairs.

Ecologic responsibility is one of the characteristics of Europe's North. In this sense, the Baltic Sea appears to be a specific challenge to the community of the surrounding nations. This community already created joint regional political institutions being far ahead of other European regions; the Council of the Baltic Sea states being just one indication of this.

The promising cooperation in this area includes also the military sphere. Nowhere in European have regional cooperative activities reached a similar stage – except for the Bosnian peace-mission. It is quite telling that in the context of the Day of the Russian Fleet in 1996, it was just the Commander of the Baltic Fleet, who regarded the cooperative actions of his fleet its outstanding achievements – in contrast to all other Russian fleet commanders who paid tribute to rather martial assessments. Admiral Yegorov is posted in Baltiysk/Pillau.

Given the recent trends, it seems obvious it will not be NATO turning down options of cooperation once reaching Kaliningrad's borderline. There is space for the creation of further cooperative links even here. In all probability the region will become a breeding-ground for elements fortifying NATO's European pillar. It is also conceivable that Russian thinking will take another twist, i.e. that NATO's closing in offers an opportunity to influence developments in a positive vein instead of operating with perceptions of ever-pending danger!

Transformation – a hidden tradition

The hinterland of Baltiysk and its capital, the Kaliningrad, do not need defence in the first place, but they need to be utilized and linked up with cooperation. They are in need of transformation in line with the changes prevailing in Western (and Northern) Europe.

This would be parallel to Peter the Great's idea of opening a window to Europe, utilized particularly in St. Petersburg. He aimed at introducing modern shipbuilding in Russia and to do away with antiquated Russian customs and plaits. For this purpose Peter was ready to transfer the capital to the new border, i.e. something opposite to the present Muscovite mentality focusing on aliens closing in on the Russian "heartland".

The specific challenges of an exclave

The British exclaves of Gibraltar, Hong Kong, Diego Garcia and others can hardly serve as examples. They do not constitute backward areas in a developed neighbourhood. The standards of the motherland do not need to be altered in order to catch up with the surrounding neighbourhood of the exclaves.

Approval of diversity

Most exclaves have a history of developing their own specific lifestyles, different from the motherland due to their exposure to the surrounding world. If this has been the case once reacting to the lower standards of the environment, incorporating only some selected characteristics, there will in all probability be quite a lot of coping when the task is one of turning in to challenges posed by a far more developed environment.

The so-called "German provinces" of the Czarist empire (the Baltic provinces) were accepted as entities of their own until the wave of russification under Alexander III. The Baltic republics were, during the Soviet reign, privileged as living areas due to their "western" atmosphere. The young generation in Kaliningrad articulated, in polls taken, a self-understanding of belonging to the most "western-like" part of Russia. There is a tradition of building on diversification altering with suppression and efforts to suffocate diversity. The later periods have also been labelled by isolation and tensions.

From a possession to a burden or a specific role

The Kaliningrad *oblast* is often conceptualized as a trophy – a conquered area. It resembles a colony and an entity which has to be cultivated and developed in order not to turn into a burden. The Falkland Islands may serve as an example of such a trend.

This insight is presumably to some extent there to judge from the effort to create the Free Economic Zone of the amber district. The fact that it took two years to provide the first directive of 1992 with concrete content clearly illustrates the mental difficulties in dealing with the exceptionality of Kaliningrad. Prior to the demise of the Cold War, the region was part and parcel of a more general politico-economic landscape serving as a major military rear mainly housing a fishing industry. The main characteristic of this design rested on an almost complete amnesia of the area's past and its specifics.

More recently, a grass-root interest in the area's history has emerged. The local authorities seem to welcome and support this as it bolsters the view that the local Russian self-esteem is an acceptance of the German or rather "Western" past of the region. It finally achieves a profile and identity of its own.

Connection – the major issue multilaterally assured

A core problem of any exclave consists of its links to the motherland. Issues of transit or corridor problems have been, on occasion, the underlying reason for war.

Tensions escalated if mutual suspicions led to perceptions of access being threatened. If hence appears that tensions arising from the sensitiveness concerning access contradict with the interests of any party. Under the present conditions the parties in question are not just concerned about the linkages but have departed from the idea of being part of a wider region. In this broader perspective assuring access appears to be of a common interest and this goes also for settling border-problems. Both issue-areas require joint efforts in order to be settled.

Under the current conditions multilateral guarantees of members of a given region or/and of states with essential interests in the region, can be helpful in solving the problem of access and fear of isolation.

Such joint guarantees do not collide with national pride or infringe upon sovereignty but serve to bolster welfare and prosperity.

Focus turning from motherland to neighbourhood

Traditionally, motherlands decide upon and determine the fate of exclaves. They shield and guarantee the security and status of those detached configurations.

These tendencies are bound to change in our globalizing world in favour of collective arrangements be they regional or transregional. The local or (sub-)regional interconnections and interdependences call for this. Common interests push aside the narrow self-interests. The division into local interests and those of the mainland becomes sensible and recognizable. Politics, and political solutions become more complex and intertwined. The centre's interests declined in priority in the context of the local Russia, as a centrally steered entity, having suffered from the costs originating from the war in Chechnia. Cost-benefit-relations between centre-related and local-related postures are bound to change.

It seems in general that exclaves will evolve into partners of the central authorities rather than stay in the role of dependencies. If refused such an option, exclaves tend to turn into costly burdens. Much points to that exclaves will gain an enhanced status, although they will remain in secondary roles in regional international affairs as well as in central decision-making. In exclaves such as Kaliningrad turning into internationally recognized components of regional affairs, their say in regional affairs will grow and their position will improve within European-wide multilateral institutions.

Kaliningrad's role in the context of the Council of the Baltic Sea States constitutes a promising start and points in the direction of further improvements.

The socio-political sphere

Kaliningrad has predominantly been discussed within a framework elevating security or economic issues, but also socio-political questions need being taken into account.

Local identity

Kaliningrad does not pose any ethnic problems at the first glance. It is ethnically Russian. However, a kind of ethnic problem occurred with the Russian Germans trying to find a safe haven, one close to their lifestyle and original culture. In old Eastern Prussia, that is among its population, no resentment took place unlike in some other parts of Russia. It could be argued that some uneasiness emerged in Germany, linked to the international sensitivity concerning the issue of re-germanization. It appears that these worries also to a certain degree existed in government circles.

In fact, the problem of Germans searching for new ground appears to be part of a larger migration in the former Soviet Union. If reaching far, it requires decisions concerning the composition of the inhabitants. In order to cope with the challenges, there has to be a local settlement policy outlining the way in which the exclave is to unfold and stay with the prerogative of the right to free settlement.

A certain settlement policy will have to be outlined according to the special needs of the exclave rather than departing, for example, from migration in Russia in general and the need to find space for migrants to re-settle. The specific demands pertaining to the exclave's needs have to be taken into account, including culture in a broader sense. The educational structures have to be able to cope with the challenges and attention has to be paid to the prerequisites for effective self-administration. This amounts to an emphasis on elites, although differently from any colonial fashion, and paying attention to the smallness of the Kaliningrad exclave.

A recognition of the specific conditions

Some unresolved issues continue to slow down the pace of reforms in Russia. These include the problems of transferring ownership of land to foreigners, special rules and regulations (taxation) for foreigners and similar issues. The smallness of Kaliningrad allows steps to be taken more easily than in Russia at large. Converting old-style enterprises into private, consumer-oriented ones is more easy to accomplish.

The same applies to the provision of residency for foreigners and their enterprises, but the special regulations pertaining to the famous "Special Free Economic Zone" may improve the situation.

The future orientation

As already indicated, the prospect for the development of an exclave depends to a large degree on whether the exclave succeeds in tuning in to the ongoing development in the vicinity and the ability to pay tribute to the specific needs of the region.

This, then, calls for the exclave to link in with the broader regional developments. Such a participation in regional development planning provides ground for the transference of special regional knowledge also for mainland Russia to utilize in its own modernization efforts. For example the working group on economic issues of the Council of the Baltic Sea states may undertake the task of coordinating various aspects of modernization.

In the sphere of culture, the Soviet period gave rise to special habits and capabilities that as a rule do not correspond with the demands of a free market system. The *oblast*, in this regard, shares the general difficulties of the mainland's reform policy. However, the smaller proportions of the exclave make a renewal less painful and allow for a exchange with the neighbouring nations.

One example may be singled out: the Polish programme of the early 1990s to prepare Soviet/Russian army officers stationed in the *oblast* with civilian professions, mainly farming. Cross-border exchange in know-how will be needed to initiate and serve economic cooperation.

Attempts to return to power politics

Obviously power political considerations would hamper any progress in the (sub-)regional relations. Fortifying the exclave's role as a bastion or stronghold against the environment will hardly contribute to further cooperation.

Russia's oscillating desires – controversial global and local goals

Russia will, in the years to come, be occupied by implementing an army reform and a restructuring of its military power. This mode of reform pertains, in part, to the way in which the external security environment is perceived. As to Kaliningrad and the Baltic Sea region more broadly, the way the West is perceived in Russian thinking has a major impact.

So far, military requirements have mainly been pitted against the need to preserve parity in the view of the US or its alleged tool, NATO. The inconsistency of such thinking continues to influence Russian security-policy designs – particularly those related to NATO's enlargement. The risk is hence there that Russian policy may be tempted to utilize regional options for other than cooperative purposes.

It has been widely discussed in the West that heavy military concentrations in the Kaliningrad *oblast* are seen as threatening and thus adverse to good relations. Hence the demands for a "demilitarization" of Kaliningrad, sometimes misinterpreted as a quest for a complete abandoning of military force in the exclave. Actually, the concept should be understood as one pointing to reasonably sufficient military strength and seen as a suggestion to scale down the over-heavy forces in the region.

Mutually acceptable solutions will have to depart from agreed levels of military presence according to "legal" interests. This "legality" stems from a legitimate right to defend oneself – and stands in conflict with the capabilities to threaten others. The reduction of conventional forces in Europe (CFE) did elaborate some measurements for unacceptably high levels of force. However, the talks also demonstrated how difficult passing judgment on such a level is.

The specific constellation in and around Kaliningrad will, however, pose less difficulties concerning decisions on the amount of military forces in the area acceptable for the parties involved.

"Inter-operated security" in the electronic age

The central point discussed here consists of the belief that future security designs have to head to technological progress as a central factor. For example, explosives and delivery means will in the future be less decisive in comparison to new means of target acquisition, targeting, fire control and communications. In the long run, electronic targeting of electronic means and key functions may prevail over physical destruction caused to the enemy.

Moreover, vulnerability will be exponentially increased and cover dimensions which have not been seen as "military" in the past. In this vein, exclaves seem to be predestined to serve as places leading the way for special new approaches, cooperative analysis and mutual agreements.

This, in turn, elevates the importance of "regional arms control", an endeavour that might turn out to be as problematic as conventional arms control in Europe was at the beginning. In any case the need to solve security issues on a local or regional level is obviously growing in importance.

4 Kaliningrad's Military Economy

CHRISTIAN WELLMANN

Many studies and articles on current developments and future perspectives with respect to Russia's Baltic exclave, the *Kaliningradskaja Oblast*, address matters of the region's economy. Extensive attention is also paid to the region's military posture and its strategic significance. However, the intersection of both these issue areas, the military economy of the region and the challenge of conversion, is rarely dealt with. This is surprising as the continuous stress on the military aspects of security undoubtedly has a direct impact on Kaliningrad's economy, its performance and future development. And if true, that the region once constituted a "garrison state", as claimed by Petersen & Petersen (1993), the process of change to a lower military profile surely influences the economic sphere as well. My aim here is to chart out some of the militarily-related aspects pertaining to the region's economy. The process analysed is one altering the remnants of a highly militarised past of a closed region and adopting to the requirements of a less militarised future, one of opening up the region to a non-Russian Europe and thereby linking Russia with the rest of the continent.

However, the analysis is mainly restricted to the role of the armaments industry within the region. The question pursued is to what extent the industry in the *oblast* has been dependent on the procurement of arms and whether the conversion currently under way has changed the previous state of affairs. The two leading arms producing enterprises in the region are in focus for closer scrutiny. Further KIA Baltica is dealt with, a project which stands not only for the most remarkable conversion endeavour, but is also a significant industrial project in itself.

The contribution also briefly touches on what has to be regarded as the possibly even more important dimension of the region's militarily based economy: the economic impact, especially on the labour market, of the deployment of strong forces in the Kaliningrad region and of their on-going reduction in scale. However, this section is limited among other reasons because of limitations in access to data.

Arms production and industrial conversion

The situation in the eighties

To what degree was the Kaliningrad region's economy dependent on military production when the processes of transition to market economy and of reducing the level of military spending gained momentum in the early nineties? What was the magnitude of the regional production capacities potentially in need of being converted to civilian use if they were not to be closed down in the course of considerably reducing military spending?

The only relevant figures available are those pertaining to employment and they date back to 1985. They are based on GOSPLAN-data and indicate that less than 19,000 employees or 15.9 per cent of the industrial labour force of the Kaliningrad *oblast* were employed in industries part of the Military-Industrial Commission (VPK). If family members are included the figures account about 7 per cent of the inhabitants of the Kaliningrad *oblast* (845,000 at that time) as being dependent on this sector of economy. These figures (all taken from Horrigan 1992) indicate the degree of dependence of the Kaliningrad economy on arms related production to be above the average for the former Soviet Union, yet far below the average for the Russian Federation (24.8 per cent of the industrial workforce; 12.1 per cent of the population).

However, to avoid a widespread misperception of the data such as these presented above, one has to take into account that the statistics used, like any other basic data on Soviet or Russian arms industry, are delimited in institutional terms. What in Soviet terminology was named the military-industry complex (MIC) was an existing organisational structure and should not be confused with the Western analytical concept of a military-industrial complex. The Soviet MIC comprised of all those enterprises, which were owned by one of the nine former ministries responsible for armament, and no other. Hence data concerning the Soviet MIC always *include* the civilian oriented production of these enterprises as well. At the same time these data *exclude* any military related production activities of enterprises not organised under the MI-Commission. This is true especially for enterprises owned by the Ministry of Defence and the Armed Forces themselves, mostly specialised in repair and maintenance activities. The "no-names" or "numerics", as they were called, belong to this category: enterprises, which for reasons of secrecy were indicated only by the number of their post-box at a centrally located address in Moscow.

Due to Kaliningrad's geographical location, in the most western part of the Soviet Union and the vicinity of the potential Central European theatre of war, strong Soviet forces were deployed in the region. It would not have been any wonder under such circumstances, if industrial capacities specialising in repair and maintenance of weaponry and military equipment would have concentrated even more in the region. Indeed, two "no-names" can be identified: number 93 and 33. The former consists of a motor vehicle repair facility in the town of Kaliningrad (*Königsberger Express*, 1(5): 14), and the latter stands for a shipyard in Baltiysk, owned by the Navy and with a workforce of – at that time – approximately 1,000 employees exclusively engaged in the repair and maintenance of naval ships (*Kaliningradskaja Pravda*, 23 May 1992: 2).

Therefore, the GOSPLAN data referred to above, even if obviously biased by also including employees engaged in production for civilian purposes, may nevertheless provide a rough indication of the degree to which the Kaliningrad regional economy was dependent on arms related production. As to this specific region, the bias is at least partly counterbalanced by a second one, e.g. the exclusion of a substantial portion of industrial repair and maintenance of military hardware. Such activities definitely existed in the region on a larger scale. Interpreted in this way, the data indicates that at minimum some 10 per cent, maybe even more, of the *oblast's* industrial activities and jobs were dependent on armament and at stake with the decline of military spending. This state of affairs drives home the point that conversion of arms industry indeed constitutes a challenge to the economic policies of the region, not to speak of the companies directly affected.

Industrial conversion as a concern of regional economic policies

Based on the federal law "On Conversion in the Defence Industry in Russia" from 1992, a regional programme "The Conversion for the Years 1992-1995" was adopted in Kaliningrad on December 23, 1992. This programme was an attempt to introduce conversion "in an orderly way" (Zverev 1996: 136) once most of the defence orders for enterprises in the region had been cut without prior warning. Nine enterprises out of a total number of 29 machine-building enterprises in the region were listed as being defence oriented and therefore subject to the programme (see no. 1-9 in the table below). It was pointed out that the responsibility for designing and implementing conversion measures rested with the affected enterprises themselves. The programme aimed at supporting the "conversion enterprises" in this task. Based on the need for improvement in the region's industrial base and its infrastructure, priority goods and services were selected as being subject to support (farming equipment, equipment for the food processing industry, pumps and valves of different types for municipal services and rural buildings, sea containers, some consumer goods etc.). Some 2.5 million USD were estimated to be enough to cover the costs of the programme.

In fact, the regional conversion programme never really came off the ground and it had only a marginal impact. Problems with the allocation of sufficient finances to the programme was only one of the reasons. Just as important for its failure was a lack of understanding by both the managers from the respective enterprises and the staff from the regional administration, concerning the nature of the conversion process as well as the mechanisms and preconditions for a successful realising of such a programme (Zverev 1996: 136-7). Nevertheless, in 1993 the conversion enterprises were, on average, able to preserve their level of overall production in view of the previous year. They did so by increasing their civilian-oriented output by 61 per cent and thus compensating the losses in military orders (an exception was *Elektropribor* which experienced a decline in its military production by 93 per cent and a decline in its civilian output by 60 per cent). The turning-point came in 1994. Throughout the first half of the year the volume of military-oriented production declined further by 50 per cent compared to the first six months of 1993 (Reymann 1995: 17). However, at the end of the year also the civilian-oriented output had fallen by 30 to 80 per cent of the previous year's level (Zverev 1996: 137).

No wonder that apart from the specialised conversion programme, the issue of preferential support for enterprises in the process of conversion occasionally also entered the agenda concerning the attempts to establish a Free Economic Zone "Yantar" on the territory of the Kaliningrad *oblast*, i.e. a process consisting of a series of steps forwards and backwards finally ending at the beginning of 1996 with the establishment of a less ambitious "Special Economic Zone". For instance, when the Head of the Regional

Administration, Matochkin, in April 1994 partially implemented an earlier decree of the Russian President by granting tax preferences for some years to specific categories of enterprises in the region, the nine enterprises already subject to the above mentioned conversion programme constituted one of those selected groups of enterprises (Reymann 1995: 32). It has, however, to be added that these regulations neither had durability nor did a few years of deferment of tax payments (a central element of the preferences granted) imply a relevant support. This is so due to the overall payment crisis in Russia. The habit anyhow is to defer payment of taxes or to avoid these altogether.

In fact, the challenge of conversion remains a pressing and an unsolved issue. The "Kaliningrad-2000" programme is one indication of this. The group of experts, which formulated this comprehensive programme for regional economic development in 1995/96 on behalf of the *oblast's* administration and the United Nation Industrial Development Organisation (UNIDO), also comprised of a sub-team especially focusing on the issue of conversion. However, the results are not yet publicly available as the programme is still undergoing evaluation by the decision-making bodies.[1]

It may, nevertheless, be concluded that until late 1996 the conversion enterprises in the Kaliningrad region had to invent measures of their own with the lack of any systematically orchestrated support scheme. They had to find their own ways to tackle the situation – and partly did so in a contradictory but yet relatively successful manner.

"Yantar": the major industrial employer and arms producer in the oblast

The Joint Stock Company (JSC) Baltic Shipbuilding Plant "Yantar", located in the fringe areas of the town of Kaliningrad, was not only the largest arms producer in the region but also the only prime contractor for the production of complete weapons systems. All the other arms related enterprises in the *oblast* only supplied separate parts for or components of military hardware, which were assembled elsewhere. Yantar was also the largest industrial employer in the region and despite its dramatically reduced labour force it still holds this position. That is why the company and its current situation will be examined in more detail.[2]

Since its establishment in 1946 the shipyard has delivered some 466 ships and vessels of various types and scales (*Königsberger Express* 4(4): 1). One hundred of these have been civilian (including ferries of the

Sachalin class and oceanographic research vessels), whereas the others have been for naval use (among these landing craft and destroyers of the *Krivak* 1 and 2 class as well as the *Udaloy* class). Towards the end-eighties military production stood for 85 per cent of the total output. By 1994 it had fallen to some 50 per cent and by 1996 to 30 per cent of an overall volume that had fallen sharply. Currently, all navy-related activities consist of repair and maintenance. Naval construction ceased once "Admiral Tschabanenko", first of a new class of anti-submarine warfare frigates, was launched in summer of 1994 (*Königsberger Express*, 2(7): 6), although the Yantar management still has vague hopes that sometime in the future the company may receive an order for the construction of a second ship of the same class.

At the end of the eighties more than 8,000 employees (4,800 of them blue-collar workers) were listed on Yantar's payroll. By the spring of 1994 the workforce had dwindled to 5,800 (3,000 blue-collar workers) and the output had dropped by the same proportion as had the number of blue-collar workers. In autumn 1996 only 2,400 persons remained employed (some 1,700 blue-collar workers and 670 engineers and administrative staff), although, about 1,000 of them had not received any payment for several months and were finally sent on compulsory vacation. Throughout 1996 Yantar experienced a severe crisis accompanied by fierce protests and strikes by despairing workers. The background pertained to the overall situation of the Russian economy as well as the conditions that any enterprise faces operating under the prevailing circumstances in Russia. This situation of Yantar is also aggravated by the specific restrictions which are not primarily caused by the necessity of conversion, but are related to the fact that the enterprise is still an arms producer and – even though privatised in juridical terms – mainly owned by the Ministry for Military Production of the Russian Federation (it holds slightly more than 50 per cent of the shares).

In its endeavour to compensate for the decline in military production Yantar mainly concentrated on winning tenders for civilian shipbuilding and repair. Diversification into non-shipbuilding activities were not on the top of the agenda. In 1993 Yantar nevertheless formed the joint venture RIK-Container for the annual production of 20,000 sea-containers together with the Kazakhstani Karaganda Steel Mill (providing the steel) and the Italian engineering company Moneta Impianti (providing know-how) (Zverev 1996: 138; Reymann 1995: 53). However, due to a withdrawal of the financial backer the undertaking was stillborn. However, with the acquisition of contracts for shipbuilding, Yantar has been more lucky over the last few years. The management can point to a record of orders that many Western shipbuilders would be happy to own: a 4,000-ton wood carrier for a St. Petersburg based shipping company, ten sea-river-ships for a company in Kaliningrad, three 18,000 ton multipurpose cargo vessels for an Estonian client, two bulk carriers for a Maltese company, two pipe carriers for the Russian Gazprom empire, ten rescue boats for off-shore installations for the British Summerwind Navigation, and six ships for the Russian fishing fleet.

This list would make even more impressive reading if there were not specific obstacles existing that hinder a smooth course of business. In the initial contract with the Estonian shipping company, for instance, the construction of five units was agreed. Later two orders were cancelled and only one of the three ships remaining was delivered; two are still under construction, although at a slow pace as liquidity to cover the costs of the production under way is lacking; Yantar as well as the Estonian client are desperately seeking credits to finance the finishing of the two ships. With the Maltese order the situation is similar: the orders amounted to six ships but finally only two were taken under contract. As only 80 per cent of the production costs are financed externally (10 per cent down payment by the client, 70 per cent credit from the banks) whilst 20 per cent have to be pre-financed by the shipyard itself, Yantar was unable to take advantage of the complete tender. What has become standard in Russian economic life in the present day, namely solving problems of liquidity simply by not paying the bills, provides no solution in the specific case where the equipment for the ships, worth about half of the whole contract, has to be imported from abroad and paid upon delivery. If the consequences of Russia's currency policies (a parity grid for the rouble exchange rate) are added to the picture, one can see that the construction of new ships for export, on the one hand, brings work to Yantar, but on the other hand ends up in commercial terms causing a loss to the company of approximately 30 per cent of the value added.

The overall situation would be less dramatic if the military client would at least pay its bills to the company. However, in autumn 1996 the debts of the Navy and the Ministry of Defence to Yantar totalled 42 thousand million roubles (approx. 8.4 million USD). This is a considerable amount in the Russian economic environment. The bill for the latest repair and maintenance work on naval vessels has not been paid, but also bills for the "Admiral Tschabanenko" remained unsettled. As a countermeasure Yantar stopped its completion soon after the frigate's launching ceremony in mid-1994. Hence, Russia's most modern anti-submarine warfare frigate was still undelivered to the Navy at the end of 1996, and has stayed at the shipyard's docks – now for some two years with "98.9 per cent" of the construction work completed. The final work on the frigate will not start again, it is emphasised, before the customer settles its accounts with Yantar.

The overall sum which the military owed the company in autumn 1996, roughly equalled the aggregate wages which at that time had been earned by the employees, although not yet paid. Most of those unpaid for a longer period and routed to a compulsory vacation are employees from Yantar's naval division. In response, the workforce not only took industrial action but workers also rallied at the Headquarters of the Baltic Fleet. In the beginning of September 1996, some 3,000 demonstrators proposed the Commanders of the Fleet that a joint "March on Moscow" should be organized as also most of the navy personnel had been waiting for their salaries. A spokesman of the Fleet, however, rejected the idea and asked the Yantar employees to be patient (*Königsberger Express*, 4(10): 5).

But the employees can obviously not live on patience and Yantar is therefore experiencing a severe brain drain. Anyone who has a chance to do so – and those are mostly the most qualified ones – opt out. For instance, a competing shipyard in Klaipeda, Lithuania, has already received some 200 specialists from Yantar. Around, 160 out of 200 of those having participated in a scheme for further professional training later left the enterprise having found more attractive jobs elsewhere.

Working for the military hampers the economic well-being of Yantar in the forms of unpaid bills, thus creating a shortage of liquidity and increasing the brain drain. Moreover the shipyard is unable to profit from the Special Economic Zone on the *oblast's* territory as arms producers do not enjoy the granted preferences.

The shipyard also lacks flexibility in competing for repair and maintenance of foreign ships because, due to its military orientation, it may sign contracts only after having the approval of the federal agencies in Moscow, a procedure much too complicated and time-consuming to allow successful bidding in the hard-nosed competition with other shipyards in the Baltic Sea area.

A further drawback is that the shipyard is not eligible for preferential credits from the European Bank for Reconstruction and Development (EBRD) despite that the EBRD consultants after four months of in-house investigations attested that Yantar has a sound and credit-worthy basic structure. The credit applied for was not granted as the EBRD statutes do not allow the handling of credits to arms producers.

The Yantar management does certainly not resist arms production as such; they even appear to dream about becoming a successful participant in the arms export business, and of constructing warships for foreign customers having some purchasing power in hard currency. The management is even prepared to obtain orders for the repair and maintenance of foreign naval ships. "This is the type of business we know best; anything else we first have to learn" they argue. Despite these dreams the management seems, however, to be realistic enough to know that the world-wide arms export market does not really provide an alternative for Yantar. For the sake of the survival of the enterprise, they have to opt for the civilian market. This they have to do even if they in attempting to meet this challenge are confronted with disadvantages of the kind indicated above, i.e. hardships derived from Yantar's present status as an arms producer controlled by the Ministry for Military Production. The company is obviously squeezed between the necessity of meeting the requirements of both, a successful re-orientation to civilian markets and the reality of its existence as a dependent supplier to a military environment which lacks the means to pay for what it demands.

In search of a way out of this unfavourable double-bind constellation, the enterprise took an initiative of its own. An attempt was made to overcome its sub-ordination to the Ministry for Military Production and to get the company regrouped becoming part of some civilian-oriented state body. Although the approach failed, the management has not dropped the idea. For the time being, only measures have been taken upon which the enterprise could decide upon on its own. Whilst all arms related activities had to remain part of Yantar, the civilian activities have been transferred to three new companies, owned and directed by Yantar: one dealing with ship building, another with ship repair and a third with wood processing. This strategy which may function to bypass some of the obstacles mentioned before, also produces a new problem. As the new branches had to be left without a capital stock of their own, they are exempt from the possibility of getting credit from the banks.

It appears, in general, that the situation at Yantar reflects a more common dilemma plaguing the conversion enterprises: A complete halt in the production of arms drastically adds to the problem of conversion, while a continuation of the production of arms, even at a lower level, hinders a re-orientation towards civilian markets. This is so as civilian and military production follow a quite different logic. Against the background sketched above the hopes of Yantar as well as of some other coversion enterprises in the region are focused for the time being mainly on a project far off rom ship-building and from anything else the enterprises have ever been engaged in before: the assembling of Korean cars (see below).

Second place: the JSC Kvartz

The Joint Stock Company Kvartz, based near to the centre of the city of Kaliningrad, is a successor to the head plant of a former "production organisation" also named Kvartz which combined a design bureau and five plants throughout the Kaliningrad region. The parts were privatised separately. Besides JSC Kvartz the newly independent enterprises JSC Avangard in Ozersk and JSC Carat in Cherniakhovsk are also subject to conversion (Zverev 1996: 135). Kvartz, an engineering works and electronics manufacturer, was the second largest arms oriented enterprise in the *oblast*.[3] With 4,500 employees in 1990, 3,000 in 1994 and some 1,000 remaining towards the end of 1996, it is one of the top ranking industrial employers in the region. As with all other respective enterprises, with the exception of Yantar, Kvartz has not been engaged in the production of weapon systems. It functioned as a supplier of semi-manufactured components and production equipment to other Soviet and COMECON manufacturers of (mainly) military hardware and to research institutes. The range of products covered quite a large variety of items with basic parts of electronic products (especially electronic circuit boards) and sophisticated automatic vacuum equipment for the application of hardening, anti-corrosive, optical and other coatings as its main lines of production. The share of arms related production (dual use equipment included) was once as high as 85 per cent, although it dropped to some 30 per cent at the beginning of 1994 and soon ceased altogether. The production equipment, on average, seems to be of high standard: a lot was installed as recently as 1988 to 1990 and has been partly imported from abroad.

In the course of privatisation in 1994, state bodies wanted to divide the plant in the town of Kaliningrad into two. There was an attempt to sell the "21st Department", as it was called, separately to an obscure Moscow-based company, publicly speculated about to function as a front for the Ministry of Defence in an endeavour to prevent private investors from gaining access to militarily sensitive technology. The workers and part of the management resisted these plans as the department in question was taken to be the most modern as to equipment and technologically the most developed part of the whole enterprise. If separated from Kvartz, the company would be unable to survive. The employees went on strike and held a demonstration in front of the regional administration building. Finally, the case was settled in court: Kvartz remained undivided. The employees and the managers received 51 per cent of the shares; however, a "golden share" remained with the Russian government, providing the Department for Electronic Production, i.e. a division of the Ministry for Military Production, the right to veto decisions (Zverev 1996: 135).

Throughout the recent years numerous conversion and diversification activities and projects as well as involving international co-operation have been announced by representatives of Kvartz. Seemingly, without providing the company with a new stable and long-term foundation, they have been effective enough for the company to survive for the time being. The company is there, although at a considerably reduced level of output. The management tries to cope with the splits that have opened up. On the one hand, it seeks long-term Western investors and customers enabling a staying in the high-tech market, and, on the other hand, tries to achieve short-term survival by manufacturing low-tech products and engage in trade and service activities. The company's information sheets resemble a department store's catalogue: apart from the equipment for vacuum coating one will find metal roof panels, circular saws, electric bells, safes, computer games, washing machines, air extractor fans, wooden furniture and many more items. Further, Kvartz is also active in the recycling of valuable metals, engages itself in wholesale and barter trade, arranges sales exhibitions, operates a hotel, a pub, a paid parking lot, and runs an exhibition hall as well as shops.

Such an extreme diversification into a broad range of activities results in the enterprise presenting itself in a way which does not allow the identification of a profile of what its competence really is about. Having to orient itself primarily on the Russian market, the management may be provided with just the current option of running Kvartz. Yet, this strategy contradicts the attempts to obtain Western capital for the enterprise's vacuum coating technologies. One surely cannot gain a profile as a high-tech company, while at the same time proudly presenting a broad list of standard products. The management of Kvartz, however, does not seem to be aware of this contradiction.

One may therefore summarise that Kvartz provides an example of another contradiction that many conversion enterprises have to tackle: the contradiction between the need to follow a long-term strategy of providing the company with a new profile that is both consistent and convincing on the markets and the need to assure contracts in the short-term. Again, as is the case with Yantar, a decisive step forward might consist of the project of assembling Korean cars in the *oblast* (see the subsection below on KIA Baltika).

EDB Fakel and other conversion enterprises

The third largest military-oriented manufacturer in the region was seemingly the Experimental Design Bureau (EDB) Fakel. Out of a workforce consisting of some 2,000 employees 95 per cent was employed in dual use space technology (mainly propulsion systems for the steering of military and civilian satellites). This field of activity had declined to 60 per cent of its shrunken total output by 1992. The company became involved in medical technology (laser surgery) (*Kaliningradskaja Pravda*, 2 June 1992: 2). Nevertheless, the enterprise has remained fully government-owned and will not be privatised as it is considered to be strategically important (Zverev 1996: 135). In the Soviet period Fakel was prevented from exporting but it managed to get some export orders in the aftermath of its first presentation abroad in March 1991. A Kaliningrad based newspaper reported this success with pride but at the same time it protested against the decision-makers in far off Moscow refusing to provide Fakel with further orders: "The White House in Washington knows more about 'Fakel' than the White House in Moscow"(*Kaliningradskaja Pravda*, 2 June 1992). Fakel continued design work on its stationary plasma thrusters, a unique technology; a new type for commercial communication satellites successfully passed durability tests in 1994/95. The tests were made within the framework of a Russian-American joint venture with International

Space Technology Inc. and Space Systems Loral, Atlantic Research (*Königsberger Express*, 3(3): 3; Zverev 1996: 133).

The JSC Stroydormash, also based in Kaliningrad city, was during the German period a main railway repair shop, whilst in the Soviet era more than 60 per cent of its output consisted of manufacturing mechanised bridges, dummies of Soviet missiles and other items of military nature. The number of employees fell from 2,500 to less than 1,000 at the end of 1994 and, even those remaining have little to do and receive wages only irregularly. Stroydormash was – together with Yantar and Kvartz -one of the three enterprises in the focus of the "Conversion 1992-1993" programme. It received priority treatment (Reymann 1993a: 5), but with little or no effect. Throughout recent years money has been earned by engagement in occasional subcontracting work of less ambitious nature. Some subsidies have been received from the regional administration. Stroydormash definitely is in bad shape. It hence attracted some public attention when the workers got an anonymous offer to sell their shares of the privatised enterprise for an unusually high price, while the management, fearing for its position, threatened those workers willing to consider the offer with dismissal. Speculations concerning the reasons why someone would be interested getting control of the enterprise despite of its dismal performance, centred on the fact that the enterprise has an unique location. It is located along the only railway line where Russian and European width of tracks meet (*Königsberger Express*, 2(10): 9). This implies, as to the future perspectives of the enterprise, that they may remain bleak as investors are mainly motivated by speculations in real estate.

The JSC Kaliningradbummash, with a workforce of a 1,000 people and formerly a manufacturer of road construction and engineering equipment, is based in the vicinity of the town of Kaliningrad and is nowadays primarily engaged in the repair of German second-hand cars (Linderfalk, 1996).

As to the other conversion enterprises listed in the table, little or nothing is reported except that most of them have totally opted out or remain only marginally involved in arms related activities. The two "no-names" on the list might be exceptions to the rule although no. 94, the motor vehicle repair shop no. 94 has cut its workforce by half in 1993 (*Königsberger Express*, 1(5): 14) and No. 33, the Baltiysk naval shipyard, had by 1992 ceased to work exclusively for its owner, the Navy. In the latter case efforts were made to diversify it into production-lines for the repair and maintenance of merchant vessels on the one hand, and into non-shipbuilding activities on the other, i.e. bedsteads, elements for prefabricated buildings. (*Kaliningradskaja Pravda*, 23 May 1992).

KIA Baltika: a way out?

On July 30 the South Korean motor vehicle manufacturer *KIA* signed a preliminary agreement with the regional administration on establishing an assembly line for eight models of KIA designed cars in Kaliningrad. With 20,000 cars to be produced in the first year and later on 50,000 cars annually (Linderfalk, 1996) the project, named KIA Baltika, has dimensions making it highly relevant for the overall economy of the Kaliningrad region. It constitutes, at the same time the largest conversion endeavour in Kaliningrad being decisive in importance for several of the conversion enterprises.

The assembly lines to be mounted at the Yantar shipyard would initially provide 1,000 new jobs.[4] Production is bound to start in mid-1997. During a first phase all components will be imported from KIA and its sub-contractors abroad and gradually imports are to be substituted by local production, which by the year 2000 is planned to cover some 60 per cent of the overall output. This makes the project important also to other conversion enterprises in the region: especially Kvartz and Kaliningradbummash are viewed as assuming the role of major local suppliers to KIA Baltika. With a regional network of suppliers in place and the indirect effects taken into account, the project, according to one estimate, will create some 50,000 jobs in the region (Linderfalk, 1996).

KIA Baltika will be run by a Russian consortium consisting of several partners, including, inter alia, the Energotransbank, a financial motor of the undertaking, Yantar which will hold a share of 20 per cent, and last but not least a Russian manufacturer of small lorries, Camas. The latter is crucial as Camas will contribute with experience in manufacturing and the marketing of cars.

If KIA Baltika becomes a reality along the lines hoped for, it would imply a turning point for the stagnating economy in the region and a major breakthrough for the Special Economic Zone. Accordingly, it has drawn much domestic as well as international attention. However, the plans have also been met with strong scepticism. Is the Korean offer to be taken seriously or is it simply an attempt to get hold of a bargaining chip for negotiations with other partners elsewhere in Eastern Europe? The announced beginning of the assembling of the first cars was frequently postponed; the Energotransbank experienced a financial crisis; and Kaliningrad Governor Gorbenko, elected in autumn 1996, rejected the idea that the Regional Administration should stand as a guarantor of credits for the project, which he had inherited from his predecessor Matotschkin. (*Königsberger Express*, 5(2): 9 and 5(4): 8). The risks involved were seen to be too large.

On the other hand, by December 1996 already 60 per cent of the assembly equipment had been shipped in 800 containers to Kaliningrad and stored on the premises of Yantar. A number of Yantar employees were at a KIA plant in South Korea for on-site technical training on how to operate an assembly line. In the view of the Yantar management this proves that KIA is serious about the project. However, it has to be added, that doubts prevail as to the production facilities shipped over (*Köningsberger Express*, 5(4): 8). They appear to be excess equipment from a Nissan plant in Greece, although having a value of some 55 million dollars (Linderfalk 1996). It has also to be kept in mind that KIA's involvement is bound to remain limited. The commercial risk rests with the Russian consortium. The role of the Koreans consists mainly of providing the technology, and selling to KIA Baltika the components needed.

This is why KIA will not suffer seriously if the undertaking turns out to be a failure in commercial terms (in 1995 KIA sold only 50 cars in Russia and expected to reach some 4,000 in 1996 (*Königsberger Express*, 5(1): 3). It is hence not KIA's commitment that constitutes the most vulnerable factor with respect to a final take-off of the project, but the core issue pertains rather to the ability of the Russian partners and the political authorities to provide the finances needed for production and marketing as well as offering a functioning infrastructure (ports, roads, railways). The project is estimated to require some 250 million USD during its initial phase and altogether 1,000 million USD over the coming five years in order to develop a network of regional suppliers (Linderfalk 1996).

The current record

The results of the recent attempts to do away with the dependence on arms procurement of core elements of Kaliningrad's mechanical engineering industries may be summarised as follows towards the end of 1996:

a. A majority of the enterprises have not received any new defence related orders for some years. Military production has in most cases come totally or almost totally to an end (at least no. 4 to 7 and 10 in the table – Zverev 1996: 137 – and no. 3 – see above).

b. In the case where production for military purposes has continued, the contractors seem nevertheless to have a problem in getting their bills with the Defence Ministry settled. As a consequence the lack of working capital is aggrevated and the employees often remain unpaid which in turn speeds up a brain drain: the most qualified employees are the first to leave the enterprise (most obviously in the case of Yantar).

c. All plants have considerably reduced their personnel. In 1994 some 3,500 persons remained directly engaged in defence production in the *oblast* (about 5 per cent of an overall industrial labour force in decline. The figure was still above 10 per cent during the mid eighties). In 1994 the share of defence oriented production had dwindled to some 3 per cent of the region's total industrial output (Kaliningrad Regional Office of State Statistics, referred to in Zverev 1996: 137). Today, two years later, the figures are in all probability even lower.

d. Void of any systematic support schemes the enterprises affected by cut-backs in defence spending have been forced to find their own ways to tackle the situation.

e. It appears at a first sight that the largest arms producing enterprises were the most successful in restructuring their activities (although a comparison is difficult as also the civilian enterprises have undergone a tough period). Moreover, the achievements did not originate with any grand design but rather from a day to day muddling through. Therefore, some of the potentials, which the enterprises in principle have, were wasted and the approach applied did not provide any long-term perspective for getting out of the crisis.

f. The project of establishing an assembly line for cars completed by a regional network of suppliers may deviate from the overall pattern. However, this project has not yet really taken off and its potential for commercial success remains uncertain.

Reduction of military deployment

Much attention has been devoted to the strength of Russia's Armed Forces in the Kaliningrad region. This has merely been discussed in terms of security policy and foreign affairs, but not as an economic issue. It is obvious, however, that any attempt to get a grip on the economic structures of the region are shaped by elements of a military economy remains incomplete if only arms related industrial production is taken into account. The larger the garrison, the stronger is the impact on the regional economy, especially the effects on the labour market and local purchasing power. The more it is reduced in scale, the larger becomes the need to substitute the possible negative effects by converting manpower and transforming military bases into civilian use. These issues, however, seem to be quite a taboo in Kaliningrad as they are regarded to be questioning the role of the military in Russian politics and society.

It has been argued that till the beginning of the nineties some 50 per cent of the region's population – family members included – earned their living through activities connected with the military, either as soldiers or civilian employees in military service, recreation facilities or in the arms industry (e.g. Hoff & Timmermann 1993: 12). Even if those employed in industry, discussed in section 1, are ignored, the figure revolves around 35 per cent to 40 per cent (this estimate being in all probability on the high side). 50 per cent definitely represents an overestimate. However, the fact that such estimates circulate, indicates that the military organisation remains a key element in the region's economy.

The number of soldiers deployed in the region has been the focus of much debate. The confusion pertains, in addition to a restricted openness on the part of the Russian authorities, to a constant flow of troops in and out of the *oblast* in the context of the withdrawal of military units from the Baltic States, Poland, Czechoslovakia and Germany between the years 1990–1993. However, the period has been an exceptional one and will hence be left outside a discussion about the economic impact of military stationing in the *oblast*. In a sense a more "normal" period started at the beginning of 1994.

According to the 1994 edition of The Military Balance, the ground forces in the Kaliningrad region consisted of some 38,000 soldiers (International Institute for Strategic Studies 1994: 117). However, this figure does not accurately mirror the number of soldiers in the region as it omits both the border troops and the internal security forces as well as the navy which in the case of the Kaliningrad region is of considerable importance (with the headquarters of the Baltic Fleet and Baltiysk as its main base). Against this background the overall number of soldiers reached an estimated figure of 55-60,000 in 1993/94.

The amount of soldiers equals to some 10–11 per cent of the region's 550,000 inhabitants of an age capable of work, and to 20 per cent of all the males within that group. If compared to the population working in the economy (i.e. excluding people unemployed, in prison and other custodial institutions, enrolled in schools and institutions of higher education or professional training, women on pregnancy leave, those on the payroll of the military, and others) the percentages would even be higher. In other words, more people in the Kaliningrad region are employed in the military sector than in any other branch of the economy, except the overall industrial sector. The latter had 99,700 employees in 1994, while agriculture, education and culture, trade, transport and communications, or any of the other branches of the economy, including government organisations, had a lower figure. (Kaliningrad Region Committee of State Statistics 1996: 21).

In addition to the direct impact of the military on the regional labour market (the military employing a considerable share of the male population), there is an indirect effect (the military acting as a consumer of local production for its everyday needs) and a multiplier effect (the soldiers and their families spending their earnings on private consumption). As there is no reliable data available on these additional average earnings, only estimates are possible, although these have to be kept in mind. It is obvious, however, that the region's economy is quite dependent on the military.

This also implies that the economy is quite vulnerable to a decline in the means allocated to the military, as has been the case in Russia during the recent years.

The amount of soldiers reduced in the Kaliningrad region remains a disputed matter, although there is agreement that a decline has taken place. Compared to the 38,000 soldiers in 1994, the 1996 edition of The Military Balance gave the figure of 24,000 (International Institute for Strategic Studies 1996: 114) indicating that there has been a decrease by a third in two years. This seems to imply that the overall figure is around 40,000 in 1996. The Deputy Commander of the Baltic Fleet claimed that some

30,000 troops were deployed in the *oblast* in 1996 (*Interfax/BNS*, 4 November 1996). However, one can safely assume that the military have added to the strains of the regional labour market by removing some 5-10,000 employment opportunities annually from the market over the past few years.

In its prognosis regarding the development of the labour market in 1993, the regional employment exchange estimated that 7,000 former military and their dependants will be seeking a new job; 4,600 were expected to contact the job centres, with 2,150 of them finally being found eligible for unemployment benefits (Reymann 1993b: 29).

Despite the considerable number of ex-soldiers entering the labour market, no schemes have been developed for re-training or re-integration of this group, although retired officers enjoy a privileged status in comparison with unemployed civilians, provided that the officers in question are not yet eligible for a pension. They have a privileged position once candidates are chosen for professional re-training courses with a duration of some three to six months. These courses are run by altogether 68 institutions in the Kaliningrad region and they are financed by the job centres. According to the Regional Employment Centre the former officers mostly have comparatively few problems in finding a new job on the civilian side, as most of them have a solid training in some relevant sphere, especially in technical professions. Only former commissars are said to be exposed to the danger of long-term unemployment.[5]

In autumn 1996 some 730 former officers were categorized as unemployed (out of a total of 23,500 unemployed) in Kaliningrad. However, this figure might be misleading. In fact, the number of retired military personnel seeking a job and registered with the employment exchange is considerably higher. The reason for this is that in Russia all those eligible for at least a minimum pension after sufficiently long service in the military, are not categorised as being unemployed, although they often have to strive for an additional income in order to earn a living. For example in the city of Kaliningrad, those former soldiers registered at the job centre, although not viewed as unemployed, outnumber those who – according to the statistics – are unemployed.

The regional pattern of former officers unemployed is quite imbalanced. In the city of Kaliningrad, housing almost half of the region's inhabitants and the largest garrison, only a few dozen ex-soldiers registered themselves at the job centre, in autumn 1996, whereas in the rural towns and districts the concentration of unemployment both was much higher in absolute and relative terms. Moreover, their period of unemployment lasted in general much longer (150 officially unemployed in Bagrationovsk, 130 in Cherniakhovsk, 50 in Sovietsk, 50 in Baltiysk etc.). This distribution reflects a particular aspect of the social situation of the ex-military, namely a housing problem. In the opinion of the Managing Director of the Regional Employment Centre, and certainly also in the view of the soldiers themselves, this is a much more pressing problem and harder to overcome than finding new employment.

In general, there is less space available per capita in the region – and the city in particular – than in Russia in general as well as in Russia's north-western districts (Reymann 1995: 26). Hence those coming from rural garrisons do not have an opportunity to move to the larger towns or even to the city of Kaliningrad, i.e. locations with a much better chance of finding new jobs. Instead, they have to remain at the place of their former deployment, detached from potential opportunities of employment in the industrial and service sectors, in the communal homes provided to them by the military (with several families sharing the same flat). When the Baltic Fleet closed all its installations on the Kaliningrad spit beginning September 1995, some 1,500 military people and their family members stayed there even when the ferry line to mainland Baltiysk came to a halt and the continuation of medical services was uncertain as the Baltic Fleet provided both of these services (*Königsberger Express* 3(12): 9). Programmes for easing the housing situation for former military personnel would undoubtedly be a central element in any strategy aiming at a re-integration of the former military into civilian life. Such a programme would also contribute to the preparedness of the military to accept further military reductions. "I invite all my visitors to bring along some bricks", said Admiral Yegorov, Chief of the Baltic Fleet (*Frankfurter Allgemeine Zeitung*, 3 March 1993).

Concluding remarks: military spending as a hidden form of subsidies

In view of the level of arms-oriented production and the level of military deployment with its direct and indirect economic effects, the *Kaliningradskaja oblast* has obviously been heavily dependent on military expenditure. Its economic structures have been shaped by this fact. As this money originated with the federal budget, it also constituted a way of injecting federal subsidies into the region, and this without having to single them out or legitimise them in any particular manner.

Nowadays these hidden subsidies (or to put it differently: the way in which federal taxes collected in the region were re-transferred to the regional economy) have largely vanished. Arms-oriented orders going to the local industry have almost completely vanished. The number of "employees" on the payroll of the Ministry of Defence has considerably declined. Moreover, due to a lack of sufficient funds, the military personnel still there in 1996 had to wait for their full salaries for months. The military institutions were unable to pay the local suppliers (electricity, foodstuffs, public transport etc.[6]). With a halt in the flow of federal subsidies via the defence budget, the crisis in the Kaliningrad economy took a dive. This may be viewed as a core reason why the region's economy, with its military emphasis, experienced more hardship than the Russian economy in general.

Obviously any attempts to re-install the former centrality of the sector are unfounded. The analysis points to that the subsidies of a military nature have to be substituted by an equal amount of non-military transfers to the region. However, the federal budget currently lacks the resources needed. Moreover, it has to be taken into account that the legitimacy of the military economy leans on the importance of providing so-called "national security", e.g. a highly self-enforcing goal, underpinned by the image that it represents a common interest. The civilian type of subsidies are, in turn, perceived as budgetary transfers and measures of economic policy serving vested (regional) interests, and hence more vulnerable in the political decision making process to competing interests. This is why local and regional politicians, hand in hand with the local military, usually prefer lobbying for "their" garrison to be maintained instead of supporting a conversion of the defence budget to civilian activities. Also the regional administration of the Kaliningrad *oblast* has frequently failed to bring Moscow finance programmes of regional economic development, including the "Conversion Programme 1992-1994".

The remaining alternative seems to consist of converting and restructuring the regional economy leaning on its own capacities. The adjustment of an economy formerly based primarily on an internal cycling and a re-distribution of resources by means of military allocation, to one linked up with an external, European or even world-wide market, is already under way in the Kaliningrad region. Obviously such a comprehensive restructuring is accompanied by a severe crisis and involves hardships for the people affected. Failures and set-backs are part of the process. A more co-operative stance on the part of the military itself, in converting additional infrastructure from military to civilian use ("base conversion") would surely facilitate the change. Considerable amounts of energy and financial resources could be saved by avoiding unnecessary projects (e.g. opening increasingly the Baltiysk harbour for civilian purposes instead of opting for the construction of altogether new port capacities outside of Baltiysk). Although considerable challenges remain to be tackled, it may also be observed that people in Kaliningrad have made some progress. The regional economy shows clear signs of strengthening its civilian side.

Notes

1   For a rough sketch of the recommendations see Zverev (1996: 140), who acted as a member of the sub-team.
2   Unless stated differently information concerning Yantar is drawn from personal conversations with the company's General Director, Leonid Y. Zmachinskij, in June 1994 and with the Technical Director, Boris Krout, in December 1996. Additionally, some items are taken from an article "Yantar is Changing its Profile": *Kaliningradskaja Pravda*, March 13, 1993.
3   When not stated otherwise information concerning Kvartz is drawn from Wellmann, 1994: 7-11, and a personal conversation with the company's General Director, Vadim A. Schepkin, and two of the Deputy General Directors in December 1996.
4   Unless stated otherwise, information concerning KIA Baltica is drawn from a personal conversation with Yantar s Technical Director, Boris Krout, in December 1996.
5   This section and the following one are based on talks with the Managing Director of the Regional Employment Centre, Anatolij A. Volick, in December 1996.
6   One example is quite telling: When the regional railway company in March 1996 was confronted with a shortage of functioning engines, and hence unable to operate all scheduled services, it ceased to run the Kaliningrad-Baltijsk line, one mainly used by military personnel. They are by law exempted from paying

fares individually, and instead the company has been reimbursed collectively by the military authorities. With one year behind in payment violent disputes occurred between conductors and soldiers (*Königsberger Express*, 4(4): 14).

References

Hoff, Magdalene and Heinz Timmermann (1993), *Kaliningrad (Königsberg): Eine russische Exklave in der baltischen Region. Stand und Perspektiven aus europäischer Sicht.* Köln: Bundesinstitut für ostwissenschaftliche und internationale Studien (Berichte 17).

Horrigan, Brenda (1992), "How Many People Worked in the Soviet Defense Industry?" *RFE/RL Research Report* 1 (33): 33-39.

International Institute for Strategic Studies, IISS (1996), *The Military Balance 1996-1997.* Oxford: Oxford University Press.

Kaliningrad Region Commitee of State Statistics (1996), *Kaliningrad Region in Figures. Concise statistical handbook.* Kaliningrad: Kaliningrad Region Commitee of State Statistics.

Linderfalk, Björn (1996), "Customs-free zone attracts South Koreans. Will KIA Motors break the deadlock of Kaliningrad investments?", *The Baltic Times*, November 14-20, p.16.

Petersen, Phillip and Shane Petersen (1993), "The Kaliningrad Garrison State", *Jane's Intelligence Review* 5(2): 59-62.

Reymann, Sybille (1993a), *Aktuelle Entwicklungslinien, Problemfelder der Wirtschaftspolitik und ordnungspolitische Veränderungen in der russischen Region Königsberg.* Hamburg: HWWA-Institut für Wirtschaftsforschung (Report 121).

Reymann, Sybille (1993b), *Die Russische Region Königsberg: Ausgewählte Probleme der Wirtschaftspolitik: Studie III.* Hamburg: HWWA-Institut für Wirtschaftsforschung (Report 130).

Reymann, Sybille (1995), *Kalininingrader Gebiet: Wirtschaftsentwicklung und -Politik im Herbst 1994 – Studie IV.* Hamburg: HWWA-Institut für Wirtschaftsforschung (Report 150).

The International Institute for Strategic Studies, IISS (1994), *The Military Balance 1994-1995.* London: Brassey's.

Zverev, Jurij M. (1996), *Russlands Gebiet Kaliningrad im neuen geopolitischen koordinatenfeld.* Köln: Berichte des Bundesinstituts für ostwissenschaftliche und internationale Studien (BiOst), no. 6.

5 Environmental Issues of the Kaliningrad Region

HELENA KROPINOVA

Introduction

The Kaliningrad region spans over 15.1 thousand square kilometres. The coastline is some 140 km long, and the maximum distance from the sea shore is nowhere more than 250 km. In addition to the coastline proper, there are also the lagoons that add approximately 280 km to the coastline. The lagoons reach far into the region itself.

The location at the Baltic Sea and the particular landscape is, however, not only beneficial. The natural conditions are in a number of ways unique and represent a diversity as indicated for example by the Kuronian spit with its rare dune landscape. Woods, meadows and bogs, i.e. uncultivated land, occupies about ¼ of the whole territory (Kucheryavy & Fedorov 1989: 54). On the other hand territorial afforestation is scarce comprising only 17 per cent of the overall area (in Lithuania the figure is more than 30 per cent, in Sweden 56 per cent and in Finland 52 per cent (*Vision and Strategies around the Baltic Sea 2010* 1994: 28).

Due to human activities, the natural vegetation in the Kaliningrad region has been altered. The forests are mainly planted and meadows have an artificial character. A developed system of roads – in view of other parts of Russia – makes the whole territory accessible for its inhabitants, this resulting in a high recreational pressure on the remaining natural areas. The prevailing situation reflects a lack of experience in Russia in dealing with the challenges and in the maintaining of a sufficient ecological balance. Success in dealing with the issues at stake is often mandatory as, for instance, many parts of the regional lands nearby the Kuronian and Vistula lagoons are below the sea level. They form so called polder lands and occupy about a thousand square km. In the case of dykes giving in, some 86.000 inhabitants could find themselves living in submerged areas.

These facts characterize the environmental features of the region. There are a number of issues in need of urgent remedy and there are problems pertaining in essence to all sectors of the biosphere. The situation is aggravated due to insufficient allocations of means for environmental purposes. The protection and rationale of nature and improvement in the use of nature resources received in 1995 just 30.9 billion roubles (some 7 million dollars) including 30.2 billions for water protection, 0.7 billions roubles for land protection, and just 16 million roubles for air protection. This comprises 3.6 per cent of all the investments, and the share remained relatively stable over time (1976 to 1980 – 5.6 per cent; 1981 to 1985 – 2.8 per cent).

The aim of this contribution is to deal with some aspects of the environmental problematique in the region by highlighting some of the most acute issues. In the vocabularies used, these are often disguised by the use of terms such as "industrial" and "antropogineous". More particularly the presentation focuses on air pollution, pollution of the hydrosphere and the lithosphere, problems connected with utilisation of consumer and production wastes as well as on the excavation and processing of minerals.

The issue of antropogineous pressure

The current environmental state of affairs pertains to a considerable degree to economic-demographical pressures. The population of the Kaliningrad region amounted in the beginning of 1996 to some 933.800 inhabitants (Kaliningradian Committee of the state statistic 1996: 158). The density is 65 persons per square kilometre. This exceeds the all-Russian average, as it comes out in statistical data, some eight times. The figure almost reaches the average ones in the Baltic Sea region, surpasses those of the Baltic and some of the Scandinavian countries (in Estonia there are 34.6 inhabitants per square kilometre), although it is lower than the one in Denmark (120 inhabitants per square kilometre) not to speak of Germany (with 225 inhabitants per square kilometre). However, the population density of Kaliningrad the territory is rather irregular and in this sense typical for the Baltic Sea region as a whole. The areas closer to the seaside are more profusely inhabited. This, then, implies that the demographic pressure on the territory variates considerably.

The distribution of consumer waste in the region is affected by the fact that every consumer produces in average some 220 kg of consumer wastes per year. There are more than 100 dumps storing solid consumer wastes in the region, occupying altogether some 160 hectares of land (Kaliningradian Committee of state statistic 1996: 164). It is a problem that more than half of them are illegal, and their use is mostly beyond control. It is also a part of the picture that the consumption of water is considerable, this having the consequence that some 40 per cent of the water contaminated originates from the municipal water companies. The population growth seems to ensure that an extensive consumption of water continues. The consumption for household purposes increased from 84.7 million cubic metres in 1990 up to 87.4 million cubic metres in 1994, that is some three per cent. The current state of the sewerage system in the region is rather arduous, but it can turn more critical taking into account that the municipal facilities have chiefly been constructed before the war and have rarely been repaired since. There is the imminent danger of the system breaking down (Krasnov 1993: 11-14).

Another factor explaining the high level of pollution in the region consists of the amount of vehicles. For the period of five years (1989-1994) this figure doubled in the region, and it almost tripled in the city of Kaliningrad. In 1994 there were 136.000 vehicles in the region, while in 1990 the figure still remained 80.700 vehicles. It appears that the Kaliningrad region turned during the beginning of the 1990s into something of a "paradise" for second hand cars. Quite often the technical condition of the vehicles was below the environmental standards as these have been formulated elsewhere in Europe. The atmospheric pollution caused by cars increased. In 1990 it comprised some 50 per cent and in 1994 it covered some 73 per cent of the overall air pollution.

Industrial pressure

A considerable concentration of some 2.900 (in 1996) industrial enterprises (Kaliningradian Committee of state statistic 1996: 7) consisting among others of five large paper and pulp enterprises, five sea ports and four fish canneries, provides a strong industrial pressure. Apart from the fact that the cities harbour large concentrations of population, they also represent centres of industry. Their urbanisation potential defines the amount of production pressure levelled on the region. This is the reason why the urban potential largely overlaps with the industrial potential. Production concentrates mostly to Kaliningrad and its suburbs (Sovetsk, Pionersk,

Neman, Chernyakhovsk, Gusev, Yantarny) and adjoining zones, and so does the appearance of industrial waste that in combination with consumer waste comprises currently 1.3 million cubic metres annually.

As to atmospheric and hydrospheric pollution, those responsible are mostly the region's enterprises. An assessment of the atmospheric condition in 1990-1995 indicates a steady drop in harmful emissions (The Amber Island of Russia 1996: 143; Kaliningrad region in figures 1996: 32). While in 1990 the amount of harmful substances was 97.2 thousand tons, it dropped till 1995 to 42 thousand tons, i.e. the reduction of air pollution comprised 55.2 thousand tons or 42 per cent. The decline in the amount of waste, that occurred as a result of some nature protection measures, comprise only 30 per cent (11.8 thousand tons) of the total. The most significant of these measures requests the use of natural gas in boiler-houses in order to reduce waste by 5.000 tons per year. The remaining 70 per cent pertains mainly to a recession and a partial or complete closing of many large enterprises. Figure 1 indicates that there is a rather close relation between trends in industrial production and air pollution.

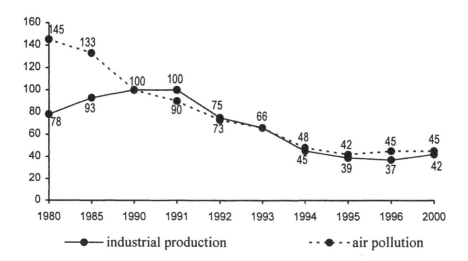

Figure 5.1 The trends of industrial production and air pollution in the Kaliningrad region

The main sources of pollution consist of pulp and paper factories, equipped with powerful heating stations and specific technologies, as well as power supply and machinery factories.

Problems pertaining to pollution of water are equally significant. There are approximately 800 major water-consumers in the region. For the past years there has been a steady decrease in the extraction from the sources of fresh water. The decline has been one of 329 million cubic metres in 1991 to 211 million cubic metres in 1995., i.e. a reduction of some 64 per cent (The Kaliningrad region in figures 1996: 32). Industrial enterprises generate half of the burden. Almost all used water is disposed into the environment in an unpurified form. The regional water purification system is far from perfect with a lack of technologies required for a full biological purification. These shortcomings do not only contribute to the pollution of surface waters, but to the contamination of subterranean and sea waters as well. On the societal side it may be observed that there are problems such as a high rate of gastric-instenstinal deceases, including dysentery, hepatitis virus and stomach ulcer.

The list of the largest polluters entails pulp and paper factories using outdated technologies, ports and machinery (Table 1).

Ports appear to have an especially harmful impact on their environment. The ports of Kaliningrad accommodate more than 1000 vessels annually. Despite the fact that the ports are specially equipped for processing litter, water containing oil and contaminated waters from the vessels, and the vessels themselves are orderly equipped to prevent such pollution, there is too much to handle. Occasionally the amount of oil-products in the ports of Pionersk and Baltiysk exceeds admissible norms in a fourfold or even eight-fold manner (*Report of the Geo-ecological department of the Kaliningrad State University*). Due to pollution, epidemics may occur, and the danger is particularly imminent during the summer and the bathing period. In a broader perspective pollution undermines the fishing and has adverse effects on the recreational potential of the Baltic Sea. The situation may become more critical, should the planned construction of new ports be commenced.

Agricultural pressure

The favourable natural conditions of the region contribute to agriculture. Agricultural lands, i.e. ploughed lands, hey-fields and pastures, make up some 55 per cent of the overall areal. This is double the average state of affairs in Russia (Fedorov 1986: 100). The use of land is, however, far from effective and mismanagement results in the loss of 15-20 thousand hectares of agricultural land (approximately 2 per cent of the whole agricultural area). The area available per person is larger than around the Baltic Rim in general, but the crop, amounting to 500 kg per capita (1987), is below the average (Knappe 1993: 7-16). As to the production of wheat, the Kaliningrad region ranks last in the Baltic Sea region (18.7 centner per hectare). The best crops – 60 centner per hectare – are harvested in Denmark, Germany and Sweden. Lithuania and Latvia reach the figure of 24.5 centner per hectare (*The Baltic Sea States* 1995: 20).

On the one hand, the usage of mineral fertilizers entails pollution of the soil. Nitrogen, phosphor and pesticides affect the quality of crops. On the other hand, reduction of their usage (by 8-10 times) afflicts the crop capacity. The capacity of crop was cut by 10 centner per hectare (from 26,2 to 16,1 centner per hectare) in 1991-1995. In order to improve the present-day situation and to secure an ecological balance, organic fertilizers (dung), available in a sufficient amount in the region, ought to be used. This would provide an opportunity to reduce both soil and water contamination that originates from animal-breeding farms.

A major part of the land in the region (90 per cent) has been meliorated (*The Kaliningrad region in figures* 1996: 100). The total length of the dams in the region is 730 km. These dams are supposed to protect some 1.000 square kilometres of land situated below the sea level. Therefore a safeguarding of a functioning drainage system appears to be of high priority. A high concentration of agricultural lands and a widely spread drainage system ensure a rapid transfer of pollutants from the fields into the rivers, lakes and the whole Baltic water area. During the last five years a sharp decline in the financing of the servicing and renewal of the drainage systems adds to the danger that the system breaks down (*Ecology of the Baltic Region* 1992: 114-24). This would entail serious environmental problems, including a swamping of agricultural lands and nearby forests as well as flooding (e.g. dispersion of harmful pollutants in submerged areas).

The impact of the economy on ecology

The current economy is not only unprofitable; it is also ecologically harmful. The most adverse effect on environment are caused by pulp, paper, kocks, asphalt and concrete production. Meat and dairy production has also a negative effect in lacking purification facilities. Pulp and paper industry comprised 12.7 per cent (1994) of the overall industrial production volume, fuel production was responsible for 13.4 per cent and kocks for 1.6 per cent (Fedorov & Zverev, 1995: 111). The state of affairs appears problematic as well, although the branches (engineering, carriage building, shipbuilding and light industry) seem less significant in theoretical terms. Tourism seems to have a minor effect.

The ports of Svetly, Kaliningrad and Pionersk also contributed to the overall pollution. If a new port is constructed, the overall cargo turnover in the Kaliningrad region would reach some 15-20 million tons per year. However, there is a reserve capacity of some 6 million tons. Moreover, due to the competition with Lithuanian (Klaipeda) and Polish (Gdansk, Gdydia) ports, Kaliningrad ports are underutilized by some two million tons per year. Reinforcement and an upgrading of the existing capabilities must therefore function as an alternative to the construction of new ports.

It can be stated more generally that the neglect of the alternative of an ecologically clean agriculture, the establishment of recreational zones and creation of national parks and other measures connected with nature protection further aggravates the situation. The presence of the military does not alter the state of affairs. A considerable amount of troops, located in the region, adds to the stress of the ecological environment and there is some contamination of the soil, water and air with a drastic effect on the various natural complexes. For the period of 1985-1990, military activities spoiled some 15 km of roads as well as 500 hectares of wrecked ploughed lands, heyfields and pastures (ing author for *Report of the Geo-ecological department of Kaliningrad State University* 1994)

The dilemmas of some specific sites

It is difficult to single out some specific sites as environmental concerns are valid for the Kaliningrad region as a whole. However, some cases seem to deserve special attention.

The Kuronian and Vistula spits are of special importance for the Kaliningrad region, not only because of their unique position, but also due to their all-Russian significance. Hence the Kuronian spit was turned into a national park in 1988. It harbours rare dune landscapes and pine woods. There is the sea and the gulfs surrounding it. Moreover, a number of rare species such as akes, deers and wild boars are found there. The territory is quite vulnerable already due to the processes of nature (frequent erosions) and various human activities such as destruction of vegetation and degradation of the dunes, adding further to the problems. The value of the Vistula spit equals that of the Kuronian one. Situated on the verge, it has been closed to tourists for a long time. Its distinctiveness and vulnerability makes protection mandatory.

The Kuronian and Vistula lagoons stand out as water areas subject to pollution, not only from the Kaliningrad region, but also the Polish (the river of Lava) and Lithuanian (the river of Neman and the Kuronian lagoon) border regions. The Vistula lagoon has lost its capacity of natural purification because of a combination of factors: its small size, shallowness (the depth is less than three meter) and unrestricted flow of polluted waters from the river Pregol. At present the Vistula lagoon belongs to the row of polluted water areas.

Centuries ago forests covered almost the whole region. However, they were cut down in order to have land for farming and agriculture. Only some isolated forest tracts are left in the Krasnoznamensk, Gvardeysk and Bagrationovsk regions, and there are some more comprehensive formations left in the Polesk, Slavsk and Nesterovsk regions. The deficit in forestry in the *oblast* (in comparison with optimum afforestation) comprises of some 50-75 per cent.

Pressure on the coastal zone is rather high and will grow further if the building of a new port and creation of recreational options hosting some 200.000 people will materialize (Fyodorov 1993: 4). The most important measures of protection consist of the building of sewage system for the towns located in the resort zone, i.e. Zelgradsk, Pionersk, Svetlogorsk and Yantarny. Such a system has been constructed, but does not function due to some construction defects.

International protection

Taking into account the present social-economic situation in the country with a shortage of subsidies and a lack of experience necessary to solve the problems encountered, there are two variants of cooperation with the foreign countries.

The first consists of transborder cooperation, for example cooperation with Lithuania in joint projects focusing on the Neman delta and the Kuronian lagoon. Projects have also been carried out between research institutes located in Kaliningrad and Poland. Some projects focus on the Vistula lagoon and others on the specific natural complexes of the Vistynets lake, a lake divided between two different countries.

The second variant leans on international support applied in the formation of joint projects. The construction of a purification plant in Gvardeysk, built with the help of Danish assistance, is one of the examples. Besides purification, the plant is to assist in personnel training and the gaining of experience needed for similar enterprises in small and middle-sized cities of Russia. There is Danish assistance also in improving Kaliningrad's sewage system as well as the restoring of the water supply and handling of consumer waste. In order to regulate and systematise available agricultural lands, a database is established with Swedish help.

The recent experiences of the three Baltic States, which for a long time used to have some of the same ecological problems and the same ecological rules, could be of interest to the Kaliningrad region. There is potential to be used in this sphere. These countries have been mapping ecologically hazardous spots and areas. The results gave ground to conclude that 42 per cent of the recreational potential located in the coastal areas was destroyed or lost as a result of previous military activities. Alternatives uses for these areas have been considered and in some cases also found (Baubinas & Taminskas 1996: 5-8).

The entering into force of the Special Economic Zone could improve the prospects for engaging into international cooperation also in the environmental field. The arrangement allows the regional administration to sign agreements with foreign administrative-local units. As soon as such agreements are registered at the Ministry of Foreign Affairs, they enter into effect. Such an option may spur the occurrence of additional international projects in the sphere of environmental questions.

Concluding remarks

No doubt, the ecological situation requires considerable attention in order for improvement to occur. This is conceivable as such, among other reasons because environmental issues are high on the agenda in Baltic Sea cooperation. The Russian Government, the states of the Baltic Sea region and many other actors are concerned with the situation and take measures in order to achieve a turn towards the better.

However, a broad range of measures are needed. As environmental issues are closely linked with economic trends, an improvement in the economy would provide additional ground for measures to improve the environmental conditions. Growth should be linked with ecological priorities, this to be reflected for example in acquiring of ecologically sound technologies and measures such as the construction of facilities for water purification.

It also seems that changes in the ecological legislation are of great importance. This applies both at the federal and regional levels. On regional level there exists a couple of examples in that local legislation may have favourable effects, but additional measures are needed. There is also a need for additional sanctuaries and protected areas, and also here both federal and regional measures are required.

An intensification of international cooperation is certainly called for, this including also cooperation in the field of research and among research institutes. Environmental issues would also benefit from a concerned and conscious public opinion, and there is space for a variety of citizen's activities here. However, this is a relatively weak dimension in the case of Kaliningrad. The environmentally oriented movement Kedr received less than one per cent of the votes in the latest parliamentary elections. There are social movements in the environmental field, but their voice and impact could grow much larger taking into account the nature and magnitude of the problems that the Kaliningrad region is experiencing.

References

Amber Island of Russia. Statistical Collection (1996). Kaliningrad: Regional State Statistics Committee Press.

Baubinas R. and J. Taminskas (1996), "Military degradation of the environment in the Lithuanian coastal area", *Coastline-EUCC*, (5), 2: 5-8.

Ecology of the Baltic Region (1992). Collection of Papers. St. Petersburg: RGO.

Fyodorov, Gennady M. (1986), *At the map of the Kaliningrad region*. Kaliningrad: Kaliningrad Publicity Center.

Fyodorov, Gennady M. *et al.*, eds. (1993), *Recreational Complex of the Kaliningrad Region*. Kaliningrad: Baltic Scientific Center.

Fyodorov, Gennady M. and Y.M. Zverev (1995), *Kalinigradian alternatives: The socio-economical development of the Kaliningrad region in the new geopolitical situation*. Kaliningrad: Yantamy Skaz.

Kaliningrad region. Essays of the Nature (1969), Kaliningrad: Kaliningrad Publicity Center.

Kaliningradian Committee of State Statistic (1996), *Socio-economical situation in the Kaliningrad region in 1995. Operative information*. Kaliningrad: Kaliningrad Committee of State Statistic.

Knappe, Elke (1993), "Der Wandel der Landnutzund in der Region Kaliningrad", *Europa Regiona* 1: 7-16.

Krasnov, Eugeny, ed. (1993), *Ways of optimization of land use: Ecologic-economical aspects*. Kaliningrad: KSU.

Kucheryavy, Pavel and Gennady Fedorov (1989), *Geography of the Kalinigrad region*. Kaliningrad: Kaliningrad Publicity Center.

The Baltic Sea States: Basic Statistical Data (1995), Warsaw: Central Statistical Office.

The Kaliningrad Regional Statistics Committee (1996), Updated information. Kaliningrad: Kaliningrad Regional Statistics Committee.

VASABS 2010 (1994), *Vision and Strategies around the Baltic Sea 2010: Towards a Framework for Special Development in the Baltic Sea Region*. Copenhagen.

6 Kaliningrad: Armed Forces and Missions

KLAUS CARSTEN PEDERSEN

Introduction

The primary analytical purpose of this brief paper is to look at what may be deduced about the possible military missions of the armed forces of the Kaliningrad Special Defence Area (KOOR) simply on the basis of their size and composition. It will also attempt to look at how relevant and realistic these missions may be under various conditions. And finally it will try to place Kaliningrad and the KOOR forces in the general context of Russian security policy and foreign relations.

An overview of the approximate size and composition of the forces serves as the necessary point of departure for the analysis. The figures are based primarily on the IISS *Military Balance 1996/97* (London, October 1996), modified slightly by input from other sources. The IISS in turn is drawing on figures reported by countries and checked under the Conventional Forces in Europe (CFE) agreement.

Before that, some definitions and distinctions are discussed. But first, two premises are lined up in order to shorten the paper.

Two premises

Kaliningrad is Russian

This may seem a superfluous statement of the obvious, but Russia's sovereignty over Kaliningrad does in fact seem to be questioned occasionally in political debate and academic discourse. It is possible, of course, for academics to question everything and anything, including this, and it seems unavoidable to have it questioned by politicians from more or less obscure corners of the political spectrum in some countries.

The territory was taken by Stalin's Soviet Union from its former ally Hitler's Germany in a war which Germany had started and lost. None of the original German inhabitants remain, and the present German Federal Republic does not have, and does not claim to have, any legitimate rights in Kaliningrad. The only neighbouring states, Poland and Lithuania, have exercised no control over the area for centuries, and they do not either have any legitimate rights there, nor do their responsible governments claim that they do. The vast majority of the population is Russian, and the only natural successor to the Soviet sovereignty over the territory is Russia.

The academic analyses of alternative sovereignty arrangements for Kaliningrad therefore seem redundant – and potentially almost as provocative as the territorial claims by some political extremists. It is difficult to see even a grain of realism or rationality in these claims, unless their sole purpose is to irritate the Russians. In this they do occasionally succeed.

The Russians are justly irritated, but they would be wise not to regard these analyses and claims as indicators of any potential outside threat or, indeed, as in any way relevant or significant. Both governments and shadow governments in all the countries that matter believe that Kaliningrad is and will remain Russian, and that it is up to the Russians to decide if, when and how to alter the status of Kaliningrad. The Russians in Kaliningrad, for example, might one day want some degree of autonomy, and the Russians in Moscow might one day agree.

The main reason that the question has come up at all is probably not that Kaliningrad is conquered territory, but the fact that it is physically separated from the rest of Russia, and the fact that Russia has tended to make this into a bigger problem than it need be.

Kaliningrad has a right to territorial defence

Since Kaliningrad is a part of Russia, its defence is unquestionably a Russian responsibility and is naturally also an element in the overall defence planning and defence system of Russia. Suggestions of a demilitarization of Kaliningrad do appear from time to time. Taken at face value such suggestions would seem to imply a total removal of all military forces and installations, which seems both unreasonable and totally unrealistic. If they are just meant as a call for a reduction of the level, quality or readiness of forces it could be seen as a call for more of what has already been done. Here, too, it is entirely up to the Russians to decide if, when and how such a reduction might take place – even if such a decision will be influenced by many factors, including external ones.

A new definition of Kaliningrad

One very easy way for Russia to de-dramatize Kaliningrad's physical separation from the rest of Russia (hereinafter the "mainland") would be to regard it as an island, *the Russian island in the Baltic Sea* rather than as an isolated exclave separated from mainland Russia by at least two foreign states (Lithuania/White Russia, Lithuania/Latvia, Poland/White Russia, or Poland/Ukraine). This would mean switching from a continental to a maritime mode of thought, and Kaliningrad might then be considered to be as easily accessible as Swedish Gotland and Danish Bornholm. There are at least two arguments for the maritime mode of thought. Firstly, it opens a way out of the most contentious and destabilizing aspect of Kaliningrad's location – the question of military transit through Lithuania. Secondly, it changes the focus of attention to a ferry link which is or could fairly easily be made to be much more economical, efficient and safe for most purposes than the land link. This, too, is a Russian decision, and it does depend on whether Russia (Moscow) wants to remove problems or prefers to nurture some bones of contention and some Lithuanian anxiety.

Viewpoints and circumstances: some distinctions

From a military point of view the location of Kaliningrad offers opportunities and presents problems – different sets of opportunities and problems depending on who is looking at them and depending on the situation.

It may be appropriate to try to distinguish between a local and a federal Russian point of view as well as between Russian and non-Russian points of view. And when it comes to the latter, there are natural differences between the small Baltic neighbours to the north and relatively large Poland to the south – as well as between these neighbours on the one hand and neutral-Nordic countries, NATO-Nordic countries, Germany and NATO on the other.

As far as the situation is concerned it may be useful to distinguish between what might be called co-operative peace, cold peace, cold war, and war. One could run through all the combinations systematically, but it will not be attempted in this paper where they will just be kept in mind.

The Russian armed forces in Kaliningrad

The Kaliningrad Special Defence Area (KOOR)

KOOR was formed in 1994 as a unique formation in the Russian defence structure. The admiral commanding the Baltic Fleet was put in charge of the KOOR, an Air Defence Area was formed and integrated into the fleet, and the ground forces constituted by the 11th Independent Guards Army were placed under operational command of the KOOR.

The forces are not only organized differently than before. They are also much reduced in numbers though not necessarily in quality. The Baltic Fleet headquarters and main base are in the KOOR (in Kaliningrad and Baltiysk respectively) and its second base is in Kronshtadt near St. Petersburg. Units move frequently, of course, between the two bases, but it is estimated by various sources that on average about two-thirds of the units and personnel of the fleet may be found in Baltiysk. Another source of variation are ships belonging to or destined for the other Russian fleets. Having been repaired or newly built at the local naval yards they normally stay in the region for a while to undergo sea trials and train their crews.

According to *The Military Balance 1996/97* the serviceable units of the Baltic Fleet number 6 submarines, 31 principal surface combatants, about 42 patrol and coastal combatants, 60 ships for mine warfare, 8 landing craft and some 118 support ships.

The sailing units are backed by naval aviation. In KOOR there are 3 fighter regiments (2 offensive and 1 defensive) with a total of about 100 aircraft plus a limited number of other aircraft and helicopters. There is also a marine infantry brigade and a coastal artillery regiment. The total number of men in naval uniform in KOOR is probably around 25.000, or two-thirds of the estimated personnel in the Baltic Fleet.

The ground forces in KOOR comprise 2 motor rifle divisions, 2 tank brigades, 3 artillery brigades, 1 attack helicopter regiment, and 1 surface-to-surface missile brigade with 18 SS-21 (which are nuclear capable but are probably not at present equipped with nuclear warheads). Between them these units are estimated to have about 850 tanks, about 925 armoured personnel carriers and fighting vehicles, and about 425 artillery pieces. The total number of men in army (and border guard) uniform in KOOR is probably about 20.000 at present, though full mobilization strength may be about 55.000. While conscripts for the Baltic Fleet come from all over Russia, the army conscripts serving in the KOOR are local boys from Kaliningrad *oblast.*

The KOOR grand total of uniformed personnel at present (late 1996) thus seems to be about 45.000 with an army mobilization reserve of 35.000 and some facilities for naval and air reinforcements from mainland Russia.

Evaluation

One immediate and necessary observation is that this personnel strength is less than it used to be and a far cry from the 100.000 to 300.000 that keep appearing in Baltic, Polish, Western and even some Russian papers – academic and others. Some of the troops withdrawn from Germany, Poland and Lithuania went home via Kaliningrad and temporarily the numbers in Kaliningrad may have been quite high, but they are low now and it is rather strange that many sources, including Russian ones, grossly exaggerate the military forces in KOOR. It is extremely important for analytical purposes as well as for the everybody's planning, that the figures be as accurate as at all possible.

These trends are interesting in themselves, but military forces do not exist in a vacuum. They are measured against other forces, and they, too, have been reduced since the end of the Cold War, though not as drastically as the Russian forces. The Baltic Fleet is much reduced in size since Soviet times, but the average age of the ships is also much lower. Some Russian military analysts have declared it desirable for Russia to have a Baltic Fleet measuring up to the combined navies of all the other Baltic Sea states. Today it probably has about half that strength, or about the same as the German fleet in the Baltic Sea. The air forces are also much reduced in the KOOR, but army tanks and artillery are only slightly reduced in numbers and not in quality. They are now of roughly the same size as the Danish Forces, but defend an area just one-third the size of Denmark.

Missions of the KOOR forces

Naval base

When the new KOOR was placed under the command of the chief of the Baltic Fleet Admiral Yegorov, it became clear that the main military role of Kaliningrad would be as a naval base, indeed the main base of the Baltic Fleet. Giving the top job to an army or air force general would have sent an ominous signal to all the neighbours, because the implication would have been that Kaliningrad was intended to become a fortress and a launching pad not just for missiles but for political pressure or worse on Lithuania and Poland.

But a naval base is understandable and acceptable and therefore reassuring. Russia is obviously entitled to a Baltic Fleet, and ice-free and forward-placed Baltiysk/Kaliningrad is the obvious choice as its main base. Of course a naval base also needs supplies from the mainland, but it is less dependent on cumbersome, politically sensitive and militarily vulnerable rail and road links transiting foreign countries. It is therefore also less of a problem for Russia and for its neighbours.

Showing the flag

This is regarded as a necessary mission by all sea powers, big and small, but especially by the big ones. It is fairly harmless and highly acceptable. What it means in practice is maintaining a highly visible presence at sea. The Baltic Fleet is very capable of doing this.

Territorial defence

This is or should be the primary mission of any defence force. Considering the limited area and coastline of Kaliningrad *oblast* and the relative weakness of all foreign forces in the vicinity, the present strength of the KOOR forces is estimated to be more than adequate for local defence. They would probably be able to move some distance into Poland to establish and hold a more easily defended line in Warmia and Mazuria – even against a reinforced attack from the west and south. Coastal defence and the Baltic Fleet also seem fully up to the task of defending the very short coastline of the *oblast*.

Defence of the links with the mainland

This is a legitimate mission which nevertheless, in the case of land and some air links, may cause great discomfort to neighbouring countries. The sea links are a very different matter – they may be secured in international waters without challenging the rights of other countries. Russia seems well able to carry out this mission.

Early warning and forward air defence of mainland Russia

The early warning mission is a realistic Kaliningrad contribution to Russian defence. But Kaliningrad's resources may not be adequate to accomplish much forward air defence of the mainland, if troubles should break out.

Area control in the central Baltic Sea and the Gulf of Finland

This is necessary to secure the sea links between Kaliningrad and mainland Russia, and it is probably the main mission of the Baltic Fleet and what it seems to be designed for. It has about half the numerical strength of all the other navies in the Baltic Sea put together, but 2-3 times as many major surface combatants (depending on how much of the German navy is counted as Baltic), and it should be up to the job.

Intelligence collection

After Soviet/Russian withdrawal from East Germany and Poland, Kaliningrad is the best spot for collecting intelligence from radio emissions and radar and may do for Russia what Bornholm does for Denmark and Gotland for Sweden. And naval intelligence gathering and surveillance units are also well placed in the Baltiysk base.

The various missions mentioned above should be more or less noncontroversial, and the KOOR forces seem to be well able to carry them out in peacetime or in the context of low-level general conflict or high-level local conflict. They seem less realistic in case of a high-level general conflict involving NATO.

Another set of missions are thinkable, but controversial and confrontational.

Political pressure and political provocation

A measure of sabre rattling may be attempted to drive home a political point. Used sparingly it may be effective. Used excessively it may end up being driven by events rather than driving them. The context could be or quickly become a new cold war.

Control over air and land links with the mainland

This mission requires total air superiority in Lithuanian airspace and control over part of Lithuanian territory. The KOOR forces seem adequate to do this in a local or low-level conflict. It would also require either an alliance with Belarus or Russian military control over Belarus. This would be an unrealistic task for the KOOR forces and would have to be accomplished by Russian forces from the mainland.

Protection of Russian seaborne foreign trade

This mission is frequently described as essential and as one of the main missions of the Baltic Fleet. But as the vast majority of this trade is shipped through the ports of Baltic states, it would be necessary to control them as well as the sea, KOOR forces alone would be insufficient but could function as an anvil if mainland forces from Leningrad Military District were the hammer. Even this would not be sufficient. It would also be necessary to control the western Baltic Sea, the Baltic exits through the Danish straits, and indeed the high seas beyond.

This is unrealistic and was unrealistic even in the heyday of Soviet sea power. But it is also irrelevant. Even the limited part of the mission of which Russian forces would be capable, would be thinkable only in a general conflict scenario which in itself would render the mission irrelevant. The point is that the trade supposed to be protected is almost entirely with countries in the Baltic Sea region or with NATO countries, and in a general conflict scenario this trade would be cut off at the source anyway, and there would be nothing left for Russia to protect.

Area denial in the western Baltic Sea

It is easier to prevent others from using the sea (denial) than to protect and secure one's own use of it (control), and it is possible that the Baltic Fleet could carry out this mission for a time as a forward defence mission against a hostile naval intrusion into the Baltic. But the context is likely to be general high-level war in Europe.

Other offensive or forward defensive missions

Taking a small part of north-eastern Poland and the southern part of the Baltic states have already been mentioned. Limited air strikes and pin-prick amphibious missions against other states in the region are possible, including attacks by the highly accurate SS-21s on a limited number of high value targets, but the scenario again is full-scale conventional war.

Conflict or cooperation

It seems that the missions for which KOOR forces are suited are essentially peacetime missions including deterrence. And Western military analysts seem to agree that although absolutely no one is planning an attack which needs to be deterred, and although the KOOR forces are probably larger than what most other countries would deploy in similar circumstances, they are not unreasonably large.

The forces seem large enough, however, to be able to handle also some missions in a low-intensity conflict or a local conflict.

Specifically, they are quite capable of creating enormous problems for Lithuania, less so for Poland and even less for Germany, Denmark, and Sweden. Finland's situation is more precarious, but not because of the forces in Kaliningrad. The military problem for Russia in this context is whether such conflicts can be controlled and contained. If they escalate into a European war it seems very uncertain that the Russian armed forces would be able to bring it to a happy conclusion. In a full-scale conventional war scenario Kaliningrad would seem particularly vulnerable. And if a war were to escalate from conventional into nuclear conflict, all bets are off.

This describes an essential flaw in Kaliningrad as a military outpost: Its chief mission is to protect the links, whose main function in turn is to support the military outpost, whose main mission etc, etc. And this merry-go-round is not harmless but leads to a catch-22, because some of the measures that may be needed to secure Kaliningrad's military links with the mainland might provoke a conflict in which Russia would not be able to hold on to it after all.

The obvious alternative would be for Russia to opt for cooperative security, and a number of possibilities – bilateral and multilateral – are opening up. Examples are the Partnership for Peace and in that framework the bilateral agreement with Denmark on cooperation in the military field, an agreement in which Russia has not so far shown a great deal of interest – in stark contrast to Poland and the three Baltic states with whom Denmark has signed similar agreements and now has very extensive cooperation. Another example is the prospective charter of cooperation with NATO.

In such a scenario of cooperation the location of Kaliningrad and its naval emphasis could be important assets in building contacts, confidence and cooperation with other military forces and security policy planners in the Baltic Sea region. And just as Kaliningrad is very exposed to any possible negative consequences of a confrontational or isolationist Russian policy, it will also be the among the first to benefit from a policy of cooperation.

In the heated debate in early 1997 about NATO's acceptance of new members, many Russian comments have been quite confrontational. NATO has been defined as hostile to Russia – as have the countries seeking membership. Most Russians have overlooked the fact that this was not originally a NATO initiative, and they have neglected to ask themselves why all their former "allies" seem to want NATO membership. And some of the suggested Russian countermeasures have included unspecified pressure on the Baltic states and casting Kaliningrad in the role of a nuclear armed fortress. However, many Russians probably realise that at the end of the day, their best and most robust friend may yet be NATO, and that their real security problems lie elsewhere.

Russia's neighbours and prospective partners will undoubtedly follow both civilian and military developments in Kaliningrad with great interest, regarding the *oblast* and its armed forces as important indicators of how Russia is going to define itself and its security interests.

7 The Region's Security: An Expert View from Moscow

ANATOLY TRYNKOV

The *oblast's* role for Russia and for Europe

The double-track NATO plan to enlarge itself and to have some "special relations" with Moscow caused a new wave of discussions in Russia and in Europe about the role of Russia's Kaliningrad *oblast's* (KO) in the European and Baltic security architecture.

The aims and the interests of the Russian Federation in the Baltic Sea area are quite compatible with those of Europe: strengthening of stability and cooperation. The Kaliningrad *oblast* may be used for achieving such a state of affairs as a large industrial and transit unit. In case of a crisis in the Baltic Sea area (for example minorities conflicts), it can become a special base for peacekeeping operations, capable to provide security for all the Baltic neighbours.

In the Presidential decree "About social and economic development of the Kaliningrad *oblast*" of May 18, 1995, a "special geographical location" of the region is emphasised as well as "its exclusive importance for the political, military and strategic and economic interests of Russia" (*Rossiiskaia gazeta*, 24 May 1995).

The KO, despite of its geographical isolation, still has great geostrategical importance for Russia. After losing the most important sea ports on the Baltic and Black Seas, with Russia becoming more isolated from Central Europe by the near foreign states, which are not always friendly towards Russia, possessing the KO is a favourable factor reducing geopolitical losses of Russia after disintegration of the USSR. In evaluating the importance of the Kaliningrad *oblast* from military-political and economic points of view, the following factors should be taken into account:

1. The unique geographical situation of the KO near West Europe and its belonging to the Hanseatic Baltic area, grant certain economic, military and strategic advantages to Russia.

2. The availability of the advanced transport infrastructure (sea, railway, river, air transport) of the *oblast*, ensures Russia's communications with the near foreign countries as well as with the western countries and creates a basis for converting Kaliningrad into an important European transport unit.

3. The ice-free port of Kaliningrad can be used for transshipment in the trade between Russia and the Western countries especially during the inactivity of the other ports.

4. Availability of natural resources (amber, petroleum, wood, fish, furs) provide additional receipts in the world market.

5. The diversified industry of the Kaliningrad region can be utilized by many Russian regions and European countries.

6. The base of Baltiysk can play an exclusively important peacekeeping role for guaranteeing security and stability in the Baltic Sea area.

NATO expansion and the *oblast*

A new hostility between East and West, erupting in case of a NATO expansion with just a formal agreement with Russia, can again turn Kaliningrad into an area, determined by military priorities. It will elevate the question of Russia's accelerated indemnification of lost positions in the Baltic Sea area, without violating the Treaty on Conventional Armed Forces in Europe (CFE).

The expansion of NATO to the East will sharpen the problem of maintaining Russia's security. The extended bloc would surpass RF, particularly by its military and technical opportunities. Tactical nuclear weapons targeted on military and industrial sites in Russia capable of destroying them in major parts of Russia's territory may appear near its borders.

In such a situation Russia should have to take adequate measures. Some Russian experts suggest deployment of nuclear systems of air and antimissile defense on its western borders and also tactical and operative missile systems, including systems already destroyed according to the INF treaty (*Moskovskie novosti*, 1 October 1995). For this purpose it would be necessary, they say, to denounce the INF treaty. At the same time Russia has without violating the CFE Treaty, the right to place 60 per cent of tanks from its quota (or 4200), more than 60 per cent of artillery (3235 systems), and one third of all its armed forces in Europe in the Kaliningrad region.

According to experts, in a case of the situation deteriorating in Baltic countries, the option of deploying of NATO's mobile forces, united naval forces and sea component of "reaction forces" of the bloc (more than 100 ships, including 50 carriers of cruise missiles, 30 ships of Poland's Navy, including 10-12 ships carrying missiles) has to be taken into account. NATO could also use a crisis situation as a pretext for deployment on Baltic Sea of operative missiles groups and marine troops for blocking forces of the Baltic fleet of RF and breaking communications. There are also prospects for the creation of some unified system in defending the Baltic countries and a development of interaction of their armed forces without Russia.

Russia in the Baltic Sea Area

Russia's Baltic fleet has during the last ten years according to admiral V.G.Yegorov, reduced its personal two times and its ships three times (*Kaliningradskaia Pravda*, 4 August 1995; *Mezhdunarodnaia zhyzn* 1995 (6): 18-22). Currently Russia's Baltic fleet, as to its fighting efficiency (not amount of ships), can be compared to fleets of either Germany, Sweden or Poland. As argued by Admiral F.N.Gromov, commander of Russia's navy, it is "almost ten times lower, than NATO's navy on the Baltic Sea" (*Voennaia mysl* 1995 (4): 9-13).

These changes in the geostrategic situation around the Baltic Rim and the reorientation of foreign and military policies of our neighbours, turn Kaliningrad into a major factor in the maintenance of Russia's security.

During 1995 the naval activities have increased significantly in the Baltic straits and close to Kaliningrad. The Partnership for Peace entailed some 20 exercises without Russia but with the participation of Poland (14), Lithuania (9), and Germany. An analysis of NATO's planning principles reveals a desire to bring them into the vicinity of the KO and shows the special role of Denmark, Germany and the Netherlands in the development of operative and tactical interaction with the armed forces of Poland and Lithuania.

The negotiations between USA, Poland and the Baltic countries regarding an air space monitoring system in the region (*Literaturnaia gazeta*, 22 March 1995) by using existing airfield networks on their territories, testifies to the special interest for this region. During 1995 NATO's activities in the vicimty of KO's air border has increased 2.5 times. In the zone of the region's air defense two thousand foreign military planes have been spotted, most frequently Germany's "Tornados", and Danish "F-16's". As to reconnaissance planes, 249 cases have been revealed, including some from Great Britain. The foreign pilots, informed about our shortage of fuel do not hasten to leave the border space, and quite often they show inclinations to provoke (*Krasnaia Zvezda*, 6 January 1996).

The aims of some neighbours of Kaliningrad to enter NATO and the progress of the three Baltic countries in developing their military cooperation (the unified air space monitoring system (in which planes "AWACS E-3A" of US Air Force, deployed on the US air base in Keflavik can be included), might require that Russia strengthens its defense power in the region. If so, they would meet collective counteractions from the Western neighbours.

During 1994-1995 "the problem of KO as a destabilising factor" was repeatedly risen in all possible West-European and Baltic fora. Hence, in mid-November 1994 in Vilnius in the documents of the Baltic Assembly it is claimed, that Russian forces in the KO considerably exceed the level of defensive sufficiency and complicate the creation of a system of collective security in the area.

The campaign for the NATO expansion and at the same time appeals for "demilitarization" of KO indicated that the Western countries may try to achieve a withdrawal of the Russian army and fleet from this strategically important security region. This is planned for ensuring NATO's irreversible military superiority and to block the Baltic fleet in the closed and freezing waters of the Gulf of Finland. In case of deterioration of international situation, an exit would depend on the position of Finland and Estonia. For the Kaliningrad region it would imply a breaking down of vital sea deliveries, interrupted fishing, losing control over fishing areas and the sea shelf, and the threat of a sea blockade.

The statements presented in some of the NATO countries, Poland and the Baltic states on excessive troop concentrations in the KO obviously had a propaganda character. They evaporated as soon as NATO's Council took a basic decision on the expansion of the bloc.

The special defense area (KOOR)

An unprecedented reduction of Russia's military presence in the Baltic region and plans of NATO expansion, made RF give ground for the creation (in view of a crisis) of KOOR. The main aim of the arrangement consists of defending the region's territory from intrusion. The strength of troops in the KOOR would probably be some 40 thousand persons in the absence of a real threat to the security of vital interests of Russia in the Baltic Sea area (*Kommersant-Daily*, 26 March 1994; *Kaliningradskaia Pravda*, 1 March 1996).

In such situation these interests are seen as:

- preservation of Russia's territorial integrity in terms of an inviolability of existing borders and an unconditional belonging of Kaliningrad to Russia;
- prevention of upsetting the balance between the armed forces in the Baltic region and a safeguarding of the transport connections between KO and mainland Russia;
- development of relations with the neighbouring Baltic Sea countries based on the OSCE principles and international law.

Such purposes can be achieved without escalating Russia's military presence in the KO, and by preserving a military partnership with the *oblast's* neighbours and other European states. There is already sufficient experience of joint military exercises, naval visits etc.

At the same time the creation and strengthening of KOOR is an important prerequisite for the maintenance of Russia's security, taking into account NATO expansion to the East. However, the arrangement is bound by problems such as the decreasing of fighting efficiency, bad social and economic situation of officers, problems of logistics, battle training, and coordination and interaction between the troops in the Kaliningrad region. According to the mass media, there are about 70000 servicemen (including 20000 officers), on the military bases of the 11th Army, Baltic Fleet, Air Defense and Border Troops.

Because of a reduction in armed forces, finding a job is a serious problem for ex-servicemen in the region. In 1996, the *oblast's* industry needed 1500 workers and the number of unemployed was of 26000. In the area 17000 officers are waiting for habitation (*Strazh Baltii*, 23 May 1995;

Krasnaia Zvezda, 26 January 1996; *Interfax*, 27 October 1995). The fighting efficiency of the army and the fleet has declined due to factors such as unpaid bills for electric power, causing in some cases breaks in delivery to military bases (*Krasnaia Zvezda*, 16 September 1995; *Vladivostok*, 26 August 1995).

Insufficient financing also complicates the problems of the border troops in Kaliningrad. According to General I.Rakhmanin, commander of the troops, the Group was only financed by 40 per cent in 1995. The servicemen of the border troops have received 400 apartments, whereas almost 1500 officers and other servicemen lack such facilities. Just one check-point has the newest equipment (*Nezavisimaia gazeta*, 8 December 1995; *Svobodnaia zona*, 1994 (94): 7).

The officers of interior forces are also under-equipped. The chief of Western department of interior forces Colonel A. Chaplygin said, that his department just has 39 per cent of the transport, and 50 per cent of the communication means needed. It is also reported that the number of crimes in railway transport only (in Kaliningrad) increased in 1995 by 22.5 per cent.

Chief of the Federal Security Service in KO, Admiral G.V.Moshkov stated that in connection with the growth in the number of cases of plunder, smuggling of weapons and due to the activation of foreign extremist and nationalist organization and intelligence services, his structure of Federal security service has some new problems (*Kaliningradskaia Pravda*, 27 February 1996).

The problem of ecological security also requires attention, including investments, especially in Baltiysk. Besides the threat of epidemics, including in the army, the absence of a safe water supply in many cities, threatens Russia, log penal sanctions damaging the Baltic Sea ecologically.

Kaliningrad's soft security

The importance of non-military forms of the KO's security is growing: problems of pertaining to transport, communication and food require solution. The creation of a transport line between St. Petersburg and Baltiysk and for sea deliveries from Belarussia would be of great importance.

Although the transport network of Kaliningrad is designed according to military needs, it remains vulnerable due to a dependency on import of fuel, on railway supplies, and also to the historical specialization of Kaliningrad ports, oriented towards a transportation of coal, wood, fish, etc.

The significance of transport also pertains to the fact that Kaliningrad's industry is far from self-sufficient. Only some 5-6 per cent of the supplies come from the region itself. In 1994 *oblast* lost about 300 billion roubles in transit fees, and 440 billion during the first half of the 1995 (*Kaliningradskaia Pravda*, 15 November 1995). With the high transportation tariffs applied by Lithuania, the activity of the Kaliningrad port has decreased to a third of the original level in 1994-1995. Despite the low fees in the ports of Kaliningrad, they were utilized only by 63 per cent in 1995.

Hence an improvement of the situation and the formation of a large transport unit is Russia's most important problem. On April 10, 1996, during a session of governmental commission on development of the KO, the Deputy Minister of Economy A.Shapovaliants emphasised, that the *oblast* should become in the long term Russia's largest commercial and transport unit (*RIA "Novosti"*, 10 April 1996).

The vulnerability as to resources in Kaliningrad is aggravated by a lack of cheap fuel and energy (*Svobodnaia zona*, 13 May 1996; *Inzhenernaia gazeta*, 1996(26): 2). New technologies for electric stations (available, for example in Sweden and offered to Estonia) have to be developed. The oil deposits in Kaliningrad can ease the problem provided that there is a refinery.

The food vulnerability (Kaliningrad alone consumes monthly imported food of some $20 million) can only be eliminated by achieving a basic self-sufficiency. Recently the production of food has increased modestly. However, during the first half of the 1995 the production still decreased by 18 per cent. Simultaneously 160 tons of imported food was of substandard quality. A considerable amount of goods remains out of control (*RIA "Novosti"*, 1 September 1995).

Exchange of experiences with the neighbouring countries, these having similar climatic conditions, is important for developing the area's agriculture. The Baltic and all-European economic cooperation can also play an important role.

Kaliningrad and its neighbours

As to links with the neighbouring states, the Kaliningrad *oblast* was separated with the demise of the Soviet Union, from Russia's territory by two independent states – Belarus and Lithuania. Under these conditions Kaliningrad became an object of increased interest to its nearest neighbours, with some political circles concluding that due to its geographic situation the region has lost its strategic importance for Russia. They nurture the idea that Russia might abandon this territory and then Kaliningrad may become an object of expansion of Lithuania, Poland or Germany.

Still some time ago the relations with Poland unfolded without Warsaw paying attention to issues of security. However, with the discussions on NATO's expansion the so-cold "danger of military oversaturation" of Kaliningrad become distinct in Polish interventions.

The concentration of Russia's troops in the area, withdrawn from Germany, Poland and the three Baltic states, had a temporary character. There never existed some "200.000 troops" in Kaliningrad, as argued by some politicians in Warsaw.

The necessity of then stationing troops in the KO pertains, in particular, to the fact that the Baltic states refused to cooperate with Russia in military issues and to allow the use of former bases in the process of withdrawal. Russia has only two bases around the Baltic Rim left: Kronstadt and Baltiysk (now they provide the fleet safe navigation into the Baltic Sea). Simultaneously Warsaw stopped financing the withdrawal of the Northern army group, which for more than 40 years had been located on Poland's territory.

Some unofficial publications disputed at the same juncture the final decision of Kaliningrad belonging to Russia. As ecological pretext was used in order to turn down the design of high-way and railway: Kaliningrad–Gusev–Goldap–Suwalki–Grodno–Russia. While Russia and Belarussia view the project primerily as an economic one, the position of the Polish side is also influenced by military and political ambitions as well as calculatious pertaining to Poland's entering into NATO.

Currently Poland is the main trading partner of the *oblast*, accounting for nearly a third of KO's foreign trade turnover. Over 400 joint ventures, that is 50 per cent of the total number, are Russian-Polish. The share of authorised capital of these joint ventures constitutes only 7 per cent of the overall figure (*Mezhdunarodnaia zhyzn* 1995(6): 66).

An important aspect of this relationship is that it rests on a quite satisfactory legal basis both at an intergovernmental and an interregional level as indicated by the agreements on co-operation between Kaliningrad and Poland's border crossings, as well as the agreements on cooperation with the Olsztyn, Elblag, Suwalki, Gdansk and Szcecin voivodships.

This legal basis has been supplemented by effective instruments of implementation. These have been a Russian-Polish round table on cooperation between Kaliningrad and Polish regions and later, a Russian-Polish Council for Cooperation between the *oblast* and the regions of the Republic of Poland has come together.

The round table specified the main areas of interests represented by respective working groups. The main groups are those for the opening and organisation of border crossings, cooperation in transportation; ecological cooperation, cooperation in agriculture, and cooperation in crime control. Subsequently they have been transformed into joint commissions headed by Russian and Polish co-chairmen.

Throughout this period the Council has focused on building new border crossings, modernising existing ones and agreeing on a regime concerning their functioning. Communications have opened up between the region and Warsaw and other cities of Poland. There is sea traffic with Gdansk, Elblag and Frombork and railroad traffic with Gdynia during summer periods. Importance has been attached to projects aiming at establishing ferry services between Gdynia, Kaliningrad, St.Petersburg, the Via Baltica highway linking in to Kaliningrad, and the option of connecting the region to transiting gas pipelines.

In the relations with Lithuania the vulnerability of KO is occasionally evidenced by attempts coming from some politicians in Vilnius to exacerbate the situation pertaining to Russia's military transit to Kaliningrad. Problems with Lithuania have been linked with the process of signing a treaty on passenger and freight transit to and from Kaliningrad as well to the demarcation of borders. The granting of most-favoured-nation status to each other in trade and economic relations provides a sound basis from which to move on in the overcoming of difficulties, towards promoting normal economic, cultural and other links between Lithuania and Russia.

Unofficial circles in Lithuania have repeatedly called on the international community to discuss the state affiliation of Kaliningrad, turn it to a neutral territory administered by the UN or to demilitarise it. Attempts to question the status of the region in the event of some change in Europe and international relations more broadly cannot be ruled out.

Right-wing Lithuanian politicians occasionally hint at what they call Russia's "indebtedness to Lithuania for damages caused by the Soviet occupation". Besides being politically questionable and unreasonable, such views also question the legal position of Kaliningrad in being prepared to receive Kaliningrad as a compensation of "Soviet debts". A minimum programme consists of promoting the *oblast's* development "without Russia's intervention", i.e. turning it to "the fourth Baltic republic" (*Kaliningradskaia Pravda*, 26 April 1995; *Inostranets*, 15 February 1995). One way of influencing Vilnius' position if such a posture would happen to gain official support, would be that Russia, as some experts (for example in Kaliningrad) suggest, could bargain by using the problem of Klaipeda (Memel) the territory having been historically part of East Prussia (*Kaliningradskaia Pravda*, 28 January 1995, 12 July 1995, 11 August 1995; *Krasnaia Zvezda*, 7 September 1995).

The climate of neighbourliness would further be improved if Lithuanian officials – both members of government and parliamentarians – distanced themselves from statements and actions by some organisations and politicians i.e viewpoints detached from political realities in virtually laying territorial claims on Kaliningrad.

Germany, for its part, does not have any "special interests" in Kaliningrad. Bonn's official position on the region may be described as proper, restrained and prudent (*Kaliningradskaia Pravda*, 22 September 1994; *Mezhdunarodnaia Zhyzn* 1995(6): 33). The German Foreign Ministry constantly stresses that the German government's policy proceeds from recognising Kaliningrad as being part of Russia. Germany does not encourage resettlement of Russian Germans in Kaliningrad, nor does it view the region as suited for German settlement. Bonn has repeatedly declared that it has no plans for any re-Germanisation of the *oblast*. Aspiring for what may be characterized as "progress by small, but effective steps" Germany is also observing with interest the process of Russian Germans migrating into region. They now constitute, depending on the source, some 6000–12000 persons.

Lately Bonn has shown more interest in Kaliningrad than before. The Ministry of Interior is particularly active. Officials have repeatedly visited the region. They have funded the construction of a German-Russian House in Kaliningrad. A substantial part of the aid delivered to the *oblast* has been financed by the ministry. The ministry's main activity is to support the ethnic Germans living in the region. While this population group is officially recognised to be relatively small in the region (mostly the Nesterovo, Neman and Krasnoznamenny districts), the German government has in the recent years allocated considerably larger funds for them than the ethnic Germans living in West Siberia. The ministry also calls for a discussion on allowing Germans to move to Kaliningrad and encourages Russian Germans to migrate to the region (*Mezhdunarodnaia Zhyzn* 1995(6): 34).

The Kaliningrad region receives humanitarian aid from Germany. in 1995 100 wagons of different agricultural machines arrived. Humanitarian aid and donations are important for the budget of the *oblast*.

KO and Schleswig-Holstein, Brandenburg, Mecklenburg-Western Pomerania as well as Kiel, Bremerhaven, and Potsdam are increasingly cooperating with each other. There are signs of a bid to gradually increase Germany's economical presence in *oblast*. German firms already account for more than a third of the total foreign investments in the region even though their share remains modest in absolute terms.

Moreover, Kaliningrad banks are stepping up cooperation with major German banks, by opening accounts, conducting interbank operations, and placing money on deposit. The Russian-German insurance business is establishing a foothold in the *oblast*.

For Kaliningrad, the role of the economic cooperation between RF and Belarussia is constantly growing. For stimulating the development of bilateral cooperation with Belarussia, Russia could use Belarussia's interest in new business ties with the Kaliningrad region, operations in Kaliningrad's ports, purchases of fishing production, etc.

Belarussia is interested in taking part in the construction of high-voltage electric lines on the territory of the KO, in producing Belarussian tractors for the *oblast*, as well as machine – tools and goods coming from its light industry. The volume of the trade between Belarussia and Kaliningrad has already reached $45 million in 1995 (i.e. a volume that Belarussia could not yet reach in relations with some states). In 1996, when a programme of economic cooperation between Belarussia and Kaliningrad was adopted in Minsk by heads of 30 joint ventures, Belarussia stands for 62 per cent of all the foreign investments in Kaliningrad (*Svobodnaia Zona*, 15 May 1996; *Interfax-West*, 13 March 1996; *Interfax-Presidential*, 14 March 1996).

Conclusions

1. Taking into account the development of the military strategic situation in the region and the previous conflicts demonstrated by the Baltic states concerning the Russian population, and keeping in mind the positions of Poland, Germany and particularly Lithuania as to Kaliningrad's future and of NATO's expansion to the East, an increase of the strategic importance of the KO for Russia is obvious. With a general weakening of Russia's positions in the Baltic Sea area after the disintegration of the USSR (the loss of four naval bases from five and 14 from 16 the Baltic fleet basing units), a strengthening of KOOR becomes specially important. This is mandatory in view of the rights of Russia, its necessary and sufficient defence and security, the dislocation of Russian troops in the region and the hardship in military transit.

2. The role and influence of Russia in the Baltic Sea area will largely depend on the fighting efficiency of the KOOR troops. Russia's position here will not be challenged if the ties with Kaliningrad are diversified and if the economic, political and ethnic expansion of foreign countries to Kaliningrad is under control.

A more intense use of KOOR within the "Partnership for Peace" and in the context of the "special relations" with NATO could strengthen confidence in the Baltic Sea area. It could include multilateral military training jointly with the Baltic countries. A detente in the military and political situation in the Baltic Sea region could be achieved by such means, with this then further adding to the prospects for development of military and technical cooperation.

3. Cooperation between Russia and Finland in the Baltic Sea region is an example of a peaceful relationship. It seems that Kaliningrad does not sufficiently participate in creating and advancing such relations. Yet the participation of Kaliningrad in such a process demonstrates Russia's aspiration to turn the Baltic region into a zone of peace and confidence, and a form of cooperation that counteracts a new split in Europe. It is most

desirable that Finland, the Scandinavian states and Germany participate in such endeavours which seem to be achievable.

4. The cooperation and partnership with neighbours must be accompanied by an unambiguous confirmation of the historical fact of Kaliningrad belonging to Russia and the sovereign right of Russia to determine the degree of its military presence in the region based exclusively on the Russia's national security interests in accordance with its military doctrine and depending on the development of the situation in Europe.

5. Given this, Russia's policy in the Baltic region should be based on the actions, aimed at preserving and strengthening international stability around Kaliningrad. Regional cooperation around the Baltic Rim should apply to all spheres and include a wide participation of Kaliningrad.

Maintenance of security in the region ought to be achieved by non-military (economic, political) rather than by military means. Compatibility and balance of economic and strategic interests with all the Baltic Sea countries would create a basis for stabilizing the regional setting and European security more broadly.

There are prospects for Russian initiatives in the context of the CBSS concerning the development of Russian ports, creation of an "electric power ring" around the Baltic Sea, cooperation between border guards in order to prevent smuggling, illegal migration, as well as weapons and drug traffic, exchange of naval visits, etc. The creation of some new bodies for cooperation between the Baltic Sea countries, including, for example, Norway and Belarus, would contribute to a strengthening of stability in the region. A new institutional centre on regional cooperation in the fields of economic, ecological and other aspects of security could be established in the context of the CBSS.

The wide participation of Russia as partner in the process of integration process in Europe and in the Baltic Sea region would create a more favourable climate for solving problems of transit, new investments, and other similar matters, these being also quite important for the future of the Kaliningrad *oblast*.

8 Kaliningrad as a Security Issue: An Expert View from Poland

ZDZISLAW LACHOWSKI

Introduction

The aim of this paper is to discuss some general (European) and (sub)regional aspects of military and political security as seen from the Polish perspective in the context of Kaliningrad's specific location and the role and place ascribed to it by Russia. Therefore the analysis starts with a general review of the Polish-Russian relations after the end of the cold war, followed by an overview of the place of Kaliningrad in Polish policy and a discussion of security and confidence building aspects regarding Europe and the region.

Origins

The former German East Prussian province was divided under the Potsdam Agreement of 1945 between the USSR and Poland, with some one-third of the territory going to the former. Unlike Poland's historical claims to the part which it acquired, the Russian rationale was of a strictly military nature. Owing to its strategic location, the Kaliningrad *oblast* took on the character of a huge garrison area, important for the air defence of the mainland USSR, basing the Baltic Fleet and stationing the follow-on forces earmarked for an attack against the West. One can guess that the location of the *oblast* in the backyard of the three Baltic republics also served as a deterrent to any possible independence drive on the part of those pretty fresh Soviet acquisitions. The specific character of the exclave effectively stymied its socio-economic development. With the end of the cold war, the rationale for maintaining the large concentration of troops evidently decreased, and the question of normalizing the situation in the area, which impinges on the regional security perceptions, including Poland's, has become a matter of urgency.

Polish-Russian security relations after the cold war

In the post-cold war period, Poland's attitude to its former main Eastern neighbour in general, and the Kaliningrad question, in particular, was subjected to the new main Polish security priorities. It also stemmed to some degree from the fact that, after the 45 years of satellite nature of Polish-Russian relations, Poland's Eastern policy has taken a back seat to its drive toward NATO membership. The priorities of Poland's security policy in its relations with Russia directly after 1989 were: getting rid of all forms of political, military and economic dependence from the Soviet Union (particularly the dissolution of the Warsaw Treaty Organization and CMEA-COMECON); establishing qualitatively new diplomatic and treaty relations with its big neighbour and other post-Soviet states; and having the former Soviet troops leave Polish territory as quickly as possible.

With the threat of attack from the East gone and the qualitatively new challenges and threats emerging instead (ethnic local crises and conflicts, the seeming menace of mass migrations, economic and social difficulties etc.) the post-communist Poland has embarked on forging new relations with its neighbours, including the Russian Federation. This was crowned with the Polish-Russian Treaty on friendly and good-neighbourly cooperation and the Agreement on withdrawal of the Russian troops from Poland's territory, both signed on 22 May 1992.

The document entitled "The tenets of the Polish security policy", adopted by the National Defence Committee in autumn 1992, stated that "[t]he fall of the USSR (...) has created an opportunity for permanent strengthening of security in the east of Europe. At present, however, it remains a politically unstable region. There is huge military potential on its territory. The possibility of the outbreak of local conflicts continues to be a serious threat. If such conflicts develop, they may also involve Poland. (...) Poland's cooperation with Ukraine, Russia and Belarus, based on the bilateral agreements, serves to reduce such threats. These agreements cover both the economic and security cooperation, including some military elements" (*Warsaw*, 2 November 1992).

In the first half of the 1990s, several major steps of military significance were taken, which contributed to an increased sense of security in Europe, and Poland's security as well. The pull-out of some 700 thousand Soviet/Russian troops and tens of thousands of heavy equipment from Germany and Central Europe has left behind only a pocket of force in the Kaliningrad *oblast*. Except for this, Russian conventional troops were withdrawn from Poland's borders. The 1990 Conventional Armed Forces in Europe (CFE) Treaty and the successive Vienna confidence- and security-building accords (1990, 1992, 1994) further constrained room for big presence of troops and equipment and military activities in Europe.

The collapse of the Soviet Union left the bulk of Russian forces either in the wrong location (in other post-Soviet republics or, domestically, due to the CFE flank limitations) or devoid of the vital military infrastructure (e.g., air defence). The Russian armed forces continue to be plagued by a variety of troubles: budgetary squeeze; contempt for institutions; absence of motivation to serve in the ranks; hazing; bribery and cheating; food shortages; weapons trading; and concomitant draft evasion. The financial difficulties have contributed to Russia's conventional forces becoming virtually obsolete. This could not but affect the army's condition.[1] Moreover the Russian forces have had to respond to serious contingencies in other parts of the Federation and the so-called "near abroad", mainly in the North Caucasus and Central Asia (Tajikistan). Obviously, even though large on paper, Russian conventional forces, including those stationed in Kaliningrad, have been weakened and their offensive capabilities have diminished along with the servicemen's morale woresening.

Poland and the Kaliningrad issue

Proceeding from the principle of inviolability of frontiers in Europe, the Polish Government has openly declared that the Kaliningrad *oblast* is and will remain Russian. Since the break-up of the Soviet Union Polish official representatives have kept stressing that Poland's policy towards Kaliningrad cannot but be impartial, "neither anti-Russian, nor anti-Lithuanian nor anti-German".[2] The region is the only part of Russia which borders on Poland after the break-up of the Soviet Union. The militarization of the *oblast*, a remnant of the cold war era, gives it a specific character, both domestically and externally. A closed area, with restricted access even for Soviet civilians in the past, along with the end of the bloc division and confrontation, Kaliningrad was expected to become a beacon and litmus test of cooperation and confidence-building in the region.

Poland's attitude towards the continuing big military presence north-east of its frontiers has for the most part been balanced and matter-of-fact.

On the one hand, Warsaw took account of the difficult technical, financial and humanitarian problems confronting Russia which had already declared to reduce its military presence in the Kaliningrad strip.[3] The Polish government also understood the complexity of Russian withdrawal, politically and militarily, from Central Europe. Moreover, it was noted that in spite of the big numbers of troops and equipment, the Kaliningrad force obviously had no longer an organized offensive capability. On the other hand, the very fact of existence of forces equalling to half of all Polish forces[4] was obviously of concern to Poland. Russia has never revealed the number of it troops in the region. Estimates of the number of troops in the area varied at that time: in the early 1990s there was talk of 90000 Janous (Hoff & Timmerman 1993: 40).

For Poland, the Kaliningrad problem in the early 1990s was more a political and economic than a military one. Various concepts concerning the future of the area, especially those of resettling Russian Germans or of intensive German investments in the region, were met with a degree of suspicion and concern on the part of the Polish political circles.[5] Seen from the present perspective, those "re-Germanization" fears proved eventually unfounded.[6] Nonetheless, in part to counter the prospect of German influence, Poland intensified the development of economic, trade and other relations with Kaliningrad (agreements on near-border cooperation, transborder crossings, the opening of a Polish consulate in Kaliningrad etc.).

Indeed, economic and trade relations as well as a range of other arrangements arrived at with regard to the Kaliningrad area have become Poland's main instrument of building cooperation and confidence in the region. The basis of cooperation constitute the Polish-Russian Treaty of 22 May 1992 and the Agreement on cooperation between the north-eastern voivodships of the Republic of Poland and the Kaliningrad Region of the Russian Federation of 22 July 1992 which are found to be satisfactory though calling for further improvements and expansion (e.g., with regard to opening the Pilawa straits for navigation of third states' ships; transit issues; flow of people and goods on the border etc.). Numerous Russian-Polish meetings and "round tables" have taken place to discuss ways and means of developing and strengthening links between the Kaliningrad area and the Polish northern provinces (Suwalki, Olsztyn, Elblag and Gdansk) in the fields of transport, agriculture, trade and banking, environment, tourism, cross-border traffic, cultural, education and sport exchanges with the aim to facilitate the flow of goods, capital and people. Kaliningrad's trade exchanges and joint ventures with its southern partner take the first place in the overall volume of the Russian *oblast's* foreign trade turnover. About 900 firms with foreign capital operate in the area, 37 per cent of them having Polish share (German firms account for 22 per cent).[7]

While Poland's attitude toward Kaliningrad issue was, as mentioned above, one of patience and understanding, nonetheless Warsaw kept voicing, via diplomatic channels, its anxiety over the Russian big military presence close to Poland's borders. This has resurfaced and been given more prominence in times of political expediency. During the domestic political battle between President Walesa and the Olszewski's centre-rightist government in spring 1992, the issue of Kaliningrad came up. Polish Defence Minister Jan Parys raised the question of "excessive militarization" in the vicinity of the Polish northern borders and called on both countries to negotiate and establish a 50-km zone of military disengagement ("military thinning-out") along the Polish-Russian frontier. The government fell soon and the suggestion has since then been quietly dropped. Later, a Polish military expert, while appreciating the seriousness of the issue, still wished this concentration would be of a provisional character in light of Russian planned military reduction and reform; also the political and economic future of Kaliningrad was hoped to determine its geopolitical standing and impact on the states in the region (Kosciuk 1993).

In the years up to 1994, a considerable part of the Russian troops and equipment withdrawn from Germany, Poland and the Baltic states had ended up in the Kaliningrad region. These developments concurred with the radical change of Russian position at the end of 1993 and in the beginning of 1994, in the aftermath of the December 1993 election showing clear shifts in the Russian political spectrum towards the nationalist and communist extremes. Moscow started to speak with a more assertive voice in matters of European security and arms control as well as on possible NATO expansion eastward. All this gave rise to some increased concern in the neighbouring countries, including Poland.

During his visit to Riga, Latvia, in February 1994, President Walesa described the number of Russian troops in that area an "alarming phenomenon" and wondered why such a powerful grouping is stationed there in peacetime; he called on the West to react to this excessive militarization of the area. Afterwards, however, in bilateral contacts with Russia, Polish officials have been reported not to press hard for that and stress that while no country is interested in "having other states' major military groupings close to its borders", Poland is not going to consider the issue a serious bilateral issue (*Izvestiya*, 9 December 1994: 3).

The Polish estimates in 1993 spoke of about 100000 servicemen, some 1300 tanks, 1500 ACVs, 700 artillery pieces, 160 combat aircraft and 60 helicopters (Kosciuk 1993: 39n). In sum, this amounted to 35-40 per cent of all Polish forces. Since then, the holdings of heavy weapons have gone further down.[8] The data given by the Russian side to the CFE Joint Consultative Group (JCG) in Vienna were in 1995 as follows: 893 tanks, 1156 ACVs, 495 artillery pieces, 32 aircraft and 52 attack helicopters.[9] The manpower figure is said to be close to 40000-45000 (Petersen 1994: 572; Yegorov 1995).

A "Militarized Status"

In the early 1990s, Kaliningrad was seen as a Russian "window" to the world. In 1991 stringent controls on foreign visitors were lifted and the "Yantar" Free Economic Zone was created. With the passage of time, however, the investment boom as envisaged by Russia has not materialized, and the *oblast* is muddling through an economic depression. The change in Russian policy towards the outside world, as witnessed since 1993/1994, has also affected the plans to hamper the level of militarization of its western exclave. Consequently, in the summer and autumn of 1994, the then Deputy Prime Minister Sergei Shakhrai published articles in which he defended the priority of Russia's military-strategic interests in the *oblast* at the cost of other development plans (*Nezavisimaya gazeta*, 26 October 1994). This reflected the view of circles close to the Russian government and the president as well as the military. It ran counter to the position of the *oblast* administration and local economic groups which strive for more economic autonomy and leeway vis-à-vis Moscow; they believe that the excessive military concentration stifles the development of economic and trade contacts, and particularly the influx of foreign capital to the area.

Generally, the Russian official arguments developed in favour of retaining the specific military character by Kaliningrad can be summed up as follows:

It is the largest and only ice-free port in the Baltic Sea, where the command of the Baltic Fleet is and will most probably be stationed permanently;

The Kaliningrad military area is the westernmost outpost to "defend the coast and territory of the region and prevent the air invasion of both the Kaliningrad Special Area and the main territory of Russia" (Yegorov 1995: 130).

Part of the former Soviet troops transfers, unprecedented indeed, from Central Europe and the Baltic republics had to be directed to the Kaliningrad area since they could not go anywhere else, both for arms control limitations (as discussed below) and socio-economic (infrastructure, housing) reasons;[10] and

Last but not least, NATO expansion to the east warrants keeping "as large a force on our western borders as is considered sufficient from the military operational point of view" (Kashlev 1995: 20).

This abnormal cold war-like situation in the tiny strip of land sandwiched between Poland and Lithuania, evidently incompatible with cooperative security arrangements made elsewhere, is worth looking closer at in the light of arms control in Europe.

Kalinigrad and CFE

The CFE treaty has radically decreased the threat of massive attack in Europe by limiting the numbers of heavy weapons that states parties can possess. The high concentration of military forces in the Kaliningrad *oblast* is not directly related to CFE implementation. Nevertheless it gives rise to concerns for the neighbouring states. As a result of the dissolution of the USSR, Kaliningrad is the only remaining tiny Russian portion of the former Baltic Military District, and under the CFE Treaty Russia is formally allowed to deploy sizeable armed forces there. The decision taken in autumn 1991 by the three Baltic states to dissociate themselves from the CFE regime, a step much regretted by Poland, resulted in sharing out the limits for the CFE rear zone between Russia (the Kaliningrad strip), Belarus and Ukraine (Sharp 1992). The break-up of the Soviet Union left Russia in a very inconvenient situation. Under the CFE terms it was prevented from deploying its forces more proportionately and adequately to its security requirements. This deployment asymmetry is illustrated by the fact that Russia could have 6 times more tanks and 15 times more ACVs in the Kaliningrad region than in the whole flank zone covering more than half the European territory of the country.[11] Russian Deputy Chief of Staff, Col.-Gen. Vladimir Zhurbenko, claimed that Russia is entitled to station in the Kaliningrad *oblast* up to 4200 tanks, 8760 ACVs and 3235 artillery systems (*Krasnaya Zvezda*, 7 December 1994). Obviously the quota is by no means used up, but cramming sizeable forces in this small exclave has created a unique phenomenon. In the Treaty context, the other CFE states parties cannot officially challenge Russia's right to keep its armed forces and armaments in the area unless they exceed the TLE entitlements for the zone. However, Russian military officials themselves have admitted that the armed forces in Kaliningrad exceed the security needs of the area and suggested that some of the troops could be redeployed into mainland Russia, preferably the Leningrad and North Caucasus MDs (belonging to the so-called flank zone) rather than beyond the Urals as suggested by other CFE parties.[12]

Russia's dissatisfaction with the flank provisions of the CFE Treaty and its persistent demands in this regard led to striking a compromise at the CFE Review Conference in May 1996, which envisaged exclusion of several military regions from the flank zone and their inclusion in the CFE rear zone, thus adding to Russia's first strategic echelon and enabling it to deploy its troops and heavy equipment more evenly. As mentioned above, the large concentration of military equipment and troops in Kaliningrad has been said to stem from the inability to redeploy them somewhere else in Russia. The Russian side also insisted on having four *oblasts* of the Leningrad MD included in its first echelon area. Due to NATO's opposition, only the flank status of the Pskov region was changed. This, however, fails to assuage fears of the Baltic states, since Russia is allowed to increase the number of armoured combat vehicles by 420 on the Estonian and Latvian borders. In this context, the statement by then Russian Defence Minister Pavel Grachev about having the "space for manoeuvring" thanks to the Kaliningrad region capabilities seems to demonstrate Russia's will to continue to maintain the special character of that region (Interview with Pavel Grachev for *Interfax*, 30 October 1995: 21). On the other hand, the extension of the area for deployment of bigger numbers of heavy weapons to parts of the former flank zone removes the reason for keeping the heavy armaments arsenal in the Kaliningrad area, and is likely to help pull out the troops and armaments stationed therein (*Rzeczpospolita*, 23-24 September 1994).

The CFE adaptation talks which started in January 1997 in Vienna provide, among other things, for the avoidance of destabilizing accumulations of armed forces. In this connection, Poland will certainly insist on a solution of the problem of Kaliningrad troop concentration.

The "Special Defence Region"

Defence Minister Grachev's announcement on 21 March 1994 of the intention to create a "special defence region" (*Kaliningradskiy osobiy oboronitelniy raion. KOOR*) in the area, (*Krasnaya Zvezda*, 22 March 1994) to be comprised of large groupings of ground forces, military aviation, air defence forces and naval units from the Baltic Fleet, added to the anxiety about Russia's plans regarding the role and tasks of such a force. Especially the air defence system is of particular concern for the special region, having been in disarray after the break-up of the Soviet Union.

The special region is subordinated to the Defence Minister and the General Staff, and its task is "to wage, if necessary, hostilities for a certain period of time in defence of the maritime coast and part of the land territory pending the arrival of the main forces from Russia" (*Krasnaya Zvezda*, 22 March 1994). Later, in explaining the rationale for the special area, the Russian military put emphasis on the need of providing a homogenous command, centralizing the supply system and reducing the costs (*Kaliningradskaya Pravda*, 28 June 1995). The KOOR, which formally was established on 1 August 1994, is under the command of Admiral Vladimir Yegorov.

Along with other developments regarding Kaliningrad, the plan and its implementation prompted a series of negative reactions from the Baltic capitals,[13] as well as from Poland[14] and some Scandinavian states.[15]

The issue of a transit corridor

The main concern of Russia, and the Russian military in particular, is the maintenance of transportation links between the Kaliningrad exclave and mainland Russia. Owing to the Russian-Lithuanian dispute over the transportation of material and other military technology *via* the Lithuanian territory, Russia has decided to consider other options, such as the development of a ferry connection between Baltiysk and St. Petersburg (so far, not effective enough) and intensification of the transportation through the Polish territory.

The plan of a Grodno-Gusev transit freeway between the Kaliningrad exclave and Belarus raised during the Yeltsin-Lukashenka meeting on 27 February,[16] evoked much concern and generated emotions in Poland in February-April 1996. Apart from Russia's genuine interest in developing and diversifying its transportation links with the region and some preliminary Polish-Russian local arrangements,[17] the heavy-handed handling of this matter by the Belarussian and Russian highest officials (especially, announcing the idea without having consulted the Polish authorities in advance) and lame explanations by the Russian transport ministry[18] evoked bad pre-World War II reminiscences and memories of the not-so-distant past. It also became a fertile ground for various interpretations and speculations, although the original message seemed to have been aimed at Lithuania. Worth noting, however, is that the question of a Polish corridor linking Belarus with Kaliningrad did not lead to a security hysteria in Warsaw, and was handled by the Polish authorities with calm and reason. Apart from the real or would-be intentions and political games of Russia and Belarus, the incident once again brought home to Poland (and others) the specific character of the exclave and political implications of its existence. The question was eventually cleared up both through unambiguous statements of the high Polish authorities and denials of the Russian side as well as during the March visit of Yevgeni Primakov to Warsaw and President Aleksander Kwasniewski's trip to Moscow in April 1996.

Kaliningrad and NATO expansion

Seen in the broader context, the question of the security dimension of Kaliningrad calls for more attention. The militant rhetoric of various political figures and groupings in Russia with more or less concealed blackmail overtones, its firm veto over Poland's and other Central European countries joining of NATO,[19] the successive steps towards a union with Belarus and the deplorable concept of a "corridor" all require taking a closer look at the security and confidence building context around Kaliningrad.

So far, there has been no clear statement of Russia's intention to use Kaliningrad as a leverage in pursuing its interests *vis-à-vis* NATO once Poland joins the Atlantic Alliance.[20] Russian politicians and mass media speculate about Moscow's possible response, hinting at various retaliatory moves, including deployment of additional weapons, conventional and nuclear alike, in the area. This, however, seems to be rather unlikely due to both political and financial consequences such decisions would imply. Instead, the Russian diplomacy and military seek to ensure that the forthcoming enlargement of the Alliance does not impair its security, worsen the balance of forces in favour of NATO and result in a large build-up of Western military equipment near its borders, a deployment of nuclear weapons in former WTO countries and an increase in Western intelligence gathering activities in the region. Some headway has already been made along these lines. The NATO allies announced in December 1996 that they had "no intention, no plans and no reason" to deploy nuclear weapons on the territory of new members,[21] the step welcomed by the Central European aspirants, too. In early January 1997, Russian Foreign Minister Yevgeni Primakov made clear that the signing of a document on special NATO-Russia relations will be conditional on an understanding reached on "updating CFE Treaty, in order to resolve our concerns about a possible advancement of NATO's military infrastructure" (*Defense News*, 20-26 January 1997: 12). Moreover, Russia claims that if the military status quo under the CFE is maintained (NATO possesses ca. 25 per cent less arms than it is entitled to in the CFE area of application), then a balance could be kept (Korzun 1997). This would mean a freezing of current holdings in Central Europe. In the meantime, during the period of negotiations (which started on 21 January 1997), the states parties have committed themselves to show restraint in relation to the current postures and capabilities of their conventional forces, in particular, with respect to their levels of forces and deployments in order not to diminish security of any state party sentence to be substituted with the one sent by fax.

The Western countries had no clear position on readjustment of the conventional arms regime by early 1997. At the same time, however, NATO and its members were reported to lend a sympathetic ear to the Russian postulates.

Poland is aware that changes in the CFE regime will affect it in the first place as a future NATO forward country. Preventing a diminution of its military potential and assuring Russia that it will not be threatened by an enlarged Alliance, are the aims Polish foreign policy has to fulfil. In this context, the Kaliningrad case is bound to be addressed, and at the same time, it is very likely to appear as either an instrument of pressure or a bargaining chip in the negotiations.

Confidence and security enhancement

The landmark arms control and disarmament agreements of the early 1990s have greatly contributed to the enhancement of security in Europe. At the same time, however, they closed the chapter of the cold war era, providing the basis for new arrangements in the new circumstances. Classic arms control, with its emphasis on the calculations of balance, is no longer helpful and sensible in a new environment with qualitatively different challenges and threats. Future limitations and reductions are more likely to become a political rather than a "bean counting" exercise. With the collapse of the bloc division, the trends and changes, mostly driven by budgetary squeezes, which are taking place in armed forces (high-tech inputs and operational developments; rapid reaction, mobile and professional forces *versus* the old-type armies) will make numerical balances increasingly unattainable and outdated. Moreover, sub-regional stability and arms control arrangements will make this even more complex and difficult. Thus, cooperative, confidence-building stability-enhancing measures are taking on prominence (Dalsjš, R. et al. 1993).

This is one of the reasons why Kaliningrad's heavy military concentration is not overdramatized by Poland and the solution to this is seen largely through political and other confidence-building and stabilizing endeavours that would gradually alleviate the situation, paving the road to broadly conceived arms control and disarmament arrangements.

In this light, also with regard to the Baltic Sea region, confidence and transparency building measures going further beyond the Vienna CSBMs are proposed. A process of informal and open-ended consultations might be launched to address (e.g. development of subregional cooperative CBMs, joint commissions, military contacts, a regional "open skies" regime etc.) regional instabilities affecting security, both of an external and domestic nature. There is a need for additional enhanced transparency measures to help lessen concentration of forces in border areas; exchange of information and dialogue in the context of naval cooperation etc.[22]

A series of naval CBMs is also called for, such as: meetings and consultations of high commanders and staffs of naval forces, visits to naval bases, various kinds of exchanges between personnel etc.; cooperation in the field of naval activities and sea rescue, including notification of planned overflights, of areas of aircraft training in the Baltic Sea, information about emergency situations of air and sea vessels, allowing emergency landings on airfields of the other party, sea rescue communications centres between Navy HQs, joint ecological disaster handling; broader information on naval forces and notification of military activities on sea and in coastal regions; mechanisms preventing incidents related to military activity etc).

Some cooperative endeavours are already said to be carried out by the Russian Baltic Fleet (Yegorov 1995: 129). However, these are in need of being expanded and instituted within an organized regime, along the above-mentioned lines in order to more effectively inject stability and predictability and stave off potential crises in the region.

Conclusion

The above analysis leads to the following conclusions:

1. The problem of Kaliningrad is an unfinished business. The area constitutes a peculiar *skansen* of Soviet-era closed society reality and thinking. In some aspects, it is a "classic" cold war remnant. Nonetheless it still stands a chance of getting out of its militarized status and ridding of its predominant garrison mentality. The *oblast* is at a crossroads: it can either join the other countries of the region in developing cooperation and regaining prosperity by taking full advantage of its location (a free trade zone, a free port, a "gateway" to Russia etc.) or spoil its chance by continuing its present condition.

2. Kaliningrad does not pose a threat *per se* to European security in general. Nor does it constitute an immediate source of domestic conflict or crisis for ethnic, religious or other reasons, as is the case with other hot spots on the continent. The pan-European security and arms control-related instruments ensure a degree of security and make it hard to prepare and launch a surprise mass-scale attack in Europe. In the subregional context,

however, the area having big stockpiles of arms weighs heavily against the regional balance of forces and constitutes a source of constant political uncertainty.

3. The area is acknowledged by Poland to be an integral part of Russia, and consequently Warsaw has developed good neighbourly relations with the Russian exclave through various forms of transboundary cooperation and contacts. Poland was and is careful not to make the situation a serious bilateral issue in the Polish-Russian relations. However, the stationing of an army-size contingent in close proximity to its borders obviously remains a matter of concern to the neighbouring countries and a potential obstacle in developing the better sense of security and building confidence in bilateral relations with Russia.

4. Kaliningrad's present and declared future status as a heavily armed area stands in stark contrast to the plans for its economic recovery and prosperity. Poland's position is to help engage Kaliningrad in the web of cooperation in various fields of common interest in order to promote mutual benefits, confidence and understanding, on the one hand, and alleviate the residual fears and concerns (such as those about calling into question its status as Russian territory), on the other. This position is generally highly praised by the Kaliningrad partners while apparently less appreciated by the Moscow government. None the less efforts made by Poland and other neighbours are not enough. The additional risk is that the continuing abnormal plight of Kaliningrad might contribute to its socio-economic reversal and ensuing backwardness as against the fast developing economies and societies in the region. As long as Kaliningrad's development is constrained by its heavy dependence on the central government, this does not augur well for the *oblast*'s prospects, and consequently for regional stability and sense of security.

5. The status of Kaliningrad stems from Russia's own sense of uncertainty rather than from genuine threats to its territorial integrity and security. On the other hand, a region with a special geographic location and bristling with weaponry may easily become a source of tension and used as an element of political game or blackmail *vis-à-vis* others in times of worsening international atmosphere. With every state having legitimate security interests, the more-than-sufficient military concentration in the area is certainly an anomaly, and no formal explanations can account for that. The enlargement of NATO to the east are being met with high suspicion and reluctance by Russia; mixed signals are coming from

Moscow, among them threats of further military deployments in the Kaliningrad forward base by way of reprisal once Poland joins the Atlantic Alliance. Such retaliatory steps would adversely affect the cooperation and security in the region, and do harm to the development projects in the *oblast*. This is why efforts should be made to continue to mutually dispel suspicions and inject more confidence, assurance and predictability in the relations in the region.

Notes

1 A report by the Bundestag's Defence Committee, as revealed by the daily *Süddeutsche Zeitung* of 27/28 January 1996, found the Russian forces to be in a "deep crisis": 51 of the 81 divisions are not operational; half of the 28 brigades are not battle-ready; only the airborne units and the two divisions earmarked for international peacekeeping missions are combat-ready. The air force and the navy are equally troubled by a lack of equipment, fuels and maintenence. In contrast, nuclear weapons are sufficiently secured and under the control of the command structures. See also *Defense News*, 15-21 January 1996, pp. 1, 21.

2 Interview with the former first Polish Consul-General in Kaliningrad, Jerzy Bahr "Problemu poczdamskiego nie ma. Sa problemy gospodarcze" [There is no Potsdam problem. There are economic problems]. *Kaliningradskaya Pravda*, 10 June 1995 in *Biuletyn Kaliningradzki number 6*.

3 Onyszkiewicz, the deputy chairman of the Defence Commission of the Sejm and former Polish Defence Minister, reasserted that "Poland is not paranoid about the Kaliningrad area. We understand that the problem arose because of the withdrawal of Russian troops from central Europe. Nevertheless, we must bear in mind the fact that, if the situation is frozen and the presence of such a heavy concentration of armaments becomes permanent, it would not contribute to a sense of security and confidence. That is why it is worth remembering why an anomaly appears in that area, we cannot treat it as a simple anomaly but should rectify it as soon as possible". Assembly of Western European Union. Proceedings. 41st ordinary session, First Part, December 1995. Minutes, *Official Report of Debates, p. 116*.

4 Some estimates even mentioned 70 per cent of the whole Polish army. See Lt. Col. Franciszek Kochanowski, "A Polish perspective on the future of the Baltic Sea region security". Presentation to the *Conference on the future of Kaliningrad and Baltic security*, held at King's College, University of London, 4 July 1993. According to Polish sources, in early 1992, the Russians had 900

tanks, 1200 armoured combat vehicles, 16 missile launchers and 900 heavy artillery pieces plus navy and air force units equipped with the MiG-29s aircraft. Border and GRU troops added to the forces of the 11th Guards Army having two armoured divisions, two mechanised divisions, one artillery division and rocket artillery units. Poland could at that time meet this huge troop and weaponry concentration with two mechanised regiments and one air squadron. Boyes, R., "Kaliningrad stirs fear among Poles", *The Times*, 15 May 1992.

5   Polish Foreign Minister Krzysztof Skubiszewski played down the fears of a "German enclave" in Kaliningrad, having admitted that the Polish side had discussed the matter with the Soviet government. *Rzeczpospolita*, 6 September 1991. Moreover, supposedly as a countermeasure, various startling (unofficial) suggestions reportedly appeared in Poland, e.g., to turn Kaliningrad into a homeland for Roma. Krauze, J., "Poland's new eastern policy takes shape", *Le Monde*, 8-9 March 1992, in *Guardian Weekly*, 15 March 1992, p. 13.

6   The lack of rules in business, restrictions in customs concessions and other factors like failing to open a German consulate in Kaliningrad have stifled the free-trade region plans and discouraged the influx of foreign capital. "Auf Wiedersehen, Königsberg", *The Economist*, 14 October 1995, p. 48. President Yeltsin signed the federal bill on the "Special Economic Zone" in Kaliningrad in January 1996. However, it did not encompass areas and installations of a strategic and defence significance, military bases as well as those of military industry, and oil and gas exploration, thus making it less attractive it the eyes of potential investors.

7   More on this, see the Polish contributions in *International Affairs* (Moscow) no.6 1995, pp 92-103.

8   Depicting the condition of the Russian Baltic Fleet in comparison with the Soviet times, Admiral Yegorov draws attention to the fact that since 1991 the Fleet personnel has been reduced by half, and its strength in ships by two-thirds; its air force has been trimmed by 60 per cent; the Fleet has lost 80 per cent (4 out of 5) of its main bases and 65 per cent (11 out of 16) of its auxiliary bases; it also has lost 30 per cent of its airfields on which 1/4 of the Fleet's air force was based, as well as 80 per cent of its coastal monitoring system; the length of the coasts has diminished by 20 km (61 per cent); and there remained only 1 (instead of 4) maintenance naval yard; 350 units have been dismantled or transferred to mainland Russia; apart from the old ships, the last cruiser has been removed; the Fleet is divided and contained to two bases in Kaliningrad (Baltiysk) and St Petersburg. The social, housing and financial conditions of the military personnel are dramatic. Interviews with Admiral Yegorov in *Strazh*

Baltiki, 14 June 1995 and in "The security interests of Russia and Europe in the Baltic" in: *Kaliningrad: Russia in the Baltic*, International Affairs (Moscow), no. 6 (1995), p. 16. Nevertheless, compared to other Russian fleets, the Baltic Fleet seems to be in pretty good shape, with most of its vessels being relatively new.

9 According to Russian data supplied to the CFE JCG, the following units are stationed at present in the area: 1 tank division plus one independent tank brigade, 2 motor rifle divisions, six artillery brigades, 1 naval infantry brigade, 1 coastal artillery regiment and 1 surface-to-surface missile brigade stationed in the area. Admiral Vladimir Yegorov, commander of the Baltic Fleet estimates that it consists of 126 ships and cutters (including 9 conventional submarines), 2 naval aircraft regiments, two anti-submarine squadrons, 1 naval infantry brigade, missile artillery units and other sub-units. The International Institute for Strategic Studies, *IISS. The Military Balance 1995-96*, p. 105.

10 See, *e.g.*, the Russian demarche of 28 September 1993 on the CFE revision, *Arms Control Reporter* (Institute for Defense and Disarmament Studies: Brookline, Mass.), sheets 407.D.85-86, and the article in *Krasnaya zvezda* by Lt.-Gen. V. Zhurbenko on 16 November 1993. In this context, Russia keeps repeating that the pullout from Kaliningrad could have taken place much faster had Poland and other states kept their promises and provided financial and housing assistance. Poland allegedly failed to pay for the withdrawal of the Soviet/Russian Northern Group of Forces; the problem of enormous environmental and physical damages made by the Soviet forces stationing in Poland was left out in this context (Kahslev 1995: 21).

11 For more on this see Falkenrath (1995), and relevant chapters dealing with arms control in Europe in the *SIPRI Yearbooks*, 1994-1996.

12 Interview with Pavel Grachev for *Moscow Interfax*, 'Grachev opposes CFE flank limitations' on 11 September 1994: 11) FBIS-SOV-95-209.

13 See, e.g., the 5th Baltic Assembly's demand to demilitarize the Kaliningrad region and convene an international round table to discuss the issue. "Calls for Kaliningrad demilitarization", Interfax (Moscow), 14 November 1994, FBIS-SOV-94-176, 15 November 1994, p. 70.

14 See Polish President Lech Walesa's remarks during his visit to Riga. *Rzeczpospolita*, 24 February 1994. One of the motives of Poland's proposal of 7 September 1994 (CSCE document CSCE/FSC/SC.29, Vienna, 7 September 1994) to launch a new agenda for arms control in Europe was to avoid excessive concentration of armaments in areas such as Kaliningrad. See comments by the Polish chief delegate to the CSCE, Ambassador J. M. Nowak, for *Rzeczpospolita*, 28 November 1994.

15 Statement by Sweden's Foreign Minister Margareta af Ugglas during her visit to Kaliningrad. Ministry for Foreign Affairs Press Release, Stockholm, 19 May 1994.

16 "We want to make a deal with the Poles and get their permission to run a section of the freeway through their territory" stated B. Yeltsin. *Warsaw Voice*, 10 March 1996: 5.

17 E.g., an agreement between the Kaliningrad authorities and the Polish north-eastern voivodships concerning the facilitating of cross-border traffic.

18 Russia claimed that they wanted a transit road built "according to Polish law and European standards". Poland's trade minister replied that all Polish border-crossing transport regulations are in line with European conventions (Warsaw Voice, 10 March 1996: 5).

19 The suggestion of introduction of tactical nuclear weapons to the Kaliningrad region to counterbalance Poland restructuring its defence system with an aim to adapt it to NATO standards, made on 1 June 1995 in *Moscow Times* by P. Felgenhauer, was later disavowed by the Russian Defence Ministry. However, such suggestions have for some time been voiced both in the Russian press and by some officials. Cf., e.g., *Komsomolskaya Pravda*, 29 September 1995, p. 2, and Sergei Shakhrai's statement for Moscow Interfax calling for desisting from arms reductions, particularly in Kaliningrad and in southern Russia. FBIS-SOV-97-008, 12 January 1997.

20 Unlike the NATO enlargement plans, Russia supports Central European aspirations to join the European Union and the Western European Union.

21 Final Communique of NAC Ministerial Meeting, 10 December 1996.

22 Some of such measures have been proposed at the OSCE Forum for Security Cooperation, e.g. in the French-German-Polish non-paper submitted on 25 September 1996.

References

Anisimov, Aleksander (1995). "The Region in the context of international relations", *International Affairs* (Moscow), 6: 26-33.

Dalsjš, Robert, *et al.* (1993), "Nordic security considerations and arms control", Stockholm: FOA pre-print, May 1993, p. 14-17.

Hoff, Magdalene and Heinz Timmerman (1993), "Kaliningrad: Russia"s future gateway to Europe?", *RFE/RL Research Report* 2 (36): pp. 37-43.

Kashlev, Yuri, (1995), "Kaliningrad as viewed from Warsaw", *Kaliningrad: Russia in the Baltic*, International Affairs (Moscow), no. 6, pp. 19-26.

Korzun, Aleksander (1997), "Russia: MFA official stresses seriousness of new CFE proposals", *Moscow Interfax in English*, 24 Jan. 1997.

Kosciuk, Leszek (1993), "Sytuacja geostrategiczna Polski na poczatku 1993 r. Bilans i prognoza" [*Poland's geostrategic situation in early 1993. The balance sheet and forecast*]. Raport o stanie bezpieczenstwa panstwa. Aspekty zewnetrzne [*Report on the security of the state. External aspects*]. Warsaw: Polish Institute of International Affairs.

Nowak, Jerzy M. (1994), "Rosyanie Zadouleni" ["Russians are Glad"]. *Rzeczpospolita*, 23-24 Sep. 1994.

Petersen, Phillip A. (1994), "Kaliningrad"s transition from garrison state", *Jane's Intelligence Review*: 572.

Sharp, Jane M. O. (1992), "Conventional arms control in Europe: developments and prospects in 1991", *SIPRI Yearbook 1992*. Oxford: Oxford University Press, pp. 465-66.

Yegorov, V.G. (1995), "Cooperative security in northern Europe", in *Vilnius-Kaliningrad. Ideas on Cooperative Security in the Baltic Sea Region*. Conference in Vilnius/Fact-finding visit to Kaliningrad, 24-27 November 1995. Helsinki: Nordic Forum for Security Policy, pp. 127-132.

Official statements

"Concern over CFE flank restriction voiced", *Krasnaya Zvezda* (daily), 7 December.

"Samyi zapadnyi forpost strany" (1994), *Krasnaya Zvezda* (daily), 22 March.

"Spory vokrug Kaliningradskoi oblasti obostryaiutsia" (1994), [Disputes around the Kaliningrad *oblast* are flaring up], *Nezavisimaya gazeta* (daily), 9 December.

"Tenets of the Polish security policy" (1992). Warsaw: Leaflet, The President"s office, 2 Nov.

"The Minister of Foreign affairs wants to see a reduction of troops in Kaliningrad" (1994). Statement by Sweden's Foreign Minister Margareta af Ugglas during her visit to Kaliningrad. Ministry for Foreign Affairs Press Release, Stockholm, 19 May 1994.

9 Russia's Exclave in the Baltic Region: A Source of Stability or Tension?

ALGIRDAS GRICIUS

Introduction

Following the collapse of the Soviet Union in December 1991, discussions about the future of the Kaliningrad region and its role in the stability in the Baltic Sea region were put into a broader perspective (Grajewski 1992: 117). The Belovezh agreements concluded by the Russian, Ukrainian and Belarussian heads of state predetermined the disintegration of the Soviet Union and confirmed Russia's status as a successor to the rights and obligations of the former union of republics. One of such rights was the one that the Russian Federation inherited with respect to the Kaliningrad region – a part of East Prussia given to the Soviet Union to administrate after World War II.

Discussions about the status of the Kaliningrad region and the future of its development continue to this day and most probably will continue into the near future. These issues were tackled at the consultative meeting of the Senate Centre for International Studies and the Foundation "Poland in Europe" on January 11, 1992. Jerzy Bahr stated in his speech that

> there is no other region on this continent whose legal, political and historical status is so undefined. What has to be considered in the first place is the elimination of the threat of German reconstitution of the region as a former 'East Prussia', and equally important, to prevent Russia from retaining it as a Russian enclave (*Krolewiec* 1992: 119).

Certainly, we can either agree or disagree with such an attitude, but this does not preclude discussions in Russia itself, in the neighbouring states in the Baltic region and beyond. For example, in March 1995, a member of the House of Representatives of the US Congress, Mr. Cox, submitted a draft resolution in connection with the withdrawal of Russian troops from Kaliningrad.[1] Among other things the draft resolution also said:

> Whereas the existence of the Kaliningrad military outpost poses a threat to the peace and security of the Baltic region and Europe, particularly to Lithuania which finds itself perilously located between Kaliningrad and Belarus, two of the most militarised regions of the world....the Kaliningrad/Konigsberg area should be made into a demilitarised zone and the Russian Federation should remove all its military forces from such area.

Recently various problems connected with the Kaliningrad region were deliberated at a seminar in Travemünde (Germany) organised by the German Baltic Academy, in Vilnius at a round table discussion "Potsdam and Lithuania".[2] and in other international events. Most of them also tackled one or another aspect of security issues of the Baltic Sea region. In recent years there appeared a number of articles about the Kaliningrad region and its future (Paleckis 1994: 115-127; Nikzentaitis 1995: 927-934; Wellmann 1996: 161-183). Thus, the problem of the Kaliningrad region is not a Russian, German, Polish or a Lithuanian issue, it is a European issue. For Lithuania, these issues are particularly urgent because through its territory the main bulk of cargo is being transported to and from this region, including military transit. Lithuania has a 295.5 km border with the Kaliningrad area. However, negotiations on its delimitation are proceeding at a rather slow pace. This issue is discussed in more detail in the chapter dealing with the Lithuanian-Russian relations. No agreement has been reached so far on the borders of the territorial waters and the economic zone in the Baltic Sea.

All these questions, plus statements of certain influential Russian political figures like Zyuganov and Zhirinovsky about a possible restoration of the Soviet Union or the Russian empire with the Baltic states included, raise understandable concern among the Lithuanian political forces about the security of Lithuania and the entire Baltic region (Kipp 73(3): 84). It is important to note that the official Russian authorities in Moscow do not support the claims of the nationalist-communist forces to the territory of the Baltic states. Likewise, the current Lithuanian Government does not have any claims to the Kaliningrad region, and relations between these two states are based on the treaty signed between

Lithuania and the Russian Federation on July 29, 1991. Nevertheless, this does not mean that discussions on the Kaliningrad issue, and especially the views of both Russian and Lithuanian politicians and political scientists about the development of this area and its future, are meaningless. The nature and contents of such discussions could have a considerable influence on not only Lithuanian-Russian relations, but also on broader political processes in the Baltic Sea region and throughout Europe.

Historical background

One of the reasons why discussions about the past and the future of East Prussia[3] and especially of its northern part (i.e., Lithuania Minor) are so complicated, is that some Russian politicians and scholars call this territory the indigenous Russian lands ("iskonno russkyje zemli"). A whole range of scientific and political studies shows that such statements do not correspond to reality. Among these studies are the second part of P. Kushner's work (Kushner 1979[1951]): a study *"Pietryèiø Pabaltijo etninë praeitis"* (The Southeast Baltic: An Ethnic History) edited by S.A. Tokarev. This study was reprinted in Chicago by M. Morkunas Press in 1979, and in the "Background and Summary" specially written for this edition Saulius Girnius says:

> Kushner drew upon the work of German scholars in the areas of archeology, toponymy, linguistics, history, ethnostatistics, geography, and anthropology, as well as countless historical documents, to powerfully argue that Lithuanians were the local inhabitants of the northern part of East Prussia.

He points out that even "until 1923, 38 newspapers in the Lithuanian language were published in East Prussia".

The book was probably prepared in order to equip the Soviet Union with additional scientific arguments about the Baltic past of the region enabling them to refute possible German or Polish claims to it. Once such a need disappeared, Kushner's work was soon removed from the circulation after its publication in 1951. As was noted by Girnius,

> ...the official Soviet line, more in keeping with its actual policy in East Prussia was expressed in 1953 in 'Bolshaya Sovetskaya Entsiklopediya'

(The Great Soviet Encyclopedia), Vol. XIX, in the article on the *Kaliningradskaya Oblast* (p.p. 426-429): 'On April 7, 1946 the Kaliningrad district (*oblast*) was created from the ancient, age-old lands of the Baltic Slavs after Fascist Germany was defeated and as eternal centre of aggression – East Prussia was destroyed'.

Girnius also pointed to the fact that the unsupportability of Moscow's claims of a Slavic history to this territory "was so evident that later editions of the Encyclopedia no longer included the sentence on the Slavic origin".

Among other works refuting the claims based on ethnicity to the Kaliningrad regions there is the Potomac Foundation's report prepared by Philip A. Petersen and Shane C. Petersen (Petersen & Petersen 1994), and a study by A. Matulevièius on Lithuania Minor (Matulevièius 1989). Both above studies and many other historical sources give no grounds for asserting that the Kaliningrad region is an ethnic Russian territory. It can be regarded a territory which was transferred to the Soviet Union, a participant of World War II, which made a weighty contribution to the victory of the allied forces.

Throughout history the Prussian lands were a strategically important territory in the Baltic Sea region. There was a time when the Teutonic Order fought for it and exterminated ethnic Prussians and other Baltic tribes akin to the Lithuanians. Later rulers of the Prussian Duchy governed by Germany sought the same goal through Germanisation of the land. And, following World War II, the eastern part of Prussia was 'cleansed' and colonised with Russian-speaking citizens of the Soviet Union, mostly Russians. Extensive material on the history of Lithuania Minor, its inhabitants and their ways of life and customs was gathered and published in the monograph "Lietuvininkø kraðtas" [*The Land of Lietuvininkai*] (Vëlius 1995).

In the course of history wars often changed borders. Without doubt the same could be expected and it actually happened in Europe after World War II. The aim of this study is not to review the Yalta or the Potsdam agreements or restore historical justice. More often than not such goals are unattainable in practice. It is by far more important to study objectively the history of nations who inhabited these lands and regions, to give realistic evaluations to a newly formed geopolitical situation, to make forecasts and to influence the further development of such regions.

The Kaliningrad area is a zone, the future development of which is of interest to many states of the Baltic Sea region, including Lithuania. Relations between Lithuania and the Russian Federation will greatly depend on how the central Russian authorities will influence the further development of this area which borders with Lithuania, Poland and the Baltic Sea, and what role it will allocate to the area in relations with the other states of the Baltic Sea region and Western Europe.

Kaliningrad: internal situation

In January 1995, a journalist of *Izvestiya*, Nikolaj Lashkevich, wrote in his article "The issue of Kaliningrad: Why is the Russian West so worried?"[4] that during the last three or four years Kaliningrad acquired many new features:

> There appeared luxury shops like Stelmann, Hitachi, Mr. Adamczyk's with splendid facades... Offices of new commercial banks and firms show off their opulent interiors. On the streets one can see self-confident young people in expensive black coats, and the streets themselves are laid with asphalt... There are increasing numbers of foreign cars. Many Germans, Poles, Lithuanians, although the tourist season ended a long time ago.

However, the journalist also presents his impressions of an entirely different nature:

> ...against the background [of these changes] there are poor old people who ask in shops to have exactly 100 and not 120 g of sausage weighed for them; middle-aged people who cannot find a niche for themselves and stand near labour exchanges. Clear features of capitalist renewal of this Russian western backwater intermingle with conspicuous details of the pre-war Soviet past which look strange in this land. In Kaliningrad Soviet monuments have not been demolished so far: there stands a chief of the world proletariat [Lenin – A.G.], the elder of the union [Kalinin – A.G.] and other revolutionary figures. According to the authorities, very soon Peter the Great, Kutuzov and other Russian military elders will peacefully join their company...

Perhaps these observations of the *Izvestya* journalist are accurate, as similar processes are characteristic of certain other cities in Russia's

European part, if not for the fact that during the election to Russia's Duma the majority of the inhabitants of the Kaliningrad region supported Zhirinovsky and Zyuganov who promised their voters to restore Great Russia within the boundaries of the former Soviet Union. The views of the population of the Kaliningrad area did not change much during the presidential elections in 1996: a considerable number of votes was cast for the leader of the Communist Party, Genadij Zyuganov.

Speaking about the political situation in the Kaliningrad region, the danger lies in that it has become a kind of politicians' Mecca often visited by the representatives of national-patriotic and national-communist forces to express their commitment to Great Russia with a strong central power and concern about the future of the region. As Kaliningrad's democratic politicians have aptly observed, upon arrival national-patriots capably use various myths: "we live worse than anyone else, Lithuanians don't let us through [having in mind the transit through Lithuania – A.G.], Germans poke their noses into our land and want to take it away from us..."..[5]

The economic situation of the Kaliningrad region is indeed far from easy. In reality, the Free Economic Zone, which has been so broadly discussed in the press, exists only on paper. An especially hard blow to the district's economy was the Russian President's decree of March 6, 1995 which annulled customs privileges that had been granted to the region in 1992. The pragmatic head of the region's administration, Yurij Matochkin, said to the news agency RIA in May 1995 that the Centre still did not understand the situation that the Kaliningrad region was put into; and, speaking about the opinion of Kaliningrad's population about the upcoming Duma elections to be held at the end of 1995, he noted that the inhabitants were going to vote for those who "understand their interests better" (*RIA-ELTA*, 5 May 1995).

The problems of Kaliningrad were deliberated in Russia's Duma in June 1996 (*BNS*, 6 June 1995). During these discussions the chairman of the Duma of the Kaliningrad region, Valerij Ustyugov, said that 60 per cent of the Kaliningrad inhabitants did not approve of the way Moscow treated the region, and 20 per cent of inhabitants supported the idea of conferring it the status of a state. During the deliberations the deputy Foreign Affairs Minister, Sergej Krylov, gave a somewhat strange answer to the heads of the Kaliningrad region and the commander of Russia's Baltic Sea Fleet, Admiral Vladimir Yegorov, saying that the agreed basis of Russia's transit through Lithuania is "temporary and unreliable". Krylov asserted that "the agreement with Lithuania on transit is practically without a time limit".[6] Such an unfounded statement of an executive official of Russia's Ministry of Foreign Affairs, who knows very well that there is only an agreement between Lithuania and the Russian Federation which can be extended annually if none of the parties announce its termination six months prior to its expiration, could be viewed as a free interpretation of the agreement in an attempt to find something between the lines.

During deliberations in the Duma a question was raised concerning a speedier drafting of the decree "On the Special Economic Zone in the Kaliningrad Region" and signing a treaty between Moscow and the Kaliningrad region on delegating authority on a mutual basis. The proposal that, in connection with the special status of the region, the head of administration of the Kaliningrad region be included into Russia's cabinet of ministers did not receive support among the Duma members. However, as a result of these discussions, gradually the situation began to improve and in January 1996 President Yeltsin signed a decree on a Special Economic Zone and a treaty under a rather complicated title "On the separation of objects of competence and mutual delegation of authorisation between government bodies of the Russian Federation and the Kaliningrad region". In the nearest future it will become clear how these decisions are being implemented and complied with.

Meanwhile, however, the economic situation in the area is rather difficult. In 1995 the level of unemployment in the region was 5 per cent, and in certain areas it reached 11 per cent (BNS, 7 September 1995). It was twice as high the average level and the highest in Russia. Although in 1995 the number of people who moved in from Latvia, Lithuania and Estonia dropped to 10 per cent of all the arriving people (in 1994 it was 15 per cent), the number of those arriving from the Central Asian republics of the former Soviet Union and Kazakhstan increased by 40 per cent (BNS, 20 December 1995). Having in mind that in 1995 there was about 20,000 new arrivals in the region and that 57 per cent of the new inhabitants are of an able age (BNS, 20 November 1995), this makes it more difficult to solve the problems of unemployment.

Speaking about the economic difficulties of the region, it should be noted that in 1995 the volume of production continued to decrease. According to the region's State Statistics Committee, in 1995 the volume shrank by 14 per cent if compared to 1994. Production of consumer goods had the biggest share in the decline: production of foodstuffs decreased by

21 per cent and non-food products by 27 per cent. It should be noted, though, that at the same time the production of pulp and paper increased more than 1.7 times (*BNS*, 31 January 1996). Although in 1995 exports grew by about 20 per cent, the trade balance of the region remained in the negative. In all the trade turnover in 1995 import constituted 60.3 per cent (501 mln USD), and exports – 39.7 per cent (334 mln. USD). Foodstuffs made up the biggest part of import. The main bulk of import came from Poland, Germany, Belarus and Ukraine. However, in the second half of 1995 there was a noticeable decrease of import as compared to 1994 (*BNS*, 7 February 1996 & 31 January 1996). In 1995 the Kaliningrad commercial port operated at less than a quarter of its capacity (1.9 mln. tons), and the workload of the state sea port was only 59.8 per cent (1.5 mln. tons). This tendency began when in Russia railway tariffs were increased twofold. Meanwhile, the ports of the Baltic states, Finland and Ukraine receive 2-2.5 mln. tons of Russian cargoes monthly. Cargoes like steel, coal, grain and oil products were diverted from the Kaliningrad ports to the neighbouring ones. A representative of the transport system of the Kaliningrad region was explaining in the newspaper *Kaliningradskaya Pravda* that largely it was the Russian railway authorities who restricted cargo flows into the Kaliningrad ports. Since they had the monopoly they established high tariffs, therefore, not only Belarussian, but also Russian cargo senders were trying to bypass Kaliningrad (*Kaliningradskaya Pravda*, 27 February 1996). Lithuania does not create any obstacles for Russia's cargo going to Kaliningrad since, according to the Lithuanian-Russian agreement, transport tariffs in one country cannot exceed those established for foreign cargo in another country.

Another problem connected with the difficult economic situation of the region was the shortage of energy supplies in the winter of 1994-95. Many schools, pre-school institutions, and other objects of the social care system were practically unheated. On February 1996 the regional Duma convened a special session on this issue as well as the problems concerning payment of salaries to the employees of budgetary organisations. The regional Duma passed an appeal where the situation was described as urgent. The appeal was addressed to the Russian President, the Government and the Parliament. The Duma proposed to the regional administration to appeal to court and sue the Russian Government for non-fulfilment of its obligations: the region's budget did not receive money it was allocated in 1995; debts grew for the accomplished work which had to be paid for from the federal budget (*BNS*, 8 February 1996). In 1995, in the region, indebtedness to energy suppliers grew considerably, the military being the biggest debtors: in February their debt to the public company "Yantarenergo" constituted 39 mln USD.

Despite the complicated economic situation in the Kaliningrad region, certain official representatives of the Russian Government believe that it is necessary to strengthen the military capacity in this area. While on a visit in Kaliningrad at the end of 1995, the Russian Deputy Prime Minister, Sergej Shakhraj, presented the main points of his "Baltic Strategic Initiative". He said:

> I have always been in favour of balancing Russia's economic and military strategic interests in this region... therefore, I shall do everything to ensure that the economic development of the Kaliningrad region strengthens and not weakens Russia's military potential in the Kaliningrad region.

Russia will not allow, continued Shakhraj, the eastward expansion of NATO, and the Kaliningrad region "has to become a brake on such an expansion" (*Lietuvos Aidas*, 8 November 1995). According to him, the other most important provision of the "Baltic Strategic Initiative" was the defence of the interests of compatriots in the Baltic states, which is a traditional statement among national-patriotic politicians. With this aim in mind, it is envisaged to create a television and radio network which would engage in an appropriate propaganda and facilitate a more effective defence of the interests of compatriots.

It is possible that the treaty of January 12, 1996 "On the separation of objects of competence and mutual delegation of authorization between government bodies of the Russian Federation and the Kaliningrad region" and the law on the Special Economic Zone passed later will accelerate economic activities within the region and have an influence on the region's relations with the neighbouring countries. Upon signing the above documents, the region's governor, Yurij Matochkin, stated that the law created a legal foundation for the region's development and that all would depend on when and what kind of bylaws would be passed. The governor expressed the hope that upon the adoption of Russia's customs code and amendments to the tax law, the Kaliningrad ports would be used more intensely by foreign exporters and that they would be able to offer a serious competition to the other Baltic Sea ports. Trying to forecast the economic situation in 1995, Matochkin said that one should not expect any significant changes in the social and economic life of the region. Real changes in industry, agriculture and trade could be felt if every year this area with the population of 900,000 received investments worth 100 mln USD. However, in 1996 the region expected to attract only foreign investments for the value of some 30 mln USD.

Although the Kaliningrad region takes a leading position in Russia as to the number of enterprises with foreign investments in mid 1995 their number exceeded 800 (*Litas*, 25 July 1996). The real volume of investments in the region does not exceed 10 mln USD (*Vneshnyaya torgovlya* 1996 (1-2): 38). The real figures of investments of various countries and the number of enterprises with foreign capital in 1996 are presented in Table 1 (*Litas*, 25 July 1996).

Table 9.1   Enterprises with foreign capital registered in the Special Economic Zone of the Kaliningrad region

Name of the country	Number of registered enterprises	Proportion of registered enterprises[1]	Foreign capital in the authorised capital stock[2]	Per cent
Total in the region	1073	100.0	23622186.6	48.4
1. France	4	0.4	5395510.0	11.1
2. Poland	363	32.1	2779627.2	5.7
3. Germany	228	20.2	2456384.1	5.1
4. Switzerland	16	1.4	2172650.0	4.5
5. Finland	5	0.4	2126353.7	4.4
6. Great Britain	11	1.0	2029746.0	4.2
7. Lithuania	183	16.2	1625857.9	3.3
8. Latvia	87	7.7	775812.6	1.6
9. British Virgin Island	2	0.2	385800.0	0.8
10. USA	20	1.8	385728.2	0.8

1: In per cent.
2: In thousand roubles.

Yurij Bedenko, chairman of the Committee for the Development of the "Yantar" Free Economic Zone in the Kaliningrad region, sees the following main problems in attracting foreign investments: unstable political situation in the country; inadequate legal basis provided by the state; flawed tax policy; recurrent changes in the legal basis of the Yantar Free Economic Zone and the absence of a fundamental law; etc (*International Affairs* 1995(6): 57).

All the contradictions notwithstanding, the year 1996 was important to Kaliningrad both in economic and political aspects. Significant documents were signed in Moscow granting the region, at least theoretically, more economic independence. Boris Yeltsin was re-elected as Russia's President, and Viktor Chernomyrdin, a person with a pragmatic view and a supporter of moderate reforms, was approved in Russia's Duma after presidential elections as Prime Minister. In Kaliningrad one could feel that economic life was becoming more vigorous. It is yet to be seen whether this positive tendency is drowned by other factors connected with Russia's military-strategic interests. A Polish diplomat – a former Polish Consul General in Kaliningrad – Jerzy Bahr, has said in reply to a question what additional guarantees are necessary to ensure a stable development of the region, that "... you don't need any other guarantees but your economic situation". He continued that "there is something else that should raise your concern: whether the Kaliningrad region will be able to integrate into the new economic environment in Europe, otherwise it will remain a 'hole' in the market's 'fabric' which covers the adjacent states – Lithuania, Poland, Sweden and others. I can't imagine how you would be able to live and develop them. Your 'guarantees' lie in a successful integration" (*Kaliningradskaya Pravda*, 23 June 1995).

Co-operation of the Kaliningrad region with the neighbouring states

Taking into account the geographical location of the Kaliningrad region, its future will be influenced to a rather great extent not only by its relations with the federal government in Moscow or its individual subjects, but also by its relations, first of all, economic, with the neighbouring states and the adjacent regions. Political stability in the entire Baltic Sea region will largely depend on the course of economic, ecological, cultural and other co-operation. Without doubt, another highly influential factor in ensuring security and stability consists of the goals and the policy pursued by the

Russian Federation with respect to the states bordering with the Kaliningrad region as well as the treatment of military issues.

Poland

At present, Poland, together with Lithuania and Germany, are the most active partners in international relations of the Kaliningrad region. Simultaneously, Poland, just like the Baltic states, seeks to strengthen its relations with the European and transatlantic structures of political, economic and defence co-operation (EU, WEU and NATO) and become a full-fledged member of these organisations. Despite the fact that these attempts, especially NATO's enlargement, are strongly opposed by Russia, the economic co-operation of the northern counties of Poland with Kaliningrad has been proceeding successfully. Poland is the most active trading partner of enterprises in the Kaliningrad region where it accounts for 20 per cent of foreign trade turnover in 1994. And it is firmly in the lead as an importer, having reached the figure of 37 per cent (Anisimov, 1955: 30).

During his visit in Vilnius in June 1995, the Marshal of the Polish Sejm, Adam Struzik, said that Poland hopes that the Kaliningrad region becomes a place for economic co-operation and not a zone of threat (*BNS*, 9 June 1995). In mid 1996, a third motorway border post between Poland and Kaliningrad "Gusev-Goldap", was inaugurated. It has a capacity of 200 cars in 24 hours (*INTERFAX*, 1 July 1995). After this post is completely finished, its capacity will increase to 1000 cars in 24 hours. Although behind schedule, the motorway Kaliningrad-Elblag is being reconstructed. In the beginning of 1996 the Polish government approved the technical project of the motorway on the Polish territory and allocated 51 mln USD for its construction (*BNS*, 22 March 1996). In future this motorway will connect Kaliningrad and Berlin. Representatives of the Polish Szczecin and the Russian Kaliningrad are planning to open a new air route linking Kaliningrad, Poznan and Szczecin. Such an air link will be important for Polish businessmen: by the end of 1995, in the Kaliningrad region there were about 800 various Polish companies (*PAP-BNS*, 23 November 1995).

On the other hand, though, there appeared some obscurity in Polish-Russian relations when the Warsaw authorities refused to grant permission to the residents of the Kaliningrad region for a transit crossing of the Polish territory with a temporary document known as a permit for return to Russia

(*ITAR-TASS*, 17 October 1995). Residents of the Kaliningrad region experience similar problems when crossing the territory of Lithuania. This obscurity grew even further when a rumour was spread from Minsk that the Belarus Ministry of Transport and Communications prepared a draft "trilateral agreement" on building a motor- and railway from Gusev to Grodno through Poland. Such a project was discussed at the meeting between President Yeltsin and President Lukashenka in Moscow (*Polish Radio*, 21 February 1996). For the Poles, such a transport corridor definitely reminds of the pre-World War II Danzig corridor and was severely criticised by high government officials in Poland, including Foreign Affairs Minister Dariusz Rosati and President Aleksandr Kwasniewski (*PAP*, 29 February 1996; *BNS*, 29 February 1996). President Kwasniewski said that there can be no transit corridor through Poland from Belarus to the Kaliningrad region. When introducing the programme of the planned visit to Lithuania (March 5-6, 1996) he said to the Lithuanian journalists that he intended to emphasise the necessity of an especially close regional co-operation, because, according to him, "only then shall we be interesting to the West". All these and other speculations about the transport corridor are hardly worth any serious attention because they are more of a propagandistic nature.

The growing number of Polish-Russian joint ventures, especially trade companies, in the Kaliningrad region, the frequent official meetings between government officials, existence of joint projects, the absence of territorial claims or problems of ethnic Russian and Polish minorities justify the conclusion that the Polish-Russian relations with respect to Kaliningrad region have taken a good course. This certainly has an influence on the Lithuanian-Russian relations which will be discussed later in this contribution.

Germany

Magdalene Hoff and Heinz Timmermann, (1995: 34) in their article "Kaliningrad: The present and future of the Russian exclave in the Baltic region as viewed by Europeans", pointed out that Germany, whose territory included East Prussia for over 700 years (this is still a debatable issue – A.G.), shows no particular interest in the problem of Kaliningrad, well knowing that it is ticklish. Indeed, for historical, political and other reasons Germany gives priority to good relations with both Russia and Poland. The twelve thousand Germans (although, according to various sources their numbers range from 4,000 to 22,000)[7] living in the Kaliningrad region, do raise problems for the region's administration from time to time when Russian national-patriotic forces begin to speak about Germanisation of the land. Old communists and war veterans in the Kaliningrad region protest against the "creeping Germanisation" and demand that even the ruins of the Königsgerg cathedral, the towers of which was restored with the help of Germans, be removed altogether (Ihlau 1995: 68-71). There is no doubt that national-communists arrive at such speculations aided by irresponsible statements and visits to Kaliningrad by German right-wing extremists who hardly represent anyone in Germany. In his article "Da werden Blasen geschlagen" published in *Der Spiegel,* Olaf Ihlau writes that

> even the Russian chauvinist Vladimir Zhirinovsky was ready a year ago to forsake Kaliningrad to Great Germany for the Russian-German alliance. Not any more, since during the last elections [to the Russian Duma in 1993 – A.G.] his party received the biggest number of votes in Kaliningrad. Nevertheless, he has not changed his favourable attitude towards the like-minded Germans.

With the anti-German moods prevailing among the "patriotically" inclined part of the society in both the Kaliningrad region and mainland Russia, government officials in Bonn, when speaking about Kaliningrad, are forced to express their full neutrality on this issue. During his visit in Vilnius, the German Foreign Affairs Minister, Klaus Kinkel, also spoke about this. He said that "Germany does not have territorial claims to the Kaliningrad region which we consider an integral part of Russia. Germany has only economic interests, and even this invokes a sensitive reaction from Moscow"(*ITAR-TASS,* 7 April 1995). A journalist from *Novoye Vremya,* Vadim Dubnov (1995: 13), wrote that when talking to people in Kaliningrad he often heard them saying that "of course, it would be ideal: German economic conditions but fully preserving all that is Russian". In other words, "with German investments but without Germans". During the press conference in Vilnius, Klaus Kinkel also said that "this region should not remain a 'white territory' within the space of the economic co-operation in the Baltic region, including the Baltic states". The Lithuanian Foreign Affairs Minister, Povilas Gylys, who also participated in the press conference, confirmed that Vilnius, too, had no territorial claims to this region.

Germany is interested that the Kaliningrad region develops as a part of the Baltic region. The German position is probably determined by economic interests and a desire to ensure stability in the region. The fact that Germany has no consulate in Kaliningrad is largely determined by Russia's reluctance to increase political tension in both Kaliningrad and Russia itself. As expressed by the German Ambassador to Russia, Otto von der Gablentz,[8] Germany

> has always wanted to open a consulate in Kaliningrad, because we think that there is quite a lot of work there. However, we are obliged to respect Russia's position which considers such a step unwelcome due to the current political situation.

The absence of a consulate does not obstruct the development of economic relations between the northern parts of Germany and the Kaliningrad region. It is true that these contacts could be more effective; however, the reason lies probably not only in the caution of German entrepreneurs but also in post-Soviet mentality which is still present in many post-communist states, and especially in an area like the Kaliningrad region. In the sphere of co-operation, the military aspect of the region plays a significant role as well, although at present it does not raise any potential threat to Germany (while the contrary is true for the Baltic states).

Belarus

Having in mind the relations between Belarus and Russia which recently grew stronger, especially in the spheres of border protection and customs control, and their goal to form in the future a union of these two states, there will be more possibilities for a broader co-operation between the Kaliningrad region and Belarus. In the beginning of 1996, the head of the Kaliningrad administration, Yurij Matochkin, offered the Belarussian President, Aleksandr Lukashenka, the option of concluding a long-term co-operation programme (*Kompaniya BelaPAN*, News Summary, 27 January 1996). Kaliningrad proposed to co-operate in the sectors of transport, communications, economy and trade, energy, agriculture and others. It was also suggested to Belarus to form its own fleet which could be based in the ports of Kaliningrad, and discuss the earlier mentioned transit motor- and railway link from Russia to Kaliningrad through Belarus and Poland. At the end of 1995, the Belarus Prime Minister, Mikhail Chigir, formed a working group to examine the expediency of using Lithuanian, Latvian and Kaliningrad ports for transporting Belarussian cargoes to other countries.[9] This was done because the Kaliningrad port became rather expensive and Belarussian companies used the services of Klaipëda and Gdansk ports with increasing frequency (*BNS*, 9 November 1995). In the beginning of 1996 in Moscow, publications appeared saying that Russia and Belarus were considering a possibility of approaching Lithuania concerning the building of a motorway from Grodno to Kaliningrad through the Lithuanian territory if no agreement is reached with Poland on a transit corridor (*INTERFAX-BNS*, 4 March 1996). This proposal is not acceptable to Lithuania, first of all, for security reasons. Moreover such a motorway and the flow of cargo it generates, would diminish the attractiveness of the Klaipëda. Although during the visit of the delegation of the Kaliningrad region to Minsk in March 1996, agreements were signed in the spheres of trade, transport, education, science and building, it can hardly be expected that economic and political relations will be intensified markedly in the nearest future. First, economic reforms in Russia and Belarus are proceeding at very different speeds. Second, political tension between the Belarus Parliament and the President prevents this country from solving many issues pertaining to economic reform. Belarus will hardly be able to develop effectively its economic ties with the neighbouring countries, including the Kaliningrad region, if it does not accelerate its own economic reforms.

The Scandinavian states

The geopolitical situation in the Baltic Sea region changed greatly after the dissolution of the Soviet empire, leading to restoration of statehood in the Baltic states, to Sweden and Finland joining the EU and to German reunification. Recently Scandinavian countries, first of all Denmark and Sweden, who earlier devoted their main attention to Nordic co-operation, have been giving more attention to the states situated on the eastern coast of the Baltic Sea. Undoubtedly, Russia's exclave – Kaliningrad – located between Lithuania and Poland, too, cannot be left without attention. As Bertel Heurlin, Professor at the Institute of Political Science at the

University of Copenhagen has observed, "Russia is considered the most unstable actor in the region" (Heurlin 1995: 72). The Baltic states are mostly concerned about the concentration of the Russian troops in two locations: the Leningrad military district and the Kaliningrad exclave. If compared with the military forces of the Baltic states, the Russian military presence is several times bigger and is not merely organised for defence purposes.

Security of the Baltic Sea region was broadly discussed at the conference "Ideas on Co-operative Security in the Baltic Sea Region", held in Vilnius in November 1994. Although the Danish Deputy Under-secretary of State for Defence, Per Carlsen (1995: 22), maintained that "for the Baltic Sea region the armed aggression has become futile", and invited everybody to develop co-operative security, a Swedish representative, Sture Ericson (1995: 17), in justification of high defence expenditure in his own country, said that

> the reason is that we do not know what military threat we will face in five, ten or fifteen years' time. More specifically, it is argued that nobody can give any credible assurances that a future new regime in Russia does not return to policies similar to the ones of the dissolved Soviet Union.

Most Lithuanian politicians and representatives of academic circles who watch political processes in Russia, support the opinion of Ericson.

Certainly, Scandinavian countries are interested not just in military security aspects connected with stability in the Baltic Sea region. They are also interested in the economic development of the region, including the Kaliningrad exclave. In the opinion of the former Danish Ambassador to Moscow, Henrik R. Iversen, the Kaliningrad region needs a special economic status (*BNS*, 6 April 1995). The Danish Defence Minister, Hans Hækkerup, holds that Russia must be included into Western co-operation both in economic and political and in military spheres (*ITAR-TASS*, 21 July 1995). An example of such policy is the agreement between the Russian and the Danish ministries of defence on military cooperation signed in September 1994.

Investments of the Scandinavian countries in the economy of the Kaliningrad region are very small, although this does not mean that they will not grow in future and this is especially true of the transport sector. This would certainly increase competition for the other ports of the Baltic states, first of all for Klaipëda, Liepaja and Ventspils. The first steps towards such a competition have already been taken. In the summer of 1995, Russian firms and a Swedish company "Bomark" founded a "Baltic Oil Transporting Company"(*BNS*, 1 August 1995).

Economic co-operation between the Kaliningrad region and the Scandinavian, as well as other countries will intensify only when the Russian federal authorities will create possibilities for a free economic development of the region and its trade with the neighbouring countries by deeds and not just by verbal statements and decrees. This conclusion is supported by the fact that the Kaliningrad region was excluded from the development programme of economic co-operation in the Baltic Sea region financed by Denmark after unsuccessful attempts to reach an agreement with Moscow to relieve the money allocated for the region from customs duties and other taxes (*ITAR-TASS*, 30 October 1995).

Lithuanian-Russian relations: the Kaliningrad issue

Lithuanian-Russian relations are based on the inter-state treaty which Lithuania, after restoring independence on March 11, 1990, signed with the Russian Federation on July 29, 1991. Since Lithuania does not have a common border with mainland Russia, a Russian-Lithuanian agreement was signed that same day on the Kaliningrad region. Article 1 of this Agreements says that both parties recognise the inviolability of the entire length of the border between Lithuania and Russia. In Article 11 Russia expressed its special interest in and Lithuania committed itself to contribute to the preservation of favourable conditions of economic, national and cultural development of the Kaliningrad region.

In evaluating current Lithuania-Russian relations it is possible to state, with some reservations, that if compared with the other Baltic states, these relations are developing along quite positive lines. During the last few years the procedure of issuing visas has been eased, transit travel by train through the Lithuanian territory (without the rights of disembarkation) has been introduced for travellers from mainland Russia to the Kaliningrad exclave. Russian citizens permanently residing in Kaliningrad and Lithuanian citizens may visit each other without visas (Songal 1995: 62). In 1995 a most favoured nation status took effect and a compromise was reached on a temporary arrangement on military transit to Kaliningrad.

Problems of the Russian ethnic minority in Lithuania are insignificant. To a certain extent this can be explained by the fact that, after regaining independence, Lithuania, the only one of the Baltic states, introduced the "zero" variant for acquiring citizenship by other nationalities who at the time resided permanently in Lithuania (*Diplomaticheskij vestnik* 1996: 39).

In 1996 the problems of the Baltic Sea region and relations between Russia and the countries of this region were analysed in the report "Russia, the Baltic Sea States and the Northern European states: The Problems and the Future of Mutual Relations" prepared by the Political Research Foundation (*Nezavisimaya gazeta*, 28 May 1996). The results of the opinion poll carried out by the Foundation in Russia about mutual relations with the countries of this region are presented in Table 9.2.

Table 9.2   How do you evaluate the level of relations between Russia and the following states? (in per cent)

Country	Good	Satisfactory	Poor	No opinion
Poland	47	29	11	13
Germany	54	36	4	6
Finland	81	14	0	5
Sweden	64	30	2	4
Norway	57	41	1	1
Denmark	46	40	0	14
Estonia	18	37	42	3
Latvia	29	46	12	13
Lithuania	46	32	10	12

The results of the poll show that the opinion of the inhabitants of Russia about the relations between Russia and the Baltic states is not very favourable, although it is much better with respect to Lithuania. In its turn, Lithuania should observe very closely and analyse Russia's relations with the other states of the Baltic region, its internal political and economic processes, and especially those linked with the policy of the institutions of the federal government in the Kaliningrad region.

Against the background of what has been said, let us discuss in more detail various aspects of the Lithuanian-Russian bilateral relations in connection with the Kaliningrad region.

Economic issues

In 1996, along the border between Lithuania and the Kaliningrad region (295.5 km) there were five international and one bilateral posts. In 1995 and in the first half of 1996 these posts were crossed by 1,321,000 and 860,000 people and by 430,000 and 219,000 vehicles respectively, excluding passenger and military transit trains.[10] In 1995 the turnover of Lithuanian goods with the Kaliningrad region comprised 551 mln Litas (138 mln USD) or 9.7 per cent of the total turnover of Lithuanian goods with the Russian Federation. When compared with 1994, it increased by 38 per cent. It should be noted that in 1995 exports from Lithuania to Kaliningrad exceeded import twofold, while the situation in the overall trade between Lithuania and Russia was quite the opposite.[11]

Entrepreneurs not only from Kaliningrad but of the entire Russia are interested not just in trade but also in investments both in Lithuania and in the other Baltic states. In Lithuania and Latvia they took the lead in the quantity of established joint ventures, and in Estonia in 1994 they came out first according to the volume of foreign investments (*Diplomaticheskij Vestnik* 1996(3): 65). Although the number of joint Lithuanian-Russian ventures in Russia and in the Kaliningrad region is impressive and is counted in hundreds, investments of Lithuanian businessmen are rather insignificant. For example, in the beginning of 1996 they did not exceed 0.5 mln USD (see Table 9.1.).

Lithuania is interested in promoting economic independence of the Kaliningrad region also because it expects to promote simultaneously demilitarisation of the region. If Russia intends to develop economic independence of the area, it will have to carry out a gradual demilitarisation. Theoretically, the new status of a Special Economic Zone applied to the Kaliningrad region in the beginning of 1996 is a very positive development. This opens up great possibilities for Lithuanian businessmen. Goods produced in the zone and confirmed by a certificate of origin are relieved from export tax. In other words, if semi-fabricated products are taken to the Kaliningrad region and if the value of their assembling or final technological processing carried out on the territory of the region constitutes no less that 15-30 per cent of the total value of the product, exports can proceed free of customs tax. Nevertheless, there is quite a number of problems in the implementation of this law, because for the law to be effective, it is necessary to change several thousands of decrees and laws in Russia. It is not realistic, in view of the situation in Russia, to expect that the status of a special zone will become fully effective in the near future. Politicians suspect that this could have been a pre-elections "gift" from Yeltsin and Matochkin on the eve of presidential elections.

The analysis of political processes and economic reform in Russia shows that economic independence is not being much encouraged. In this regard one may recall how Moscow, when the Free Economic Zone "Yantar" was just beginning to recover, stopped this process in 1995 (Matochkin, 1995: 11). In Lithuania's economic relations with the Kaliningrad region there exists a problem of double standards. If Lithuania makes some concessions to the Kaliningrad region, usually no corresponding action is forthcoming from Russia. Russia should remember, in this regard, that the European Parliament promotes integration of the transportation network of the Baltic states and the Kaliningrad region into the European system (*DPA-ELTA*, 14 July 1995).

Recently a Kaliningrad trade mission was opened in Vilnius. Lithuania is planning to open a similar trade institution in Kaliningrad. Co-operation agreements have been signed between the Kaliningrad region and the bordering Lithuanian counties. The prospects of the regional co-operation project "Nemunas" between Lithuania, Poland and the Kaliningrad region in the fields of trade, transport, the environment and in other spheres are being closely examined. All this should intensify economic relations between the Kaliningrad region and Lithuania, as well as other neighbouring states, on the basis of market economy. However, positive changes in this sphere are hardly possible if Moscow does not constructively settle various military and political aspects of the region's development.

Military and security issues

These issues are viewed to be urgent by the Baltic states and especially Lithuania, which, albeit it does not have a direct border with mainland Russia, does have a common border (295 km long from the border with Poland and up to the Baltic Sea) with the Russian exclave – the Kaliningrad region. According to various sources, in 1995 this small territory of 15.100 square km housed about 60-100 thousand Russian troops (Redman 1995). Although in the publications of the newspaper

Segodnia it was maintained that only 26.000 troops remained in the region (*Segodnia*, 17 June 1994) (which is hardly credible), this raises understandable concern of the neighbouring states about the future of this region. It is difficult to assess the level of militarisation because very often it is not clear what exactly is taken into account, i.e. land force, navy, air force, border troops or even logistic support services. Therefore, it is also not surprising that time and time again in the neighbouring states, including Lithuania, discussions arise, at various levels and of a different scale, about the demilitarisation of the area.

Demilitarisation of the Kaliningrad region does, probably, take place in a quantitative sense, by reducing the number of troops; however, from the qualitative point of view, no such process can be observed. For example, in 1996 in the Baltic Sea, of the altogether 100 surface and submarine vessels, fifty belong to Russia. The vessels of all the other Baltic Sea states are designed only for coastline defence and not to wage war against Russia. Poland has three submarines, a torpedo boat and a few patrol boats, and the Baltic states which own 16 per cent of the land along the coastline, have only two naval ships (Lithuania). The biggest air cushioned landing craft "Zubr" was built in 1994 in the Kaliningrad region and handed over to the military. The same year the Baltic Navy was given one of the most modern missile carriers "Samu".[12] As was observed by the Lithuanian Deputy Foreign Affairs Minister, Albinas Januŏka, such a powerful Russian navy is able to control not only the eastern part of the Baltic Sea but practically the whole sea.[13] On the other hand, the current balance arround the Baltic Sea can hardly pose any threat to stability in the region, although, if political tension increases, this balance would originate much concern in the Baltic states.

The militarised Kaliningrad region can be and probably will be used as Russia's card in its attempts to stop the integration of Lithuania, Latvia, Estonia, as well as Poland into Western economic, political and security structures. This was stated, by the Deputy Foreign Affairs Minister of Russia, Sergej Krylov, in May 1995 in Kaliningrad, during his meeting with Russian ambassadors to the countries of the Baltic region (*BNS*, 30 May 1995). "The Kaliningrad region must become Russia's fortress", said Gavril Popov, the Russian leader of democratic reforms while visiting this region (*BNS*, 31 May 1995).

Yurij Voyevoda, a Duma deputy, elected from the Kaliningrad region, has voiced an opinion that the Russian navy should be deployed also in the

Baltic states (*BNS*, 22 August 1995). Such statements are also encouraged by strong anti-Baltic attitudes among the Russian military. The opinion poll conducted by German Ebert Foundation in 1994 among the Russian military elite showed that 49 per cent of those polled considered the Baltic states as the principal enemies of Russia: Latvia being on the top, Lithuania ranking third (after Afghanistan) and Estonia taking the forth position; only then followed the United States (Vares, 1995: 54). Similar pronouncements about Kaliningrad as Russia's military forward position on the Baltic Sea were voiced by other Russian politicians and military officers: a Duma deputy and leader of the political movement "Russia, Forward", Boris Fyodorov (*BNS*, 13 September 1995), Vice Admiral Viktor Kravchenko (*BNS*, 4 September 1995) and others.

A document entitled "A Concept of Actions Against Threat to National Security of the Russian Federation" prepared by the Defence Research Institute in Koroliov (formerly Kaliningrad) and published in *Segodnia* (a newspaper based in Moscow) was met by a strong reaction in Poland and the Baltic states (*PAP-ELTA*, 20 October 1995). The document proposed to deploy Russia's tactical nuclear weapon in Belarus, the Kaliningrad region and on the ships of the Baltic Navy.[14] One could draw a conclusion that this was yet another way to intimidate the West and the Baltic states.

Another urgent issue for Lithuania's security consists of the railway and air military transit of the Russian Federation through the Lithuanian territory carried out in compliance with the temporary agreement between both parties. Clearly, the military transit by rail has not provoked conflicts of any significance. According to unofficial data, in 1995 the number of carriages to and from Kaliningrad did not exceed 5000, and in the first half of 1996 this number was declining. This could be explained by the increasing volume of military cargo transported by sea from St. Petersburg to the ports of Kaliningrad. It should also be noted that the main cargo in the military transit contains supplies for the troops – goods and fuel, and not military material. Lithuania's right to allow or not to allow military transit can be politically beneficial to Lithuania, although, abuse of this right can seriously complicate Lithuanian-Russian relations. Until Lithuania joins the Euro-Atlantic economic and defence structures, the best option would be to internationalise military transit for a certain period of time to be observed by representatives from foreign countries or such international organisations as the WEU or NATO. The definite solution will primarily depend on further political developments in Russia. Due to the huge influence of military officers and the military-industrial complex in Russia, it is hardly possible to expect a speedy demilitarisation of the Kaliningrad region and a prompt solution of related problems.

Political co-operation

Following parliamentary elections in Lithuania in 1992, won by the left-wing Democratic Labour Party, the opposition – supporters of the leader of the restoration of independence, Vytautas Landsbergis – began to argue that the new Lithuanian government will endorse a fully pro-Russian policy, one risking Lithuania's independence. Statements of opposition politicians about such danger became more frequent once in the leader of the Democratic Labour Party, Algirdas Brazauskas, was elected the President of the Republic, the beginning of 1993. However, the evolution of Lithuanian-Russian relations during the years 1993-1996 shows that such fears have been unfounded and rather propagandistic. The very fact that in almost four years no summit was held between the Lithuanian and Russian presidents proves that pro-Russian orientation does not prevail in foreign affairs and the relations between the two countries. Despite certain achievements, bilateral relations are still problematic due to Russia's reluctance to settle them constructively. These problems range from the refusal to return buildings of the Lithuanian embassies in Paris and Rome, unilateral statements of the Russian representatives about intentions to begin the exploitation of an oil field between Lithuania and the Kaliningrad region in a disputed Baltic Sea zone (*INTERFAX-BNS*, 17 January 1996), procrastination of the delimitation of the land border with the Kaliningrad region (*ELTA*, 24 February 1995; *Kaliningradskaya Pravda*, 20 October 1995), and a refusal to return hard currency savings of the Lithuanian citizens in the banks of Moscow.

Another very urgent issue in the Lithuanian-Russian relations consists of the conclusion of an agreement on readmission. Unfortunately, Russia has not been willing to negotiate and sign such an agreement. Moreover, inefficient Lithuanian-Kaliningrad region border control favours smuggling. Mutual efforts are necessary if one wants to come to grips with this issue. Yet there are also achievements in the Lithuanian-Russian relations allowing the relations between these two states, despite some disagreements, to develop positively. During the recent years there has been only a limited number of meetings between prime ministers or parliamentary delegations, on visits of high government officials. As a result, an agreement was reached on a most favoured nation status, a temporary agreement has been with the Kaliningrad region on military transit, and an arrangement was made for the inhabitants of this region for a visa free stay covering up to thirty days in Lithuania. A further easing of border crossings is not possible as Russia has not been willing to discuss the issue of readmission and sign an appropriate treaty. Furthermore, the negotiations on border delimitation with Russia have progressed slowly as Russia has proposed to solve this issue in package, including the issue of delimiting an economic zone in the Baltic Sea. Lithuania proposes that the issue of border delimitation is solved in stages as the delimitation of the maritime economic zone may require quite some time. However, Russia does not agree with such an approach.

Political co-operation between Lithuania and Russia is for a large part connected with the issues of the Kaliningrad region. This aspect is discussed by Aleksandr Songal (1995: 66), head of the Directorate of International Affairs in the Kaliningrad Regional Administration, "I wish to conclude by expressing the deep conviction that most problems involving our region have to do with difficulties in Russian-Lithuanian relations". From the Lithuanian point of view it is clear that most of the problems are there because Russia finds it difficult to come to terms with the fact that Lithuania is an independent state and that, when solving existing problems, it is necessary to take into account Lithuania's legitimate interests.

However, the political co-operation between Lithuania and the Kaliningrad region is rather intense despite these difficulties. Kaliningrad officials, including head of the administration, Yuri Matochkin, often visit Lithuania. An additional stimulus to the political and economic co-operation between Lithuania and the Kaliningrad region was given by the decree signed by President Yeltsin in May 1995 granting the right to the head of the regional administration to hold negotiations and conclude agreements with administrative-territorial units, ministries and other institutions of foreign states (*BNS*, 21 May 1995). At the same time the administration of the region was instructed to submit proposals to the Russian Government concerning the establishment of an institution for regional co-operation between the Kaliningrad and Lithuania. Such a co-ordination council will, in the best of cases, be established in 1996. Political co-operation with Lithuania could be made more effective if it were not for the somewhat ambiguous position of the Kaliningrad authorities concerning the economic future of the region. This position is largely influenced by frequent visits of politicians from Moscow to Kaliningrad and their national-patriotic statements about the regions future. Although it is obvious that the main decisions concerning the relations of the Kaliningrad region with the neighbouring states and their regions, including Lithuania, are taken in Moscow.

Final remarks

The political and economic situation in the Kaliningrad region and relations pursued by this region with the neighbouring states, although strongly influenced by the restrictions imposed by the politicians in Moscow and the federal government, give reason to assert that the region does have some limited degree of independence. Lithuania, like the other Baltic Sea states, is interested in a free development of the economy of this area and decline in the level of armaments. Obviously they are, in this respect, rather modest. The question can be posed as follows: does responsibility for the current situation in the Kaliningrad region lie with neighbouring countries who do not show enough initiative for a closer co-operation with this Russian exclave in the Baltic region, or on Moscow and the Kaliningrad authorities that do not want to let too many foreigners in as they could then influence the region's economic, political and cultural development.

When examining the co-operation between the neighbouring states and the Kaliningrad region, one can notice that most of these states endeavour at promoting an all-round co-operation with the region and at the same time watch closely the activities of other states the area. Undoubtedly, such efforts pertain to the general background consisting of relations between these states and Russia. This is fully understandable and can be easily discerned in the Lithuanian-Russian relations as well.

No matter what aspects are being examined of the links between the Kaliningrad region and the countries of the Baltic region, everything will eventually come down to the question about the future of the region. Questions like "Who does the region historically belong to" or "What is the legal status of the Kaliningrad region?" can be left aside; as the main question reads: "What is the further development pattern of the Kaliningrad region: a 'merchant's' or a 'warrior's'?" scenario. "Calls on Russia to demilitarise the Kaliningradskaya *Oblast* are often heard – but they are not combined with any indication of what the neighbours are willing to offer in return", maintains Christian Wellmann (Wellmann 1994: 209). However, having in mind the present extent of militarisation of the region, such a statement may be challenged. Demilitarisation, economic prosperity and political stability are interconnected processes. Changes at any one of these levels will certainly induce changes in the other two. In his interview to the Latvian daily *Diena*, Zbigniew Brzezinski stated that "it would not be good if Kaliningrad remained a militarised, impoverished and a forsaken land" (*Lietuvos Aidas*, 9 February 1995).

Political, economic and social forces currently at work in Kaliningrad and Moscow will ultimately drive the Russian exclave down one of two paths of development – either as a prosperous commercial centre, or as a reinforced military stronghold (Redman 1995).

At present they are at a crossroad. Russia will have to choose: either a minimal military contingent in an economically advanced region, or a small number of not very successful joint ventures with the neighbouring states. Lithuania is certainly not interested in the latter option. A major military contingent located within limited space can hardly co-exist a prospering private business. In other words, a choice has to be made between "Hong Kong" and "Gibraltar".

The former Swedish Premier, Carl Bildt (1994), stated a while ago that the Baltic states are a litmus paper which will help to know Russia's intentions in its foreign policy. It seems that the same can be said about the Kaliningrad region. Moscow's policy towards Kaliningrad will be a clear indication whether Russia is prepared to restore itself as a democratic and economically powerful actor in Europe or it will return to the traditional role that it held in the past – a military power ill at ease in the 21st century Europe. If the latter turns true, then no one will be sure about stability and security in Europe.

Notes

1 An unofficial translation of the draft was published in the newspaper *Kaliningradskaya Pravda*, April 28, 1995.
2 The material of these discussions was published in D. Bakanienė (ed.),

Potsdam and the Königsberg Region (Vilnius: Science and Encyclopaedia Publishers, 1996).
3 Now the main part of East Prussia is the territory of the Kaliningrad region.
4 Reprinted in *Lietuvos Rytas* (a Lithuanian daily), 21 January 1995.
5 Ibid.
6 Ibid.
7 Ibid., p. 35.
8 At a conference in Vilnius 24-27 November 1994 arranged by the Nordic Forum for Security Policy.
9 *Lietuvos Rytas*, 12 December, 1995.
10 Data of the Border Police Department of the Republic of Lithuania presented to the Foreign Affairs Committee of the Seimas of the Republic of Lithuania.
11 Preliminary data of the Lithuanian Customs Department presented to the Ministry of Industry and Trade of the Republic of Lithuania on March 26, 1996.
12 All these facts were presented in the Lithuanian monthly newspaper "Donelaièio þemë" (The Land of Donelaitis), June 1996, in a resume of the discussion about Konigsberg/the Kaliningrad region organised by the Lithuanian National Union in May 1996.
13 Ibid.
14 According to the newspaper, this institute is not known in Moscow, although, it is unofficially known that Anton Surikov, an adviser at the institute, located in one of Moscow suburbs, works for Russia's military intelligence.

References

Bildt, Carl (1994): "The Baltic Litmus Test", Foreign Affairs, 73 (5) (Sept./Oct.), pp.80-81.
Carlsen, Per (1995): "Opportunities for Cooperation", Nordic Forum for Security Policy (1995), *Vilnius/Kaliningrad: Ideas on Co-operative Security in the Baltic Sea Region.* Conference in Vilnius 24-27 November. Helsinki: Nordic Forum for Security Policy (22-26).
Ericson, Sture (1995): "Changing Security Scenarios in the Baltic Sea Region", Nordic Forum for Security Policy (1995), *Vilnius/Kaliningrad: Ideas on Co-operative Security in the Baltic Sea Region.* Conference in Vilnius 24-27 November. Helsinki: Nordic Forum for Security Policy (16-22.
Grajewski, Andrzej (1992), "Regional Co-operation of the Baltic Region", *Polska w Europe.*

Heurlin, Bertel (1995), "Security Problems in the Baltic Region in the 1990s", in Joenniemi, Pertti and Carl-Erik Stålvant (eds.), *Baltic Sea Politics: Achievements and Challenges*. Stockholm: Nordic Council, pp. 55-76

Ihlau, Olaf (1995), "Da werden Blasen geschlagen", *Der Spiegel* (17): 68-71.

Kipp, Jacob W. (1994), "The Zhirinovsky Threat", *Foreign Affairs* 73(3): 72-87.

Kushner, P.I. *(1979[1951]), Etnicheskyje territorii i etnicheskyje granitsy* [Ethnic Territories and Ethnic Boundaries] in *Pietryèiø Pabaltijo etninë praeitis* [The Southeast Baltic: an Ethnic History]. Chicago: M. Morkunas Press.

Matulevièius, A. (1989), *Maþoji Lietuva XVIII amþiuje. Lietuviø tautinë padëtis* [Lithuania Minor in the 18th Century: Lithuanians' Ethnic Situation]. Vilnius.

Nikzentaitis, Alvydas (1995), "Das Kaliningrader Gebiet im Spannungsfeld internationaler Interessen. Unter besonderer Berucksichtigung der deutsch-litauischen Beziehung", *Osteuropa* vol. 45, no. 10: 927-934.

Nordic Forum for Security Policy (1995), *Vilnius/Kaliningrad: Ideas on Co-operative Security in the Baltic Sea Region*. Conference in Vilnius 24-27 November. Helsinki: Nordic Forum for Security Policy.

Paleckis, Justas (1994), "Fast unser Land oder Nachbarland?" pp. 115-127 in Muller-Hermann, Ernst (ed.), *Konigsberg/Kaliningrad unter europaischen Perspektiven*. Bremen: H.M. Hauschild.

Petersen, Philip A. and Shane C. Petersen (1994), *The Security Implications of and Alternative Futures for the Kaliningrad Region. Final Report*. Washington: The Potomac Foundation.

Polska w Europe (1992), "Kaliningrad 1992 – A Diagnosis", *Polska w Europe*.

Redman, Nicholas H. (1995), "Kaliningrad: Russia"s Baltic Exclave", *Briefing paper* No. 25. London: The Royal Institute of International Affairs.

Songal, Aleksandr (1995), "Searching for More Effective Cooperation Mechanisms", *International Affairs* (Moscow), no. 6: 62-67.

Vëlius, Norbertas (ed.), (1995), *Lietuvininkø Kraðtas* [The Land of Lietuvininkai]. Kaunas: Litterae Universitatis.

Wellmann, Christian (1994), "Demilitarisation as a precondition for economic development" in Lähteenmaki, Kaisa (ed.), "Dimensions of Conflict and Co-operation in the Baltic Sea Rim". *Research Report No. 58*. Tampere: Tampere Peace Research Institute.

Wellmann, Christian (1996), "Russia's Kaliningrad Exclave at the Crossroads. The Interrelation between Economic Development and Security Politics", *Cooperation and Conflict* 2: 161-183.

10 Kaliningrad: Visions of the Future

LYNDELLE D. FAIRLIE

Introduction

Two images from 1996 events are symbolic of the contrasts in Kaliningrad. At the strategic level, Russian officials have said they might install missiles in Kaliningrad as part of Russia's protest against NATO enlargement. At the level of economic regionalism and globalization, the South Korean vehicle manufacturer, KIA, has signed an agreement to manufacture vehicles in Kaliningrad. The images of missiles and cars symbolize the contrast in scenarios for the future of Kaliningrad. Analysts frequently see these alternatives as mutually exclusive options characterized as "the garrison state" versus "the marketplace" (Joenniemi 1996: 3, quoting Lange 1993; Wellmann 1996).

Contrast is also illustrated by election results for both the presidency and the governorship. In the first round of the presidential election in June 1996, Yeltsin led in Kaliningrad with 34 per cent of the vote but Zuganov received 23 per cent, Lebed received 20 per cent, Yavlinski 13 per cent and Zhirinovski 7 per cent.[1] This division of opinion was a harbinger of things to come. In the run-off election for Governor in October, the incumbent, Yuri Matochkin who was a Yeltsin-appointed reformer, was defeated by Leonid Gorbenko, Director General of the fishing seaport who was supported by a combination of reformers and Communists. Following Gorbenko's election, the firing of some leading reform-oriented administrators fueled speculation that Kaliningrad might be retreating from its opening to the west and returning to a focus on the "garrison state" role it played during the Soviet period.

This author does not subscribe to the dichotomous scenarios for the future of Kaliningrad. In my opinion, the "garrison" or "marketplace" scenarios are a false dilemma. In principle, the Kaliningrad of the future could follow the example of Hawaii and develop the garrison and marketplace roles simultaneously. Hawaii shares with Kaliningrad the advantage of being located on a double periphery. In the Hawaiian case the interface of the North American and Asiatic economies gives the islands unique opportunities. Kaliningrad's location on the periphery of both Europe and the former Soviet Union may offer it niche opportunities. These possibilities for the future will be discussed later in this analysis but before looking too far into the future, one must take account of the extent to which the short-term future will be occupied with the resolution of issues emerging from the past.

The old agenda, yet to be finished, is the dissolution of the Soviet Union. This is too often forgotten in the west, which is all too quick to jump the gun on the closing phases of dissolution of the Soviet Union. In the west's well-meaning attempt to please the Baltic states and give them some reassurance of welcome into western economic and political systems, the west is too quick to start up new institutions and arrangements, forgetting that old business from the Soviet period is still on the agenda and needs to be resolved so that Russia's interests can be accommodated along with those of the Baltic states. One example is air traffic control. Western talk about unifying Polish and Baltic air traffic control and defense may sound efficient to western ears but naturally offends Russia which is well aware that Vilnius still runs the air traffic control approaches to Kaliningrad. This legacy from the Soviet period is one illustration of the west's overly eager efforts to open new agendas without paying adequate attention to resolution of old business.

Disappointment is likely in the Baltic Sea area unless the west improves not only the attention paid to old business but also the resolution of conflicting signals given to the area. On one hand, the EU bureaucracy continues with the "structured dialog" which encourages EU applicants such as the Baltic states and Poland to harmonize their economic and legal systems with the EU. On the other hand, at the most recent meeting of the World Economic Forum, "Virtually every German official in Davos, from parliamentary majority leader Wolfgang Schauble on down, drew the East-West line along the border of the former Soviet Union. When asked if they would not include the Baltics in the western community, they demurred, citing Russian sensitivity on the issue. They definitely ruled out Baltic membership in NATO, and several ruled out even the less controversial EU membership because of the security commitment it would imply and because of Russia-Baltic tensions over Russian minorities, especially in Estonia" (Pond 1996: 23).

The dissolution of the Soviet Union and the resulting separation of Kaliningrad from mainland Russia has left other unresolved issues such as lack of agreement on the border between Kaliningrad and Lithuania and uncertainties about transit access to Kaliningrad from mainland Russia across Belarus, Poland and Lithuania. When viewed from the perspective of these issues, Kaliningrad has a new role in the post-Soviet period. In the politics and economics of the reconfiguration of post-Soviet and East European space, Kaliningrad now sometimes plays a role similar to that of Berlin during the Cold War. In the Berlin case, transit access issues sometimes flared as a symbol of Cold War politics between East and West. In Kaliningrad's case, transit access and other issues are sometimes issues and symbols which can be used by Russia, Lithuania, Belarus and Poland as they re-organize their political and economic relationships in the post-Soviet period. This is a totally new role for Kaliningrad, because in the Soviet period only Moscow's view really mattered for these actors.

From the perspective of Kaliningrad's role in the reconfiguration of post-Soviet space, even the psychological and political/economic location of Kaliningrad may be changing. The conventional view is that it is separated from mainland Russia by some 400 kilometers. However, Russia's relationship with Belarus may be so close that there is little independent policy on the part of Belarus. As a result, realistically speaking, Kaliningrad may be not 400 kilometers from Russia but less than 100 kilometers away, if one considers the Polish and Lithuanian borders with Belarus to be the *de facto* border with Russia. This analysis will explore the issue in more detail later.

When the Soviet Union dissolved, Kaliningrad's separation from mainland Russia caused anxiety in Kaliningrad, Moscow, and the West about whether Kaliningrad would be viable as an exclave. As a result, in the immediate post-Soviet period, there were a number of future scenarios put forward which speculated about the possibility that Kaliningrad might become part of Germany, a condominium run by several countries or a fourth Baltic Republic. These statist-oriented scenarios have fallen out of fashion now that several years have passed and the anxiety about Kaliningrad's viability has dissipated. Analysts now see that while Kaliningrad's situation may be unusual, its problems are not insurmountable and could even be transformed into opportunities. While it is possible that these statist scenarios might be considered again in the future, they do not seem like short-term options.

In addition to the statist issues which arose as a result of the dissolution of the Soviet Union, economics also changed. Prices in Kaliningrad rose above the Russian average due to transit costs from the mainland and border-related fees. Partly for this reason, Kaliningrad was given various advantages first in the Free Economic Zone and later in the Special Economic Zone in order to compensate for inflation and give the *oblast* a foundation for new economic opportunities bridging East and West. In fact, later in this analysis, it will be argued that if the speculation about smuggling is correct, one can speculate that powerful economic interests who benefit from the smuggling have great incentive to retain the Special Economic Zone privileges which Kaliningrad now has. These privileges determine the economic relationships with the mainland which in turn make the smuggling profitable. As a result, the sectoral prosperity which is due to Kaliningrad's relationship with mainland Russia solidifies Kaliningrad's connection with Russia rather than encourages separatist tendencies. Thus, ironically, the smuggling which reduces Russia's revenue from customs charges nonetheless has the advantage of reinforcing statist unity. These relationships are explained in the section on lack of transparency in the Kaliningrad economy.

The smugglers and legitimate business interests have already moved beyond the Cold War between East and West and have moved beyond the cold peace rivalries within post-Soviet space. They and other legitimate businesses have already de-securitized and de-bordered the Kaliningrad region and routinely integrated the economy of post-Soviet space with that of the western world. It is time for western and Russian policy makers and academics to catch up with daily life in contemporary Kaliningrad and recognize that the military/security scenarios are no longer the only game in town. Now the military and security issues are only one sector operating simultaneously with other de-securitized sectors.

This essay focuses on changes in the center-periphery relationships as one important variable which affects the future of Kaliningrad. The analysis starts from the assumption that as of now two center/periphery entities are the most important actors – the Moscow-dominated entity of Russia/Belarus and the Brussels-led EU. This essay raises questions about how Kaliningrad will function in a regional context on the double periphery of these two political/economic entities. First, I consider the future scenarios related to change on the periphery of post-Soviet space. This requires focus on Kaliningrad as part of a region. Attention is paid to Russia's changing relationship with Belarus. Secondly, I consider how changes on the European periphery might affect Kaliningrad as neighboring Poland and Lithuania attempt to join the EU and NATO. At the end of this essay I review the criticism which scholars have made about the appropriateness of center-periphery paradigms.

Change in the periphery of post-Soviet space: dissolution of the Soviet Union – an ongoing process

Russia-Belarus Community?

The dissolution of the Soviet Union led to the conventional view of Kaliningrad's geo-strategic location in relationship to "mainland" Russia. Former Kaliningrad Governor Matochkin articulated this view by saying that "the distance to the nearest region of the Russian Federation exceeds 300 kilometers and the shortest sea route from Kaliningrad to the nearest Russian port makes 1,100 kilometers" (Matochkin 1995b: 18). This author argues here that another interpretation of Kaliningrad's location may be coming into being due to Russia's changing relationship with Belarus.

In historical perspective, what is now western Belarus belonged to Poland up to the end of World War II. After the war, Belarus acquired its current borders and became part of the Soviet Union. Because Belarus has a border with Poland and Poland is likely to be a member of NATO and the EU soon, Belarus now must be considered by western analysts who analyze regional issues. This point was emphasized by Aleksandr Lebed, Russia's former chief security official, when on the eve of his recent visit to Belarus, he described the Belarus-Polish border as "Russia's national border with NATO".[2]

In April, 1996 Yeltsin and the Belarus President, Aleksandr Lukashenko, signed an agreement creating the Russia-Belarus Community. One of the questions regarding this union is whether it is essentially a merger of the two countries or whether it was primarily election rhetoric intended to gain Yeltsin supporters who might otherwise have voted for more nationalistic candidates during the presidential election. *The Economist* (10 August 1996: 36) characterized the Community as a "charade devised by Mr. Yeltsin to please Russian nationalists keen on rebuilding the Soviet Union".

The election rhetoric hypothesis is one possibility which gained credence after Yeltsin's re-election. Within three weeks of Yeltsin's reelection Lukashenko began accusing Moscow of behaving "extremely incorrectly" toward Belarus and of failing to implement – or even of "grossly violating" – bilateral economic agreements and the CIS customs union treaty.[3]

If the relationship between Russia and Belarus does become closer, then there may be several implications for Kaliningrad and for countries bordering Belarus. From the Kaliningrad perspective, if Russia and Belarus become united on major political and economic policies, it would mean in part that Kaliningrad is not hundreds of kilometers from "mainland" Russia but is only approximately one hundred kilometers from the Russia/Belarus Community. This would have several implications.

The most publicized issue at the moment is NATO's enlargement to include Poland. From the optimistic perspective, Kaliningrad could benefit from the resolution of the NATO enlargement issue by means of a Charter which takes account of the interests of Russia as well as Central and Eastern Europe. Pertti Joenniemi has argued that the NATO enlargement issue has toned down Baltic controversies:

> NATO has made it clear that it is not going to accept new members that have open, unsettled issues with their neighboring countries. This condition, once it has been understood and reflected upon, has in all probability tuned down any border disputes as well as the insistence on renaming Kaliningrad (Joenniemi 1996: 11-12).

One could argue, however, that while the NATO and EU values have set the agenda for the Baltic states and reduced their options for creating contentious issues with Russia, Moscow is not as limited by NATO and EU values because Russia does not realistically expect to join either institution in the near future.

In fact, when Yeltsin visited Kaliningrad in June 1996 and spoke about NATO expansion, he said that "Its advance to the frontiers of the community of Russia and Belarus is alarming our peoples. They do not want a new confrontation, new lines of division on the continent".[4] In response to a possible expansion of NATO, former Russian Defense Minister Grachev mentioned in early 1996 the possibility of "creating a powerful Russian-Belarus military group on the territory of Belarus".[5]

A second implication of Russia's changing relationship with Belarus is that Russia and Belarus have a political incentive to try to improve access to the sea for Belarus via Kaliningrad. In February, 1996 Yeltsin said that "Russia will also help boost Belarussian trade by providing access to a sea outlet, ... Kaliningrad". He said "We are planning to reach an accord with the Poles to build a stretch of road across their territory".[6] This caused a political problem because Moscow and Minsk referred to the idea as a "corridor" which reminded Poland of Hitler's invasion to link Germany with East Prussia.

If better access to the sea could be achieved for Belarus through Poland rather than through Lithuania, it would be a political bargaining chip for Moscow in its relationship with Lithuania. Moscow could use its influence to channel trade from Belarus through Poland to the Kaliningrad port, diverting cargo away from ports in the Baltic states and Poland. Moscow's enthusiasm for this scheme may decrease once Poland is admitted to NATO and the EU.

Some western skeptics dismiss these plans as political rhetoric but agreements have been signed between Kaliningrad and Belarus[7] which envisage enabling Belarus to use part of a Kaliningrad port and to apply its own trade and customs policies in its portion of the Kaliningrad port. In addition, former Kaliningrad Governor Matochkin led a delegation to Belarus in part to suggest the possibility of Kaliningrad and Belarus forming a financial-industrial-group in the shipping sector. These plans are reported to be regarded seriously at high government levels in Minsk.

The possibility of a separate customs system for Belarus at the Kaliningrad port may come as a surprise to western observers because Russia and Belarus have supposedly agreed to form a customs union, applying the EU model. Basically, the definition of a customs union is that member states reduce trade barriers among themselves and construct a common external barrier against non-members. Because of this definition of a customs union, westerners would normally expect that if Russia and Belarus are forming a customs union, the implication is that they would have one common policy for trade and customs. The news that Belarus wants its own policies at the Kaliningrad port raises questions about what Russia and Belarus mean when they say they are forming a customs union.

The route by which Belarus accesses the Baltic Sea may be affected not only by the issue of transit access across Poland or Lithuania but also by obstacles such as visas. At present Belarus citizens need a visa to go to Lithuania but they do not need a visa to go to Poland. The bureaucratic inconvenience of getting a visa may give Belarus people a special incentive to go to Poland rather than Lithuania.

Relationships between Poland and Belarus are affected in part by the thousands of Poles who live in Belarus and the Belarussian minority in Poland. This population distribution is understandable considering that the territory which is now part of western Belarus was part of Poland until the end of World War II. It is easy to understand why Belarussians would go to Poland. It is more difficult to understand why they would go through Poland to Kaliningrad rather than simply use Polish ports.

Access to the sea is also an issue on the Russian Pacific coast and the Tumen River Economic Development Area might offer a model of cooperation. Under U.N. auspices, the project links Russia, North Korea and China with the goal of creating a major port centered around the Tumen River. At present, China has no access to the sea at this point because the Chinese border is a few miles inland along the banks of the Tumen and only North Korea and Russia have territory on the banks of the river as it empties into the Pacific. Port politics in the area plays a role, as both the Chinese port of Dalian and the Russian port of Vladivostok are skeptical about more competition.

In the Baltic area, port competition among Kaliningrad and the ports of Poland and the Baltic states is also a factor. Björn Linderfalk reports that "From Tallinn to Klaipeda, the trend of 1996 has been to lure foreign investment to ports with the bait of free economic zones" (*The Baltic Times* (40) 19 December 1996 – 8 January 1997: 11). All of the ports need improvements and Kaliningrad will need to show promise on a regular basis if it hopes to compete for business coming to Baltic ports. The concern about "access to the sea" reflects the dynamics of the cold peace among the constituent parts of the former Soviet Union. In western Europe, people in landlocked countries such as Switzerland choose to use ports for economic reasons. The politics of "access to the sea" is an old agenda issue which is not a problem in modern western Europe.

Does the Russia-Belarus community change the strategic value of Kaliningrad?

It is possible that the potential union or alliance of Russia and Belarus might have the subtle implication of either raising or lowering the strategic value of Kaliningrad to Moscow. The following factors may be at work.

In the past there has been some thought in the west that Kaliningrad is important to Moscow partly because it is the only Russian ice-free port on the Baltic Sea and partly for psychological reasons. When speaking about Kaliningrad, Russian leaders often say that historically speaking, Peter the Great sought access to the sea for Russia in the Baltic and that if Russia lost Kaliningrad, it would be back to the situation it was in before Peter the Great. According to this interpretation, what is at stake is a psychological sense of loss on the part of Russia. The sense of loss is magnified because of the loss of the Baltic ports which Moscow controlled during the Soviet period.

For this reason, westerners sometimes wonder if Kaliningrad is important to Moscow partly because the Russian presence there is one of the few remaining factors which gives Moscow credibility as a political power in geo-strategic issues in the central/eastern European area. If Russia does indeed unify or ally with Belarus, Kaliningrad would no longer be the only Russian presence in the eastern European area. Kaliningrad would have to share that distinction with Belarus. Kaliningrad's value to Moscow might be lowered because Belarus and its border with Poland give Russia credibility as a European power with or without Kaliningrad.

Kaliningrad's value might also be lowered if its economy is closely linked in the future with Belarus and if political and economic instability in Belarus becomes worse. Thousands of people have demonstrated in Minsk against the union with Russia. The opposition leaders, Belarus Popular Front Chairman and Vice-Chairman, have asked for political asylum in the United States. In August, 1996 President Lukashenko described "the economic situation as one of "free fall" and expressed deep concern over social tensions approaching a critical point".[8] The issue of asylum, now an issue in countries such as France and Germany, could become an issue in the Baltic and central and east European area if conditions in Belarus continue to deteriorate and Belarusians become asylum-seekers.

On the other hand, a Russian union or close alliance with Belarus might increase the credibility of Russian interest in Kaliningrad. The conventional wisdom which says that Kaliningrad is separated from "mainland" Russia by two foreign countries and hundreds of kilometers is one of the factors fueling western speculation that Russia cannot be seriously interested in Kaliningrad. If Kaliningrad were not hundreds of kilometers away but only approximately one hundred kilometers from a Russia/Belarus alliance or union, Russian interest in Kaliningrad would seem more plausible.

Center-periphery relations: what kind of federalism?

Within the Moscow-dominated post-Soviet paradigm, center-periphery relations involve Kaliningrad's relationship with "mainland" Russia or is it Kaliningrad's relationship with the Russia-Belarus Community? For the purpose of this section of the essay, the starting assumption will be that Kaliningrad is part of Russia rather than the Russia-Belarus Community. Although this may sound like a theoretical distinction, it could quickly assume importance if the Kaliningrad economy were to blossom as a result of the KIA deal or other improvements in the economy or deterioration in Belarus.

Representation

One of the problems of center-periphery relations involves the formalization of federalism. One of the questions is how should the interests of Kaliningrad be represented in Moscow and how should Moscow be represented in Kaliningrad? Presently, Yeltsin has a presidential representative[9] in Kaliningrad. In addition, the Governor and his regional Administration are customarily assumed to be the local implementation apparatus of Moscow but the Governor has been appointed in the past and was elected for the first time in October, 1996. Kaliningrad has representation in the Duma and Federation Council as well as a lobbyist in Moscow and separate lines of influence through the military and through personal connections within the Kremlin.

Analysts do not agree on basic ideas such as whom the Governor represents. For example, former Russian Vice-Premier S.M. Shakhrai accused the former *oblast* administration of "continually balancing among the interests of the region, the interests of Russia, and the 'attractive no-cost' pastries of the European community" (Fyodorov & Zverev 1995: 45).

Unfortunately, this accusation against the administration did not take into account the realities of any federal state. Speaking from the northern German regional perspective, for example, Werner Jann (1994: 184) said about German regions that "it is dangerous to wait for the center to take care of your interests, because the center is preoccupied with many different regions". One of the questions for the future is how the new Gorbenko administration will interact with the Federation Council, Duma, Kremlin, military, *oblast* Duma and other Russian officials to produce policy affecting Kaliningrad.

The argument which Kaliningrad usually makes to Moscow is that it has a disadvantage because it is separated from "mainland" Russia by three borders of sovereign states and therefore it needs special privileges to compensate for these disadvantages. According to presidential representative, Tamara Poluektova, this argument has been especially hard to sell in the Federation Council where representatives of other regions are trying to look after their own interests and can argue that any expense which Kaliningrad causes for the federal budget may be disadvantageous to their own regions.[10] In a slightly different perspective on the issue, the Ministry for Nationality Affairs and Regional Policy was concerned that other regions might seek privileges comparable with whatever was granted to Kaliningrad (Current Digest 1995: 4).

Changes on the periphery of Europe: NATO and the EU at Russia's border?

In thinking about NATO and the EU, one must remember that both organizations are themselves moving targets. The EU is considering changes in its own organization during the IGC conference. Regarding NATO, *The Economist* (20 April 1996: 39-40) observed that the future of NATO may be "a consensus on the need for fewer levels of command and smaller headquarters; for greater flexibility and mobility; and for the ability to sustain more forces outside the NATO area". In this section, I will consider the military and de-securitized issues which are arising in the post-Soviet period as NATO and the EU consider expansion to the Baltic area.

"Demilitarization" of Kaliningrad?

During the Soviet period Kaliningrad served as the base from which Soviet troops in East Germany and Poland were supplied. Only Soviet ships visited the port. The border even to neighboring Poland was closed except for infrequent diplomatic use. For this reason, Kaliningrad was essentially unknown to most non-Soviet people in the Baltic area.

After the dissolution of the Soviet Union and the Warsaw Pact, Kaliningrad needed a new role. The Kaliningrad Special Defense Region (KOOR) was intended to streamline administrative efficiency and its direction by Admiral Yegorov probably indicates that maritime duties will be its principal focus. The focus could be changed or enhanced by the addition of tactical nuclear missiles. This is one policy option some Russians have considered in response to the potential enlargement of NATO. Some western experts warn that the signal and symbolic effect of such deployments would be disastrous: "Regionally, we would be back in a Cold War situation or next thereto" (Joenniemi 1996: 9, quoting Huldt 1996: 21). From a more optimistic perspective, one should note that even a Russian test of a Tochka surface-to-surface missile in Kaliningrad at a training ground only fifteen kilometers from the Lithuanian border in October, 1995 was not worrisome to Lithuania.[11] The overall political climate was good, so missile tests were not a problem.

Demilitarization is sometimes regarded by foreigners as a necessary prerequisite to Kaliningrad's participation in the Baltic and European economy. In addition, the Baltic states, Poland and other voices have sometimes advocated the "demilitarization" of Kaliningrad as a part of reducing security risks in the Baltic area. This provokes Russia to reply that outsiders should not interfere in its internal affairs and to remind everyone that Russia will not tolerate encroachments on Kaliningrad.

Demilitarization seems like a very unrealistic suggestion to Russian policy-makers who contemplate the possibility of Kaliningrad being surrounded by NATO and the EU. In protesting NATO's enlargement, former Russian Defense Minister Grachev expressed this concern saying "We would not want to be cut off from the special defensive district of Kaliningrad by NATO states".[12] Due to security concerns, former Deputy Premier Shakhrai urged the development of Kaliningrad as a military asset rather than an international commercial port. He apparently initially took this position because of a 1994 European Parliament resolution which in his view was "a proposal to work out a special international status of the territory and in perspective to establish in fact a fourth independent Baltic government" (Fyodorov & Zverev 1995: 46). Shakhrai presumably regarded this resolution as a threat to Russian sovereignty in Kaliningrad.

In the opinion of this author, there is no inherent justification for such false dilemma thinking. In principle, the example of Hawaii illustrates that it is not necessary to choose between militarization and commercial activity. In Honolulu, substantial Japanese investment co-exists with the large U.S. Navy base at Pearl Harbor. This situation exists in spite of the fact that the U.S. and Japan went to war during World War II because of the Japanese attack on Pearl Harbor.

Applying the Hawaii example to the Kaliningrad case, one can argue that a substantial Russian military presence could be compatible even with German investment. Independent of the appropriateness of German investment, Russian officials are now moving in the direction of accepting the idea of shared use of the deep-water port by both military and commercial interests. During Yeltsin's visit to Kaliningrad in June 1996, he said at a meeting "with the residents of Baltiysk that he supports the idea of setting up a state-of-the-art commercial port on the territory of Kaliningrad Region" and that "he had agreed with the local authorities on financing the construction of the commercial port and intends to allocate large sums of money for it".[13] The new Governor, Gorbenko, has also indicated support for the co-existence of both military and commercial sectors. Referring to the Russian military base in Baltiysk, Governor Gorbenko expressed the view that "in Gibraltar and Panama, too, both [military] bases and free economic zones were present. Therefore it should pose no obstacle in Russia".[14] The potential billion dollar deal with KIA illustrates the potential compatibility of militarization and economic development in Kaliningrad.

In the future, it may be that one of the debates among Russian policymakers may be just how much of a garrison Kaliningrad should be. A recent analysis in *Survival* said that some Kaliningrad military officers "are already beginning to question whether its value is worth the cost" (Asmus & Nurick 1996: 138). The future will depend a great deal on the assessment within Russia of just what role Kaliningrad is supposed to play: coastal defense, a political playing card in geo-politics, or a commercial gateway? The answers to these questions will determine what Russia is comfortable with in the future. If Russia eventually concludes that Kaliningrad is not much of a military asset and if Kaliningrad became a fourth Baltic

Republic or a region with autonomous status similar to the Åland Islands, Russia might theoretically agree to shared use of Baltiysk just as it is now reportedly considering letting Belarus share in the Kaliningrad port. Would this be a harmonious arrangement with well-integrated borders or a potential hot spot similar to the presence of the U.S. base at Guantanamo in Cuba?

The Åland Islands, culturally Swedish but located within Finnish sovereignty, are de-militarized so any suggestion of the Åland Islands model raises the question of what would happen if Kaliningrad were de-militarized. Even if Kaliningrad were de-militarized, one can ask how Poland and Lithuania would assess security risks. Would the two countries then feel safe? One could guess that they would not feel safe because of the ability in modern times of countries to move mobile forces around quickly. If Russia wanted to, it could quickly change its military presence in Kaliningrad or even increase threats to Poland and Lithuania via its ally, Belarus. It is probably for that reason that a NATO briefing team said that Kaliningrad's border with Poland and the current state of Russian activity there is not regarded as a risk for NATO.[15] Alternatively, perhaps the most extraordinary scenario for the future of Kaliningrad which has been suggested recently by a Russian analyst is the idea of NATO guarantees for Russia's territorial integrity, including specifically for the exposed Kaliningrad salient (*The Washington Post*, 18 August 1996: Op-Ed C7).

Potential EU enlargement brings de-securitized issues

The idea of NATO and the EU at Russia's border is not a new idea. Norway shares a border with Russia and was one of the key NATO members throughout the Cold War. Finland is a member of the EU and shares a border with Russia. What is a new idea is the possibility that Kaliningrad might become a Russian enclave within the EU and NATO if Poland and Lithuania become full members.

This section of the essay introduces de-securitized issues which might arise for Kaliningrad if Poland and Lithuania, now associate members, join the EU as full members. Brussels now has a "pre-accession" strategy for EU associate members such as Poland and Lithuania which want to enter the EU. The Commission prepared a White paper which was designed to assist applicants such as Poland in harmonizing their economy with the EU on a sector by sector basis (Commission 1995). This was considered an essential step in preparing to enter the internal market. Such preparation is regarded as a prerequisite to adoption of the *acquis communitaire*. The "structured dialog" which is part of this strategy guides aspirant members in their efforts to harmonize their economy, government and legal systems with the EU. In the future, there is the theoretical possibility that there might be enough harmonization to enable Poland and Lithuania to decide to merge, repeating a configuration in their past histories. This idea recently appeared in a humorous but thought-provoking story in *The Economist* (31 August 1996: 44).

The EU Commission has been asked to write an opinion on the progress applicants states have made towards EU membership. As part of this process, each of the Baltic states reportedly received a 300-page questionnaire from Brussels designed to measure the progress they are making towards the possibility of entering the EU. The Lithuanian answer reportedly was thousands of pages long. The answers to the questionnaires should be studied partly from the perspective of implications for Kaliningrad. The plans for harmonization of government and legal systems with the EU illustrate James Rosenau's point that institutional isomorphism is one mechanism of globalizing dynamics (Rosenau 1996: 11). If Poland and Lithuania do eventually join the EU, Kaliningrad will find that increasingly decisions are made which affect them over which they have little influence. This was one of the arguments made in Scandinavia when voters were urged to approve admission of their countries to the EU.

In addition to examining the effects of having the EU as a neighbour, one could examine the effect of the proposed Neman Euro-region. Its goal is to facilitate cross-border cooperation. Some sources say it will include Kaliningrad, Poland and Lithuania and other reports say Belarus will also be included. Some think it will be a serious project while others think it is mostly rhetoric. The Neman Euro-region might provide a useful forum in which to practice multilateral cooperation.

The issue of air traffic control is an example of the need for co-ordination in the re-organization of central/eastern Europe and post-Soviet space. Vilnius still runs Kaliningrad's air traffic control above 20,000 feet as it did during the Soviet period.[16] Rivalry between East and West in the area of air traffic control may arise in part because there is talk of blending air traffic control with air defense. A recent article in the British journal *Survival* made policy recommendations which were reportedly under serious consideration in the U.S. State Department. One of their suggestions included the idea that "Baltic airspace should be integrated with that of the West in a fashion akin to the Central European Regional Airspace Initiative" (Asmus & Nurick 1996: 131). This is the sort of suggestion which Russians normally find to be provocative or uninformed.

While westerners think about integrating Baltic air space with the West, there is talk about the union between Russia and Belarus involving air defense. Because Kaliningrad is part of Russia, one wonders what role it would play in unified air defense of Russia and Belarus and how that would work under the current situation whereby Kaliningrad's air traffic control is run not by Belarus but by Lithuania. Overall, one has the impression that people in both the west and in post-Soviet space toss out suggestions on subjects such as air traffic control without giving adequate consideration to detail. As with other sectors, the Moscow and western processes will have a lot of detail to negotiate in regularizing relationships in post-Soviet and East European space.

In addition to air traffic control, agriculture and transport are sectors which cause concern. It is possible that EU agriculture and transport policies might affect Kaliningrad if they are applied to potential new members like Poland and Lithuania. In both sectors, Kaliningrad is concerned with what it believes are subsidies which its foreign competitors in Poland and Lithuania are getting. Lithuanian agricultural producers may outdistance Kaliningrad producers even more now that the Baltic states have formed a free trade area in farm products effective January 1, 1997. Subsidies to foreign producers have been an issue in Kaliningrad elections. Because these policies are primarily determined in Brussels and the capitals of the EU members and Associates, they may become an issue again. In the future, the need to negotiate subsidies may be one of the reasons why the Kaliningrad of the future might want more autonomy.

EU transport policy may affect Kaliningrad in the future. One of the questions will be how the EU's forum for negotiating transport issues interfaces with the CIS Council of Railway Transport. Established in 1992 and joined by the Baltic countries as observers a year later, it "regulates the work of railways at the interstate level and drafts common principles for their operation" (*The Baltic Times*, 19-25 September 1996: 9). Kaliningrad may also be affected by the Commission's Baltic Ports Memorandum of Understanding and by the recently adopted Communication "Shaping Europe's Maritime Future". The Commission hopes to extend the MARIS program to the Baltic area including the sub-projects: MARTRANS,

SAFEMAR, MARSOURCE and MARVEL. Because SAFEMAR involves international conventions on safety and MARSOURCE is "aimed at aiding the creation of a fisheries and oceans information network"[17] Kaliningrad may be affected. It has a fishing industry and Lloyds List reports indicate from time to time that ships originating from Kaliningrad have had safety problems. Does it have enough autonomy to negotiate these issues itself with its neighbors or is it dependent on Moscow to take up its issues with Poland and Lithuania?

In the EU and in the Baltic area, urban policy and the separation of cities from their hinterland is also a concern. Because the Soviet Union was an integrated state, its dissolution has left not only Kaliningrad but also other areas separated from their hinterlands. For example, Daugavpils in Latvia, formerly served regions which are now in Belarus and Lithuania. In the post-Soviet period, non-tariff barriers such as requirements for visas disrupt what were formerly integrated areas. In Kaliningrad's case, it used to be part of the Baltic Economic Zone. Kaliningraders could travel easily to the Baltic states. Now Kaliningraders can go to Poland and Lithuania without a visa but they need a visa to go to Latvia and Estonia. Kaliningrad proposed the elimination of visa requirements by those states in return for the right of citizens from those states to pass through Kaliningrad without a visa on their way to Poland rather than circumventing Kaliningrad. Latvia and Estonia rejected their proposal.[18] The need for visas may be one reason why the train from Kaliningrad to Riga has been discontinued.

The EU has similar problems in what Ohmae (1995) would call "region states" which cross nation-state boundaries into non-EU territories. The Swiss cities of Basel and Geneva are examples. In Basel's case, it is located in Switzerland, outside the EU but its suburbs are within the EU member states of Germany and France. Similarly, the Swiss city of Geneva is almost entirely surrounded by France. In the future, if Poland and Lithuania join the EU and/or NATO, Kaliningrad might find that like Basel and Geneva, it is surrounded by something to which it does not belong.

In the case of the European Union, the idea that there will be internal freedom of circulation within the EU implies that it should have an external border. The EU is trying to implement this idea with the Schengen agreements which aim to have no internal EU border but a defensible external border against non-member states. Anyone who has visited the Polish-German border is likely to think this is a very illusionary objective. The Oder River is a pleasant small river which could easily be crossed by any person with some initiative and a small boat. Unless Brussels plans to build a wall around the EU, they probably would not be any more successful at keeping people out than is the U.S.

If Poland and the Baltic states join the European Union, Kaliningrad may resemble the U.S.-Mexico border where there is a flourishing *maquiladora*[19] industry as well as a market for false documents and smuggling of prospective illegal aliens. In this scenario, Kaliningrad could easily become a conduit for prospective Russian refugees who could be smuggled into the Baltic states where the large number of ethnic Russians legitimately in the area would make it easier for illegal aliens to take on falsified Baltic citizenship and later obtain an EU passport.

This scenario could become even more probable if the Russians succeed in getting these changes: "automatic dual citizenship for Russians abroad; Russian to be an official language; and treaties guaranteeing the rights of 'Russian-speakers', a wider category than Russian citizens or ethnic Russians" (*The Economist,* 27 August 1994: 48). This sort of scenario would cause a lot of concern for the EU. The Schengen agreement tries to set up a clear external border on the outer perimeter of the EU. If the Baltic states joined under the conditions noted above, it would be almost impossible to realistically set up a border which separated Russia and Russians from the Baltic EU members.

Even without the attraction of the possibility of Polish and Lithuanian membership in the EU, the dramatic fluctuation of the rouble in October, 1994 and the resulting end of rouble convertibility during this period in the Baltic states gave Kaliningraders a powerful incentive to leave the rouble zone if they could. What if this problem occurs in the future? Kaliningraders' former links to the Baltic states probably give them opportunities to see that the life of the Russian minorities in the Baltic states outside the rouble zone is likely to be more promising than is their own future as presently envisioned. Yeltsin's presidential representative in Kaliningrad noted that young people from Kaliningrad now visit neighboring Poland for the price of a disco ticket and can observe what life is like there.[20]

How many currencies: are the Euro and the rouble optimal?

Within Russia, regions develop at different speeds. One corollary of what the EU calls "variable geometry" is that the state experiencing variable geometry may not find it optimal to have one currency for the entire area. Within the EU, the debate over the desirability of a "Euro" single currency for all member nation-states is under way. Martin Feldstein (1991), an economist, argues that one currency is optimal when all the areas within a currency zone are at the same place in the business cycle at the same time. If all areas are not in the same place in the business cycle at the same time, then separate currencies and separate policies determined by regional financial authorities may be optimal. This is the argument made against the Euro by those who wish to retain national currencies within the EU and policies for each member state set by the central bank of each member state. When applying this logic to Russia, one wonders if the Russia of the future will need different currencies for different areas of the country. Kaliningrad may need a currency compatible with European and Scandinavian economies and European Russia and Belarus whereas the Russian Far East may need a currency compatible with its major trading partners in Asia.

With or without separate currencies, the increasing harmonization of the economies and legal systems of Poland and Lithuania to fit the EU's internal market and *acquis communitaire* and developments such as the Baltic states' free trade area in farm products, indicate that serious analysis is needed about how these economic systems will affect Kaliningrad. Some theoretical guidance can be gleened from the work of Ronald J. Wonnacott (1996) who analyzes free trade areas in comparison with bilateral arrangements which he calls hub-and-spoke systems. Future-oriented Kaliningraders should put high priority on such a study in light of Wonnacott's observation: "How will outside countries compare a H & S with an FTA? While outsiders will face discrimination in competing in either an H & S or an FTA, this problem will be greater in an FTA because the discrimination will be in competition with all members, not just the hub. This is just one example of a more general observation: The more that countries in a region liberalize trade among themselves, the greater the problem outsiders will face in competing in this regional market" (Wonnacott 1996: 250).

Life on the double periphery: does the Kaliningrad economy need more autonomy?

In light of the new problems and opportunities discussed in the previous section, it seems reasonable to ask if Kaliningrad needs more autonomy in order to be consistently responsive to opportunities and problems. Kaliningrad economic geographers note that important legislation for the financial support of the *oblast* passed in the Duma in December 1994 with only one vote to spare (Fyodorov & Zverev 1995: 45). When considering the future, this small majority makes one wonder if Kaliningrad will be successful in continuing to get favorable legislation adopted. If the KIA deal comes to fruition, legislators from other Russian regions could argue that Kaliningrad is getting too many advantages and they may argue that it is time to level the playing field and reduce some of Kaliningrad's privileges. Reports of smuggling and the resulting customs revenue lost to Russia may also prompt demands for reduction of the privileges which make the smuggling profitable.

On the other hand, the former administration of the *oblast* reportedly noticed

> a change of tone in Moscow as it becomes more apparent that NATO will expand to the East. The Government will be more amenable, understanding that the changing geo-political situation demands increased attention to the western outpost of Russia (*Commersant Daily*, 13 September 1996: 152).

Perhaps this explains why "the Russian federal budget has assigned *R226bn* for the needs of...Kaliningrad to be distributed through the regional support fund. The sum is 65 per cent larger than allocations provided for 1996".[21] Even though the 1997 budget projections from Moscow look promising for Kaliningrad, adverse changes are always possible, particularly in the light of the moves of the "donor regions" to increase their influence, presumably at the expense of the regions such as Kaliningrad which are not net contributors to the Russian budget.

In the future Kaliningrad might want more autonomy because in the past it has sometimes experienced policy reversals by Moscow. Policy reversals cause frustration at the local level and may deter foreign investment but they are not unique to Kaliningrad. Policy reversals have happened in both Kaliningrad and the Russian Far East. In the Kaliningrad case, former Governor Matochkin wrote that

> In these past years, however, we have seen Moscow time and again present us with a decree with one hand and take it back with the other almost the following day. This was the case in the spring of 1994, when the State Duma amended the presidential decree granting the Yantar FEZ residents tariff preferences. And it happened again in the spring of 1995, when a presidential decree dated March 6 and the Federal law 'On Some Questions of Granting Preferences to Participants in Foreign Economic Activities' abolished the preferences granted for ten years by the 1993 presidential decree (Matochkin 1995a: 12).

A policy reversal also took place on Russia's Pacific rim. In the Free Economic Zone in the port of Nadhodka near Vladivostok, benefits were withdrawn with a negative impact on foreign investment. For example, in the early 1990s when customs and tax privileges were granted, Chinese builders leased large plots of land for a period of fifty years in order to build hotels but "all the privileges were canceled antidate. Now the Chinese will have to give one of the hotels free of charge to the city to pay for the accrued taxes".

Inaction or policy reversals by Moscow forces Russians and Russian regions to fend for themselves when they find declining subsidies, defense contracts, wage arrears and reversals in laws and decrees from Moscow. In such circumstances, people begin to learn that they cannot count on Moscow and must take care of themselves. An economic geographer reported in Kaliningrad in 1994 that it was estimated that Kaliningrad had approximately 2 per cent unemployment because many people had four or five jobs.[22]

In some ways, this trend of making each individual into a self-employed entrepreneur who will hold several jobs rather than one lifetime career with the same employer is a trend in developed countries as well. Thomas Peters' book, *Liberation Management*, discusses these trends in business. In the Russian case, the creativity, adaptability and entrepreneurial initiative displayed by people in peripheral areas such as Kaliningrad and Vladivostok when they are forced by Moscow to fend for themselves should make clear that peripheral areas near dynamic trading blocs may have options. Continued slow policy action and policy reversals by Moscow may gradually convince people in peripheral areas that Moscow is increasingly less important in their daily lives.

From the Russian perspective the West also has what appear to Russians to be contradictions in policy. Fyodorov and Zverev start from the position that the FEZ was ended in response to IMF guidelines which required Moscow to cut expenses such as the revenue loss due to customs exemptions received by Kaliningrad. According to Fyodorov and Zverev, when Russia complied with this western suggestion, they were penalized by a different western institution: the EU put the TACIS program on hold due to the elimination of the FEZ (Fyodorov & Zverev 1995: 52). From the Russian perspective, the IMF and EU should coordinate to avoid policy reversals themselves. This is not easy because organizations such as the EU and NATO are themselves changing.

What will the Kaliningrad perspective be in the future? If Kaliningrad had more autonomy or even independence, there are some policies which they could decide for themselves without reference to Moscow. Some Kaliningraders say they would like to be a visa-free territory or at least a territory where visitors could get a visa on arrival which would be valid for Kaliningrad but not for other parts of Russia. It is also said that they would like to have amber reclassified as a precious gem. Also, shuttle-traders are now regulated by Moscow in terms of how much merchandise they can import without duty. With more autonomy or independence, these policies could be locally regulated.

Protection from foreign competition might also be an issue which would be more likely to be addressed if local policy-makers were in charge rather than Moscow officials. Kaliningrad politicians who are critical of some aspects of the previous Free Economic Zone say that Kaliningrad is the victim of dumping by foreign producers who benefit from subsidies (*Kaliningrad Pravda,* 9 September 1995). Protectionism was an issue in the regional elections on October 6, 1996 for the Governor and for the *oblast* Duma. Governor Gorbenko's election campaign promises to aid Kaliningrad workers may be reflected in future protectionist policies.

Before the election, reports indicated that there are "quantitative restrictions on the import of some particular types of foodstuffs, building materials, petroleum products and excisable goods. Goods brought into the region within the established quotas will not be subject to customs duties, excise and value-added tax, but on condition that the goods will not be taken beyond the bounds of the Kaliningrad region.[23] Duties will be charged when goods are imported in excess of the quotas. The list of goods is reportedly compiled by the Regional Administration. The case can be made that this gives needed flexibility" (*Kaliningrad Pravda,* 9 September 1995). On the other hand, skeptics argue that there is potential for arbitrary decision-making which makes it difficult for businesses to make decisions based on predictable ground rules.

Transportation subsidies are another controversial aspect of protectionism issues. Kaliningraders say their port loses business because Lithuania subsidizes transportation costs of shipping to its Klaipeda port, which Kaliningrad sees as a competitor. If Kaliningrad were a fourth Baltic Republic or had comparable autonomy under Russian sovereignty, perhaps they would be able to negotiate these controversies over subsidies within the framework of the EU if Poland and Lithuania join the EU.

Future potential disputes about subsidies may place Kaliningrad at a disadvantage because according to the agreements between Russia and the EU,

> Russia will still fall under the rules for state-trading countries as far as anti-dumping and safeguard measures are concerned. These afford the EU much greater discretion in the imposition of protective measures (Bustin & Krylov 1996: 34).

In addition, the economics of the Special Economic Zone are dependent in part on "rules of origin" (ROOs), meaning that goods such as the projected vehicles made by KIA in Kaliningrad are eligible for duty-free export to mainland Russia depending on how much local content is added in Kaliningrad. Because the EU and Russia have no agreement on rules of origin, some experts think that "this is likely to lead to disputes and controversies between the EU and Russia as far as rules of origin are concerned, until Russia accedes to GATT (WTO)" (Bustin & Krylov 1996: 34). For these reasons, Kaliningrad might prefer autonomy so it could negotiate relevant agreements with the EU independent of Moscow. Sector by sector, one increasingly sees that the future will involve a lot of negotiation about the detailed interface of the two dominant center-periphery paradigms based in Moscow and Brussels.

Another policy which Kaliningrad might prefer to control itself in the future rather than defer to Moscow is policy involving immigrants. If Kaliningrad were to become a place which resolved its own unemployment problems and attracted labor from other areas to jobs, then a little-noticed provision of the recent Special Economic Zone law might take on controversial importance. The SEZ law specifies that immigration preference should be given to native-speakers of Russian who wish to emigrate from the Baltic states.[24] However, the treaty with Belarus expresses the intention to have free movement of labor.[25] Is there a contradiction in these agreements? If jobs became available for outsiders, who would get preference: Belarusians or Russians from the Baltic states?

Questions about whether Russia as a whole and Kaliningrad would benefit or lose from more autonomy or independence in the future would in most western countries be based in part on a thorough economic analysis which would be dependent upon transparency of the economy. To the outside observer, the lack of transparency about the economy appears to be one of the obstacles to analysis of the Kaliningrad situation. The transparency issue arises because observers are puzzled by the contrasts which they observe in Kaliningrad. Analysts speculate that the Kaliningrad economy may be one in which several economies are operating in largely unrelated sectors. A segmented economy might be one way of explaining why Kaliningrad appears to observers to be a land of contrasts.

An impressionistic sketch of contrasting images includes some of the following elements. One observer reported that the prison appeared to be busy but it was silhouetted against a skyline showing a port which was still. Agriculture is stagnant and people have been reported to be digging in the fields for fragments of amber. Yet the CNN report of Yeltsin's visit to Kaliningrad commented that "the new bank directors have armored limousines".[26] Two military personnel committed suicide reportedly due to bad conditions[27] but there are more satellite dishes on the side of apartment buildings. Big dogs are well-kept and large stuffed animals are for sale. Casinos prosper and the florist shop is crowded but a farmer has not been paid in a year. New kiosks draw shoppers and reports indicate there are a lot of fur coats around town in winter.

The sectors of the economy which are declining are comparable with other regions of Russia. Fishing, defense and agriculture are all down due to declines in the budget and changes in the economy. On the other hand, there are also success stories. Foreign investments in the zone increased twofold last year (1995) as compared to 1994.[28] The Tass report indicated that investments were more than thirty million dollars in the sectors of telephones, oil and chemical sector and road and hotel construction.

Tourism blossomed when Kaliningrad was opened to foreigners. Elderly Germans who had left *Königsberg* in the war returned to visit their homeland. Now most have done so and tourism is diversifying.

Some of the economic success stories are worth noting partly because it is important to learn why they are successful. The Swedish chemical company, AGA, manufactures gases such as oxygen and is successful in Russia because raw materials are no problem and the prime costs are those of energy and labor.[29] The crane manufacturer, Baltkran, is a German and Russian company which created more jobs last year and workers receive pay that is higher than the Kaliningrad average. The Yantar Shipyard still gets orders for ships because its construction costs are ten per cent below that of Poland.[30] At the port a new multi-million dollar fertilizer terminal is operating. In the past, most Russian fertilizer was shipped to the West via ports in the Baltic states and Black Sea. Russia has wanted to shift some of these cargoes away from the Baltic states to bring the business to Kaliningrad and this terminal may be part of that plan.

Kaliningrad has also been participating in the Baltic regional economy. There is a vigorous cross-border trade with Poland and Lithuania. As is the case in many Russian border areas, there are "shuttle-traders". The title covers an estimated 20 million Russian citizens who supplement their incomes by buying inexpensive consumer goods abroad and re-selling them at home.[31] Reduced duties have led to the situation whereby "thousands of petty traders have been traveling to Poland, Lithuania and Germany to stock up on jeans and liquor. They are up to twice as cheap here as in Moscow".[32] This "shuttle-trader" activity may be affected by the new government resolution which says that beginning in August, 1996 the maximum value of goods that a private individual will be allowed to bring into Russia without paying duty will be cut from $2,000 to $1,000.[33]

The sectors of the economy noted above are reasonably transparent. Yet observers are skeptical about whether the amount of economic activity which is transparent accounts for all the pockets of apparent prosperity in the city. Analysts look for additional explanations of the prosperity and see reports of a shadow economy typical of that found throughout parts of post-Soviet space. The June, 1996 issue of *Jane's Intelligence Review,* reported that "Russian gangs are also strong in the Baltic states, which – like the lawless Russian exclave of Kaliningrad – are above all used as routes for smuggling and money-laundering...".[34] The clearest hypothesis about the problems which have occurred in the past appeared in this report from *The Moscow Times* (3 September 1996: 12): The Lithuanian transport ministry says whole trainloads of oil are being "stolen" or just vanish as part of widespread scams designed to avoid paying Russian export taxes. Lithuania is a special focus for oil smuggling because of its uncertain status as a corridor between the Russian enclave of Kaliningrad on the Baltic Sea and the rest of Russia. The nature of smuggling through Lithuania is simple. Trains of oil must travel across Lithuania to get to Kaliningrad from Russia. But because Kaliningrad, the final destination, is Russian territory, Russia does not levy its high export taxes on oil delivered there. In fact, shipments of oil products to Kaliningrad are often simply covers for smuggling, usually with the connivance of the companies in Kaliningrad that are listed as the official receivers in Russian customs declarations. Whole trainloads of such cargo are "stolen" and then exported to international markets tax free. But Lithuania is not the only conduit for smugglers. Customs officials have exposed similar scams in Ukraine and Belarus.[35]

Because Latvia is also a transit state between mainland Russia and Kaliningrad, similar allegations come from Latvia. In September, 1995 Tass reported that people who operated at most of Russia's oil refineries, used false papers to organize fuel deliveries to non-existent companies in the Russian enclave of Kaliningrad. The accounts were paid at a preferential rate, as Kaliningrad is part of Russia. On their way to Kaliningrad, the shipments suddenly changed direction to Latvia from where a lion's share of diesel, mazut and petrol was shipped by sea to the west to be sold at world prices.[36]

Other resources such as amber, timber and aluminum have been mentioned in reports. At the Kaliningrad amber mine, deputy manager, Stanislav Romanov, was quoted as saying that a worry "is organized theft within the plant, losing 30 per cent or perhaps more of output".[37] In 1995 *Moscow News* said that "Whole trains loaded with aluminum 'evaporate' on their way to the sea ports of Kaliningrad and Tallinn".[38] During the period 1992-1993 the Russian Interior Ministry reportedly commented on the smuggling of natural resources out of Russia saying in part that such activity involved "up to a trainload a day passing through Lithuania and into the port of Kaliningrad alone".[39]

Summary data in 1995 indicated that as a result of verification of more than 6,000 organizations which exported goods from Russia to Kaliningrad in 1993-1994, it was found that not less than half of the exported goods were "left" in Belarus and the Baltic states.[40] In attempt to deal with these kinds of problems, a 1994 report said that "A new rule now requires oil purchasers in Kaliningrad to deposit enough money to pay the export duties if the oil is being sold outside of Russia. If the oil arrives, the deposit is refunded. Now smugglers must either bribe customs officers, use false documents or transport their cargo by truck on back roads, a much less efficient method of smuggling".[41]

In 1997 reports suggested that Kaliningrad "is believed to be a major center for alcohol traffickers due to its special status as a Free Economic Zone. Imported pure alcohol from Western Europe is converted in secret factories and shipped for sale across the former Soviet Union, while vodka produced in Russia is often sent to the enclave for repackaging so that producers can take advantage of the region's tax breaks. Kaliningrad customs officers seized 11 tons of alcohol in the first half of December alone" (*The Baltic Times*, (41) 9-15 January 1997: 11). For this reason, authorities "have banned the import of pure spirits and vodka from the start of the year" (*The Baltic Times*, (41) 9-15 January 1997: 11).

There is also speculation that "a considerable amount of illegalities have occurred including smuggling of drugs, weapons and refugees...the combination of demoralized, poorly paid troops and masses of inadequately guarded arms, ammunition and related equipment has turned Kaliningrad into one of the biggest black-market arms bazaars in Russia" (Joenniemi 1996: 16, quoting *Guardian*, 21 May 1992; Redman 1995: 3).

The viewpoints of Kaliningraders about how much autonomy they might want from Moscow might depend in part on the source of their income. On one hand, people who are doing legitimate business based on the local economy and its legal relationships with Poland and Lithuania might favor or oppose autonomy depending on whether or not their business is linked to the privileges which have been granted because Kaliningrad is separated from "mainland" Russia. If they receive their income from Moscow subsidies which are still important and which may in some sectors of the economy not be easily replaced by private sector economic activity, they would want to retain a close connection with Moscow. Other Kaliningraders who would want to retain a close connection to Moscow would be those who profit from a shadow economy which may be prospering because Kaliningraders can obtain natural resources cheaply from "mainland" Russia and then illegally re-export them to the western world under the circumstances indicated in the section on the shadow economy.

Kaliningrad's alleged shadow economy should be kept in perspective. Recent analysis of Russia as a whole indicates that "about 90 per cent of private sector income and about 40 per cent of all wages are never reported to Goskomstat and are therefore not reflected in the official reports of Russia's GDP and PCI" (Shama 1996: 112). In the future, models such as the Åland Islands will need to be studied if serious analysis becomes possible under conditions of economic transparency.

Competing paradigms?

In looking at the future, one can say that the reconfiguration of post-Soviet space, the former Warsaw Pact and the Baltic region in the post-Cold war period is somewhat analogous to the big bang theory of the origin and subsequent development of the universe. It is not clear how territories will congeal into viable regions. Both globalizing and localizing changes occur simultaneously (Rosenau 1996).

In the years ahead the question is how Kaliningrad and the area around it will congeal into what kind of configurations: a political and economic version of the reconfiguration of the universe after the big bang. Will the Russia-Belarus Community in effect become one state? Will Kaliningrad remain part of Russia? Will Kaliningrad and parts of north-west Russia become a state separate from the rest of Russia? Will Kaliningrad become a fourth Baltic Republic? If Kaliningrad becomes independent, would Kaliningrad have shared use with Russia of the Baltiysk base in a variant of plans now on the drawing board for a possible Belarus portion of the port at Kaliningrad? If Kaliningrad becomes independent, would Russia have exclusive use of Baltiysk in an arrangement reminiscent of the U.S. base at Guantanamo in Cuba? Will neighboring Poland and Lithuania enter NATO and the EU? Will Poland and Lithuania unite to form one country? Any of these possibilities and still other possibilities might be part of re-configuration of post-Soviet space in the future.

In trying to understand this process, scholars have noted that both fragmentation and integration are occurring simultaneously. Werner Jann cautions analysts to avoid limiting themselves to only one paradigm such as a center-periphery conception or the "banana" growth corridor future scenarios. Jann writes that the center-periphery perspective is what he calls the "Brussels Perspective" which is based on a hierarchical and concentric classical conception of the state. In this view

> there is a center and there is a periphery – both in political and economical terms. Some areas are more European than others...Some people like this perspective, i.e. in France and Germany, some may fear it, like quite a few in Britain, but they still share the same perspective. In this perspective Northern Europe is the periphery... (Jann 1994: 182-183).

It is not only Brussels but also Moscow which has a center-periphery perspective. Moscow sees itself as the center and the "near abroad" as those new states which formerly belonged to the Soviet Union. In this paradigm, the "far abroad" is territory in a concentric circle beyond the "near abroad". Moderate conservatives in the Russian foreign policy elite think that Russia "should develop its sphere of influence, particularly in the 'near abroad'" (Kerr 1995: 977). This center/periphery paradigm may be useful as a way to conceptualize some of the relationships among the Soviet successor states but it may not be useful as a comprehensive way of assessing the situation in Russian border areas such as Kaliningrad and Vladivostok.

For these areas, either the "evolving regions" or "banana growth strip" conceptions of political and economic change may be most relevant in the future even though neither paradigm necessarily has Moscow at its center. Insofar as Kaliningrad becomes increasingly involved with Europe and Vladivostok with Asia, both the regionalism and banana growth corridor concepts are challenges to Moscow's idea that it is the center and the "near abroad" and "far abroad" are peripheral circles[42]. At present, Kaliningrad still looks to Moscow as the center of its universe partly because of the *oblast's* dependence on subsidies. However, in the future, Moscow may be located less at the center of a viable economy and more at the peripheries of the dynamic European and Asian trading blocs.

Analysts who are not persuaded of the utility of a concentric concept of Brussels at the center of an orderly institution prefer what they see as an alternative concept of a collection of regions which does not necessarily have a center. However, the collection of regions idea is not necessarily in opposition to a Brussels-centric paradigm. One interpretation of the Brussels response to the EU member states' attempt to assert themselves via the "subsidiarity"[43] concept was the idea that Brussels deliberately encouraged regions in the hope that the regions will put pressure on their own capitals to delegate more authority to regions, thereby undermining the strength of the nation-states.

Weaker states may allow Brussels to increase its power but the EU's IGC conference which was called to revise the Maastricht treaty illustrated that the discussion about how to structure power and authority is not limited to post-Soviet space and Brussels is not invincible. The EU concept of "variable geometry" acknowledges that different parts of the EU are progressing economically at different speeds. Variable geometry is also a concept which applies to regions of Russia which are developing at different speeds. The problems of the EU today may be the paradigm most applicable to the future of Russia. The issue of whether or not there should be one currency for each member state or a single currency, the Euro, may be questions for Russia in the future. The post-Soviet period has already seen the use of multiple currencies inside Russia (Olshansky 1993: 17).

While it is fine to suggest theoretically that a region without concentric circles is plausible, Marshall R. Singer's analysis suggests that a dynamic center is a hard concept to challenge. In his book, *Weak States in a World of Powers: The Dynamics of International Relationships (1996)* and in his recent application of this principle to the former Soviet Union in his paper "After the Collapse of the Soviet Empire: *Weak States in a World of Powers revisited*" Singer makes the basic point that powerful economies are attractive to the regions on their peripheries, even when those peripheral areas are in other nation-states. Peripheral areas do not even have to be in weak states to experience this relationship. California belongs to the powerful American economy but all of its leading foreign trade partners other than Mexico are in Asia.

In the European region, one need only to look at the pattern of trade with Germany by countries which once belonged to the Warsaw Pact or Soviet Union to illustrate rapid change and the important role of a dynamic source of economic energy. Due in part to the prominent role of export credits which give customers an incentive to purchase from German suppliers, Germany has become the leading trading partner of most of the Warsaw Pact and the Baltic countries. Drawing on World Bank, U.N. and Russian data, Singer concludes that "Whereas the Soviet Union used to be the major trading partner for all of the Soviet bloc countries, by 1992-1993, Germany became the major trading partner for every one of the countries of Eastern Europe, with the exception of Bulgaria (for which we have incomplete data) and Slovakia (which trades most with the Czech Republic). Not only that, but with the exception of Bulgaria, none of them now has even 10 per cent of their total trade with Russia" (Singer 1996: 19-21). The overall message is that a Brussels or German-based center-periphery paradigm has not been challenged by any competing paradigm if one measures the strength of paradigms in conventional variables.

When the Brussels-centric paradigm is applied to Kaliningrad, one can see that Kaliningrad has been included in future plans for major roads in the Baltic area and Kaliningrad also participates in the assistance program which the EU has for Soviet successor states. The EU program, known as TACIS[44], is already in Kaliningrad and new efforts are underway to coordinate TACIS and the EU PHARE[45] program because TACIS applies to the former Soviet Union and PHARE applies to central European states such as Poland and the Baltic states. PHARE and TACIS interface at the Russian border with Poland, located at Kaliningrad. Coordination would be helpful from a regional perspective. If such coordination is achieved, whose power, authority and influence will probably increase: that of Brussels? Warsaw? Vilnius or Moscow?

In spite of the EU's internal differences expressed in the IGC conference and even without new coordination of PHARE and TACIS, it is now clear that the influence of Brussels is increasing in the countries which border on Kaliningrad and even in Belarus. For example, the *Baltic Times* recently reported that in discussing border bottlenecks, "problems on the Lithuanian-Polish border have been exceptionally serious...a special $2.5 million EU PHARE grant has been received to finance the final expansion phase at the [Lithuanian-Polish] Kalvarija border station on the Via Baltica. Another PHARE grant for the same amount will be directed to further upgrade customs equipment at the [Lithuanian-Belarusian] Medininkai station" (*The Baltic Times*, 19-25 September 1996: 9). In Baltic space, the EU center-periphery paradigm appears to be the process which is beginning to interface most significantly with a Moscow-centered paradigm.

Any alternative paradigm of change in the area such as the idea of a collection of regions without a center will need to make a lot of substantive progress fast in order to have any credibility as a rival to Brussels in terms of increasing influence in the Baltic region. For example, one might ask if the Baltic Sea Area is a substantive alternative paradigm. Its documents raise interesting questions. For example in a section on "Main problems with respect to spatial planning", in the "Standards and norms" category, Kaliningrad is listed as "adaptation to EU standards" and Belarus is listed as "needed harmonization with EU standards" (*Visions and Strategies around the Baltic Sea Area,* 1994: 6-7). What does that mean? How could Belarus adapt to EU standards and to standards in a Russia-Belarus Community unless the Community was also going to adapt to EU standards. If Russia plans to adapt to EU standards, what does that mean for the Russian Far East? Although Baltic regional institutions raise interesting questions, they do not seem to have the resources or promise of future economic benefits which would compete with Brussels.

Of course Brussels is not the only power center which has influence over Belarus and Lithuania. Because Russia still supplies energy to Lithuania, it could apply the same sort of political pressure to Lithuania as has reportedly been applied to Moldova.[46] Lithuanian focus on both Russia and the EU may be compatible in that the clear EU priority on avoiding ethnic and border problems implies that no serious Lithuanian government or political party would attempt to implement any policy which would be disruptive to Lithuania's relationships with Kaliningrad or "mainland" Russia. If this proves to be an accurate prediction, it will be an illustration of Pertti Joenniemi's point that "regionality seems to have positive effects on softening the impact of (neo)nationalism and ethnicity, the two principles competing with regionality in organizing political space in post-Cold War Europe" (Joenniemi 1994: 33).

Conclusion

To keep problems and opportunities in perspective, one should note that Kaliningraders report that historically they had some of the exclave mentality even during the Soviet period. This attitude came from their position in the Baltic Economic Zone. Kaliningrad researchers explained that in the communist party hierarchy, Republic bosses had more influence than bosses from *oblasts*. Partly for that reason, they felt that from the Moscow perspective, Kaliningrad was in a lower priority position vis-à-vis the Baltic Republics. Kaliningraders also seemed to feel that the Baltic Republics had been favored in the allocation of resources. Thus, to some extent, Kaliningrad felt like an exclave of Russia even during the Soviet period. Not that Muscovites would sympathize with these complaints. One jealous Muscovite said that during the Soviet period Kaliningrad had six TV stations while Moscow had two and Kaliningrad had access to consumer products from the Baltic states that were not available in Moscow.

In the Soviet period the role of Kaliningrad and of the Baltic states and ports was clear and their economies were integrated. The dissolution of the Soviet Union changed the map and legal formalities such as sovereignty rather quickly but the intricate economic and social inter-relationships are understandably still being reorganized much more slowly. Thoughtful analysis of these intricacies is not helped by simple slogans which run along the lines of "Russia is sovereign in Kaliningrad". It would be more useful to start from the reality that Kaliningrad's sovereignty is especially porous[47] given its prior connections to the Baltic states and its new quasi-free trade area with neighboring Poland and Lithuania. The core of Kaliningrad's problems is that there has so far been no definitive consistent plan outlining Kaliningrad's role. The clarity of the Soviet period is gone.

Nonetheless, Kaliningrad has proven that it can survive and even attract major foreign investment because of its unusual situation. The anxiety about the status of Kaliningrad which was expressed at the time the Soviet Union dissolved has passed. The threats which do exist are not necessarily due to conflict among states but are the kind of problems which arise in a globalized world where non-state actors play an important role. The 1994 explosion in Lithuania which destroyed part of the railroad linking Moscow and Kaliningrad was an example of a problem which arose even though the destruction was not overtly committed by any state.

In the past, western academic analysis has largely focused on the Cold War interpretation of security and has been devoted primarily to counting military personnel and equipment in Kaliningrad and contemplating implications. This is understandable given the situation in the Baltic area during the Cold War. Denmark and Germany belonged to the EU and those countries as well as Norway belonged to NATO but Sweden and Finland were neutral and belonged to neither group. To the east and south of them were the Soviet Union and the Warsaw Pact.

This explains why the dialog in the Baltic area lags about fifty years behind the dialog in western Europe. Fifty years ago Europe emerged from the ruins of World War II and the founding fathers of the EU talked hopefully about developing peace and prosperity by means of regional cooperation. They hoped that low-level functional cooperation would spillover into long-standing peace. The meeting of the Baltic Prime Ministers in Visby, Sweden in May, 1996 discussed low level issues and avoided traditional security. The reasoning sounded very much like the reasoning expressed by the EU founders almost fifty years ago. This essay argues that it is time for academic analysis to follow the spirit of Visby and catch up with contemporary Kaliningrad. Although traditional security issues can be important issues if tensions flare, they need not necessarily be problematic.

Many Kaliningraders have essentially "de-securitized" themselves and are now involved in the regional economy with all of its problems and opportunities. Kaliningrad's cross-border cooperation with neighboring states involves the same issues which are considered in relationships between the EU and associate EU members: crime, migration, the environment, and barriers to economic activity. If the Europort and KIA projects come to fruition, Kaliningrad may be moving towards the Hawaii model faster than most skeptics would have imagined possible.

The danger for western policy makers may lie in the risk of Euro-centric analysis. It is commendable to want to include Kaliningrad and northwestern Russia in European and Baltic regional arrangements. However, in doing so the west may be accidentally jeopardizing the cohesiveness of Russia as it exists today. Kaliningrad may experience one of the future scenarios which I previously suggested is also a possibility for the Russian Pacific rim: prosperity in peripheral areas may be inversely related to the cohesiveness of Russian federalism (Fairlie 1993). The efforts of Kaliningrad and many other regions to obtain agreements which give them more autonomy vis-á-vis Moscow have led some analysts to ask whether Russia is now one state governed by a constitution or an area governed by a collection of treaties.[48]

It may be that in the future Russia may end the same way the Soviet Union ended – with a suggestion from Moscow. Mikhail Gorbachev has recently suggested that one solution to the Chechnya problem would be for Chechnya to become an "associate member"– rather than subject – of the Russian Federation. Gorbachev cited the model of the Kingdom of Poland (before 1863), Grand Duchy of Finland, and Emirate of Bukhara within Tsarist Russia.[49]

Equally divisive are ideas voiced even by Yeltsin – ideas which would have been unthinkable in the past, including the idea that Russia should join the EU.[50] In the future Moscow may think that its own future would be more promising if the Moscow area and northwest Russia became a separate state. As such, it might some time in the future have the possibility of some kind of closer arrangement with the EU. One analyst, with a background in the Baltic states, suggested: "Why should we not imagine several Russian-speaking states? We had them in the Middle Ages. There are several English, French and German-speaking ones, after all" (Rebas 1994: 39).

In its present configuration the idea of Russia in the European Union is puzzling given that the Russian Far East would not tolerate using a European tariff against its best foreign trading partners in Asia. Similarly the idea of Russia as a future member of NATO causes skeptics to ask whether that would imply that European NATO members would be obligated to defend the Russian border with China.

Russian peripheral areas such as Kaliningrad and Vladivostok experience the future possibilities of being part of what Ohmae calls a region state, a dynamic economic unit which crosses international borders. For Vladivostok, the "far abroad" is much closer than the "near abroad" and this perspective illustrates the need for a new orientation in which Russia accounts for the fact that the economic centers of power are in Europe, Asia and the U.S. and that Russia is on the outer periphery of these trading blocs. In this conceptualization, Russia is on the periphery, not in the center as is the case when one perceives the region as having Russia at the center with the "near abroad" as the next outer ring. In the Kaliningrad case, the region is closer to both the "near abroad" and the "far abroad" than it is to "mainland" Russia.

The different needs of European and Asiatic Russia illustrate the fundamental problem noted by Gunnar Lassinantti (1994: 17): "the regional level is only capable of dealing with low politics". One of the results is that in the future states such as Russia and Canada which appear to be too large to deal effectively with the problems of all of their regions will be under more pressure to divide and become smaller states so that they can deal with both low and high politics. Russia may be so big that Kaliningrad, Moscow and the rest of "mainland" Russia may not have enough compatible interests. This principle was illustrated in Shakhrai's opinion that Kaliningrad's integration with foreign economies might be at the expense of Russian security. In the future, public policy makers may need to either form smaller states or to make some choices between traditional security and trans-boundary economic progress. Pertti Joenniemi posed the problem this way (1994: 32)

> If security is a major concern, then political space is better organized according to different and more statist principles. In that case, principles would be required that do not allow trans-boundary cooperation in the first place.

Such questions imply that although the politically correct rhetoric in the West now is that there must be no new dividing lines such as the Berlin wall and Iron Curtain, more subtle dividing lines are almost taken for granted as valid underlying assumptions. The questions about NATO and EU's possible enlargement to the Baltic states raises the question of whether or not there is a grey area in the Baltic states which is a buffer between Russia and the West. If there is no dividing line or grey area in the Baltic states, is there a line anywhere? If one believes *The Economist*, one would conclude that if people must become reconciled to a dividing line somewhere, perhaps it is clear and commonly assumed that although there may be ambiguity about the Baltic states there is little ambiguity that Belarus lies on the Russian side of a gray area at best or a dividing line at worst. *The Economist* (24 August 1996: 39) speculated: "If more of Mr. Lukashenka, and union with a Russia that has precious little to offer them, turn out to be what Belarussian voters want, the rest of the world will have little choice but to nod its head sadly". What then would be the implication for Kaliningrad?

It may not only be Belarus which draws dividing lines but also the EU. The basis of the Schengen agreements is the idea that while there should be freedom of circulation within the EU in the future, there should also be an outer border against non-member states. If Poland and Lithuania join the EU, the challenge for Kaliningrad will be to avoid marginalization and turn its peripheral status into the more positive image of a gateway or bridge. The KIA deal is an indicator that the gateway possibility may become a vibrant reality.

Schengen notwithstanding, the current hope is that it will be possible to avoid or minimize dividing lines, or at least dividing lines west of Belarus. There are always hopes that regional cooperation will produce spillover effects which will lead to peace and prosperity. The Hawaii model gives hope that zero sum game choices can be avoided. However, the difficulty of achieving "detente from below" (Lassinantti 1994: 18) when working within the context of states in their current form is illustrated by the 1996 controversy over the proposed Polish "corridor" linking Kaliningrad to Belarus via Poland. Creating "detente from below" and making other changes may not be easy but effort should still be made. Linear progress should not be expected, as the history of policy reversals such as ending of the FEZ and subsequent creation of the SEZ illustrates.

Moscow should not be signaled out for all the blame. Part of the problem is that Russia has too much to do. The neat bi-polar world has become a messy multi-polar place. No country can reasonably be expected to do a good and linear job of simultaneously adjusting to the end of the Soviet Union and Warsaw Pact as well as adjusting to the introduction of democracy and a market economy. When westerners puzzle over Russia's alarm at its loss of influence they should avoid Euro-centrism and reflect upon the changes in post-Soviet space. Suggestions that the "whole Russian Federation join in a unified European space" (Müller-Hermann 1995: 42) appear to ignore the concerns of Asiatic Russia and change throughout the former Soviet Union. For example, Presidents from the new states on Russia's southern border have been meeting with regard to the planned "transit corridor" of highway, railroad, and pipeline links from Uzbekistan, Turkmenistan, and Kazakhstan via Azerbaijan and Georgia to the Black Sea and Turkey, bypassing Russia.[51] When confronted with this kind of change on a daily basis in various parts of post-Soviet space, it is no wonder that Russia would be anxious about a loss of influence.

Many of the changes being experienced by Russia are also experienced by other countries. Theoretically speaking, post-Soviet Russia is a case study of the relationships described by James Rosenau in his book, *Turbulence in World Politics: A Theory of Change & Continuity.* According to Rosenau (1993a: 19-20)

> the core of the theory posits every region and country of the world as experiencing continual tensions between decentralizing and centralizing pressures, between conflictful tendencies toward fragmentation within groups, states, and societies on the one hand and cooperative tendencies toward coherence among states and within regions on the other.

In summary, future scenarios for Kaliningrad range from continuation of the status quo to Kaliningrad becoming part of a genuine Russia-Belarus

Community or part of a state consisting perhaps of northwest Russia and Belarus. Alternatively, it might become a fourth Baltic Republic flanked by a Poland and Lithuania which have either joined to form one state or which may both join the EU. In any case, the common denominator will probably be extensive detailed negotiations to facilitate as smooth an interface as possible between two center-periphery paradigms: Brussels and Moscow. The new SEZ may have already made Kaliningrad essentially part of a free trade zone linking foreign states with Russia.

The fact that a lot of Kaliningrad's trade and SEZ relationships involve neighboring Poland and Lithuania, neither of which are now members of the EU indicates that there may be utility in conceptually broadening the center-periphery paradigms to include Wonnacott's comparison of free trade areas with bilateral arrangements and Robert Scalapino's concept of arcs. Scalapino suggests that "in connection with domestic or sub-regional crises, the parties or countries most directly involved frequently interact through a series of concentric arcs, with one's position dependent upon one's degree of involvement and sense of national interest" (Scalapino 1995: 100). In his analysis of Asia, he uses the "term 'arcs' rather than 'circles' because at every level there must be an open-endedness to facilitate interaction between and among the various involved parties" (Scalapino 1995: 100). In the Baltic area political change will involve active participation by the Baltic states. Their interactions with Russia and with Brussels fall within the theoretical scope of Arie Kacowicz who wrote that some of the factors which influence the relationships are asymmetry among the powers involved, regime differences and shared norms and values (Kacowicz 1994: 219-254).

If Brussels-centered and Moscow-centered paradigms and their proximate arcs are the most likely paradigms of importance in the immediate future for Kaliningrad, it follows that one important aspect of the dynamism of these systems is the issue of who the important players are in decision-making within Russia and within the EU. Events within Russia are largely outside our influence, but within the EU change might be more easily affected. Consistent with the idea of proximate arcs, Sweden and Finland should take a larger role in the EU. From the perspective of micro-management of institutions, perhaps they should encourage more coordination in the TACIS program for example. If reports are accurate in indicating that the EBRD rejected a plan for a modest upgrade of the Kaliningrad airport because the project cost too little, $5 million, and fell below the EBRD minimum of $6 million projects, then Scandinavia could take the lead in asking for a review of EBRD policies or the creation of new programs which would allow incremental development projects to be funded.

EU members such as Britain, which has a tendency to keep a low profile on Kaliningrad issues, should stop deferring to what the British assume is a German sphere of influence. Germany does its best to multilateralize its interest in Kaliningrad within the EU context. It would be in the interests of Germany and the EU generally if Britain and the others stopped deferring to Germany. Such a policy change would also help to relieve Russian anxiety over German influence in that part of post-Soviet space.

If in the future, the patterns of interaction in the EU today become the paradigm for relationships within Russia, one should expect that progress will not be linear. James Rosenau speculates that globalization and localization will occur simultaneously. Pertti Joenniemi and Pierre Hassner caution against believing in a European security architecture which will make life orderly and predictable (Joenniemi 1994: 28-29; Hassner 1996).

In speaking of the Baltic and eastern European area, Hassner thinks that the future will be decided on a case by case basis. Given the history of the area, uncertainty is understandable. David Lake argues that it is even preferable. He recommends an "ad hoc approach to foreign policy" (Lake 1996: 1). His reasoning is that "local conflicts risk becoming global conflicts not through superpower competition or the clash of vital interests, but through the application of broad principles of international rectitude" (Lake 1996: 3).

Anne Applebaum's recent visit to the Baltic and east European area is set in historical content and she introduces readers to the area by saying "The borderlands lie in a flat plain, crushed between the civilizations of Europe and those of Asia. East of Poland, west of Russia, their lack of mountains, seas, deserts, and canyons has always made the borderlands easy to conquer" (Applebaum 1994: ix). Future scenarios for Kaliningrad do not imply that any foreign government presently poses a threat to Kaliningrad. "...Russia's focus should not be on external threats. The Olshansky analysis of separatist trends in Russia shows that the greatest threat to Russian territorial integrity comes not from outside but from Russia itself" (Fairlie 1996: 166). Policy reversals will try the patience of Kaliningraders of the future. For the present, however, the apparent prominent role of smuggling, based on the economic links between Kaliningrad and mainland Russia, is one factor which will temper separatism and strengthen statist links with Moscow.

This author concurs with many Kaliningrad and Moscow experts who say that what the area needs is stability and consistency. In the interests of stability, Fyodorov and Zverev argue that it is not helpful to hear ideas which question the viability of Russian sovereignty. However, a historical view of the area which spans centuries would lead cautious observers to avoid the current politically correct view that Russian sovereignty will prevail forever without question. Perhaps the Kaliningrad of the future will be forever part of Russia or is it the Russia-Belarus Community? If so, will it be viable as an exclave just as Alaska is an exclave of the U.S. and Greece is viable as an exclave of its fellow EU states? Perhaps Kaliningrad's future will remind analysts of some model we already know: the Åland Islands? Hawaii? Berlin in the Cold-War period? the U.S. base at Guantanamo in Cuba? international cooperation similar to the Tumen project linking Russia, North Korea and China?

By extrapolating the present to the future, one can see Kaliningrad provides a learning environment for multilateral cooperation. In the military sector, Russia has already cooperated with NATO in the BALTOPS and Partnership for Peace exercises. In the future, the Neman Euroregion might offer another multilateral regional cooperation learning experience. Moscow should also learn more about how the EU's internal market and *acquis communitaire* might affect Poland and Lithuania. More learning is required in these de-securitized sectors which have come to prominence in the post-Soviet period. Lack of learning would mean that Russia would be continually surprised by developments in neighboring states and the result would likely be discontinuous temporary solutions. The objective in this survey has been to attempt to account for a wide range of scenarios so that whatever happens, analysts will be able to say in the future that we gave careful consideration to all of the possibilities which we can imagine at this point in time.

Notes

1   Election results are rounded to the nearest whole number. This author was an

official observer at the election and received the official results from the staff of Peter A. Voropaev, Chairman, Electoral Commission of Kaliningrad Region.

2   "Lebed on costs of NATO enlargement", *Monitor* Vol. II, No. 171, 16 September 1996. [Online]. Available: Jamestown Foundation.

3   "Belarus: Unfulfilled Promises", *Fortnight-in-Review* Vol. 1 No. 3, 26 July 1996. [Online]. Available: Jamestown Foundation.

4   Oleg Shchedrov, "Yeltsin woos military vote in Baltic enclave", Reuters, Limited sec.: Money Report. Bonds Capital Market, 23 June 1996 BC cycle. [Online]. Available: NEXIS Library: EUROPE File: ALLEUR

5   "Russia, Belarus may set up force if NATO expands," Reuters, Limited, 14 May 1996 BC cycle. [Online]. Available: NEXIS Library: EUROPE File: ALLEUR.

6   Brian Killen, "Russia, Belarus strengthen links, write off debts", The Reuter European Business Report, 27 February 1996. [Online]. Available: NEXIS Library: EUROPE File: ALLEUR.

7   Vladimir Kozyrev, Deputy Head, State Management of Transport Complex, Kaliningrad Region Administration and Anatoly Demenok, Head of Marine Department, State Management of Transport Complex, Kaliningrad Region Administration, interview by author, interpreted by Vladimir Lissniak, Kaliningrad, Russia, June 1996.

8   "Belarus Economy in 'free fall' – will Moscow bail it out?" *Monitor* Vol. II, No. 151, 2 August 1996. [Online]. Available: Jamestown Foundation.

9   The official title is The plenipotentiary representative of the President of Russia in Kaliningrad region.

10 Tamara Poluektova, The plenipotentiary representative of the President of Russia in Kaliningrad region, interview by the author, interpreted by Vladimir Lissniak, Kaliningrad, Russia, June, 1996.

11 Siditas Shileris, Consul-General of Lithuania in Kaliningrad, interview by the author, interpreted by Vladimir Lissniak, Kaliningrad, Russia, June, 1996

12 "Russia, Belarus may set up force if NATO expands," Reuters North American Wire, 14 May 1996 BC cycle. [Online]. Available: NEXIS Library: EUROPE File: ALLEUR.

13 "Yeltsin's visit to Kaliningrad: Yeltsin tells Kaliningraders he will support Russians in Baltic states", BBC Summary of World Broadcasts, 23 June 1996, sec. Part 1 Former USSR; Russian Election Special; EE/D2646/A citing source as Interfax news agency, Moscow, in Russian 0928 gmt23 June 96. [Online]. Available: NEXIS Library: WORLD File: ALLWLD.

14 "Poles sign cooperation agreements with Russia's Kaliningrad Region", BBC Summary of World Broadcasts, 16 December 1996, sec. Part 2 Central Europe,

the Balkans; Central Europe; Poland; Internal Affairs; EE/D2796/C citing source as PAP news agency, Warsaw, in Polish 2357 gmt 13 December 1996. [Online]. Available: NEXIS Library: EUROPE File: ALLEUR.

15 Stephen C. Maloney, Commander, U.S. Navy, NATO, Supreme Allied Command, Atlantic and Lieutenant Colonel T.W. Loveridge Strategic Concepts, Policy and Organization, SACLANT headquarters, interview by author, San Diego, California, spring 1996.

16 "Baltic uprising", *Flight International*, 16 June 1993. [Online]. Available: NEXIS Library: NEWS File: MAGS.

17 "EU/Baltic States: technology the key to maritime renaissance?", European Report 11 September 1996 sec. No. 2156 and "Bangemann speech to Baltic Sea Conference", 10 September 1996, The Reuter European Community Report. [Online]. Available: NEXIS Library: EUROPE File: ALLEUR.

18 Yuri D. Rozhkov-Yurjevsky, International Relations Department, Kaliningrad Regional Administration, interview by the author, interpreted by Vladimir Lissniak, Kaliningrad, June, 1996.

19 Plants which assemble component parts.

20 Tamara Poluektova, The plenipotentiary representative of the President of Russia in Kaliningrad region, interview by the author, interpreted by Vladimir Lissniak, Kaliningrad, Russia, June, 1996.

21 "Baltic agency reports big increase in Russian budget for Kaliningrad in 1997", BBC Summary of World Broadcasts, 14 January 1997, sec. Part 1 Former USSR; Russia; other reports; SU/D2816/B citing source as BNS news agency, Tallinn, in English 1855 gmt 12 January 1997. [Online]. Available: NEXIS Library: EUROPE File: ALLEUR.

22 Valentin Korneyevets, Economic Geographer at Kaliningrad State University, interview by author, interpreted by Vladimir Lissniak, Kaliningrad, Russia, July 1994.

23 "Laws and Resolutions", *Moscow News* 15 August 1996, sec. Documents; No. 32. [Online]. Available: NEXIS Library: EUROPE File: ALLEUR.

24 The Russian Federation Federal Statute "On the Special Economic Zone in the Kaliningrad Region" Chapter VIII The Procedure for entry, exit and staying on the territory of the Kaliningrad region. Social and Labor Relations. Article 22. The Procedure for Entry, Exit and Staying on the Territory of the Kaliningrad Region. "The bodies of state authority of the Kaliningrad Region shall provide preferential conditions for migration to the territory of the Kaliningrad Region and settlement on this territory of persons currently residing or staying on the territory of Lithuania, Latvia or Estonia who were heretofore citizens of the Union of Soviet Socialist Republics and whose native language is Russian".

25 Peter Rutland, "Russo-Belarusian Union: New Beginning or Dead End?", 29 March 1996, Vol. 1 No. 46 OMRI *Analytical Brief.* [Online}. Available: OMRI.

26 Cable News Network, Inc. CCN SHOW: NEWS 8: 12 am ET June 30, 1996 Transcript #65-2, CNN's Senior European Correspondent, Richard Blystone. [Online]. Available NEXIS: Library EUROPE File ALLEUR

27 "Defense chief to work for no pay", *The Herald* (Glasgow), 6 September 1996, sec. p. 15. [Online]. Available: NEXIS Library: EUROPE File: ALLEUR

28 Robert Serebrennikov, "Law on Kaliningrad free trade zone approved", 10 January 1996, The Russian Information Agency Itar-Tass. [Online]. Available: NEXIS Library: EUROPE File: ALLEUR.

29 Ivan Cheberko, "Swedes Set To Make Money Out of Think Russian Air", RUSSICA Information Inc. RusData DiaLine-BizEkon News, sec. News, 10 October 1995. [Online]. Available: NEXIS Library: EUROPE File: ALLEUR.

30 S. Azarova, "Yantar shipyard stays afloat by fulfilling Estonian orders", Reuter Textline, Novecon, 23 November 1995. [Online]. Available: NEXIS Library: EUROPE File: ALLEUR.

31 "Russian government to crack down on 'shuttle-traders'", 24 July 1996 *Monitor* Vol. II, No. 144. [Online]. Available: Jamestown Foundation.

32 Vladimir Zhukov, "Russian enclave dreams of emulating Hong Kong", Agence France Presse, 4 September 1996, sec. Financial pages. [Online] Available: NEXIS Library: EUROPE File: ALLEUR.

33 "Russian government to crack down on 'shuttle-traders'", 24 July 1996 *Monitor* Vol. II, No. 144. [Online]. Available: Jamestown Foundation.

34 "Mafiya: Organized crime in Russia: The Mafiya and the World", *Jane's Intelligence Review*, 1 June 1996, sec. Special Report No., pg. 18. [Online]. Available: NEXIS Library: EUROPE File: ALLEUR.

35 Geoff Winestock, "The Slippery Business of Russian Oil Exports", *The Moscow Times*, 27 May 1995, sec. No. 720. [Online]. Available: NEXIS Library: EUROPE File: ALLEUR.

36 Galina Kuchina, "Investigation ends into oil smuggling case in Latvia", ITAR-TASS, 20 September 1995. [Online]. Available: NEXIS Library: EUROPE File: ALLEUR.

37 Benoit Thely, "Amber fever grips enclave", Agence France Presse, 20 June 1996, sec. International news, 20: 11 gmt. [Online]. Available: NEXIS Library: EUROPE File: ALLEUR.

38 Dmitry Ukhlin, "Corruption in Defense Ministry Continues", *Moscow News*, 11 August 1995, sec. Politics; No. 31. [Online]. Available: NEXIS Library: EUROPE File: ALLEUR.

39 Ariel Cohen, Ph.D., Senior Analyst and Salvatori Fellow in Russian and Eurasian Studies, The Heritage Foundation, before the House International Affairs Committee, prepared testimony "Crime and Corruption in Russia and the new independent states: Threats to markets, democracy and international security", Federal News Service, 31 January 1996, sec. In the news quoting "Russians Smugglers Gain Strength", The Wall Street Journal, March 30, 1994, p. A12. [Online]. Available: NEXIS Library: EUROPE File: ALLEUR.

40 "Internal affairs: Interior Ministry board discusses smuggling situation in Russia's northwest", BBC Summary of World Broadcasts, 14 March 1995, sec. Part 1 Former USSR: Russia; Su/2251/B citing source: Interfax news agency, Moscow, in English 1339 gmt 10 March 1995. [Online]. Available: NEXIS Library: WORLD File: ALLWLD.

41 Julie Corwin, Douglas Stanglin, Suzanne Possehl, Jeff Trimble, "The looting of Russia", U.S. News & World Report, 7 March 1994, sec. World Report; Vol. 116, No. 9, p. 36. [Online]. Available: NEXIS Library.

42 This chapter is part of a larger research project on comparative analysis of Russian borders. See, for example, Lyndelle Fairlie, "Center-periphery Issues in the Russian Far East". (This manuscript was later published in English and in Italian and the title was changed without consultation with the author. The published titles were "Longing for Autonomy in the Russian Far East", ("Voglia di autonomia dell'Estremo Oriente russo"), *Relazioni Internazionali* June 1993, Institute for the Study of International Politics, Milan.

43 Subsidiarity is the idea that decision-making within the EU should whenever possible take place in the capitals of member states rather than in Brussels. The burden of proof is on the Commission to demonstrate that policy initiatives at the state level would be inadequate and that policy by Brussels is necessary.

44 TACIS is the acronym for Technical Assistance for the Commonwealth of Independent States. The program "provides technical assistance in a number of key areas to underpin the transition to a market economy and a democratic society", *Europe in a Changing World: The External Relations of the European Community*, Commission of the European Communities, 1993, p. 34.

45 PHARE (Poland Hungary assistance to reconstruct the economy) was later extended to the Czech Republic, Slovakia, Bulgaria, Romania, the three Baltic states, Albania and some states in the former Yugoslavia.

46 "Russia uses Moldovan debt for leverage", *Monitor* 19 September 1996, Vol. II No. 174, [Online] Available: Jamestown Foundation.

47 For analysis of porous sovereignty, see Ivo D. Duchacek, *The Territorial Dimension of Politics Within, Among, and Across Nations* (Boulder, Colorado: Westview Press, Inc., 1986).

48 "...constitutional lawyers who warn that Russia is ceasing to be a constitution-based state and becoming a treaty-based (and therefore less stable) one". "Opposition to Russian scheme for 'Rebuilding the federation from the ground up'", *Monitor*, 14 June 1996, [Online] Available: Jamestown Foundation.
49 "Chechnya's Political Status Under Consideration", *Monitor* Vol II. NO. 160 29 August 1996, [Online]. Available: Jamestown Foundation.
50 "Help Russia join the EU, Yeltsin asks Finland", Agence France Presse, 20 January 1995, sec. International news. [Online]. Available: NEXIS Library: EUROPE File: ALLEUR.
51 "Three Presidents discuss oil export, transit corridor", *Monitor*, 19 September 1996, Vol. II No. 174. [Online]. Available: Jamestown Foundation.

References

Note: Sources below are books and articles. On-line sources and interviews appear in notes.

Applebaum, Anne (1994), *Between East and West: Across the Borderlands of Europe*. New York: Pantheon Books.

Arvedlund, Erin (1996), "Hong Kong On the Baltic?" *The Moscow Times*, 3 September.

Asmus, Ronald D. and Robert C. Nurick (1996), "NATO Enlargement and the Baltic States", *Survival* 38 (2): 121-43.

Azarova, Svetlana and Vadim Bardin (1996), "Yuri Matochkin between Vladimir Shumeiko and Victor Chernomirdin", (in Russian). *Commersant Daily*.

Bebriss, Peteris (1996), "Baltic, CIS railways to cooperate: Russia says tariff hike was an economic decision", *The Baltic Times* 19-25 September.

Brzezinski, Zbigniew (1996), "Voice of Reason From Moscow", *The Washington Post* 18 August.

Bustin, G. L. and Krylov, A. V. (1996), "Russian law heads for EU compatibility", *International Financial Law Review* July, no. 7: 34.

Commission of the European Communities (1995), *White Paper: Preparation of the Associated Countries of Central and Eastern Europe for Integration into the Internal Market of the Union*. Brussels.

Fairlie, Lyndelle D. (1993), "Voglia di autonomia dell'Estremo Oriente russo" [Longing for Autonomy in the Russian Far East], *Relazioni Internazionali* June vol. no. , 1993: 30.

Fairlie, Lyndelle D. (1996), "Kaliningrad: A Russian Exclave in Search of New Roles", in Gansler, Paul *et al.* eds., *Border Regions in Functional Transition:*

European and North American Perspectives on Transboundary Interaction (Regio Series of the IRS no. 9). Berlin: Institute for Regional Development and Structural Planning, pp. 213-37.

Feldstein, Martin (1991), "Does One Market Require One Money?", in *Policy Implications of Trade and Currency Zones: A Symposium Sponsored by the Federal Reserve Bank of Kansas City*. 22-24 August. Jackson Hole, Wyoming: Federal Reserve Bank of Kansas City.

Fyodorov, Gennady M. and Yuriy Zverev (1995), *Kaliningrad Alternatives: Social-economic development of the Kaliningrad oblast under the new geopolitical conditions*. Kaliningrad: Kaliningrad State University (Translated by Irving J. Kern).

Hassner, Pierre (1996), Lecture at the University of San Diego, CA. Spring, 1996.

Huldt, Bo (1996), "Kaliningrad as a strategic hub – after the Cold War?" in *Forum Kaliningrad* 1996. Karlskrona, Sweden: The Baltic Institute, pp. 18-22.

Jann, Werner (1994), "Common Security in the Baltic Sea Region", in Bäcklund, Gunnar ed., *Common Security in Northern Europe after the Cold War: The Baltic Sea Region and the Barents Sea Region*. A report from the Olof Palme International Center Seminar, Stockholm 18-20 March 1994. Stockholm: Olof Palme International Center.

Joenniemi, Pertti (1994), "Regionality in the New Europe: The Baltic and Barents Sea Projects", in Bäcklund, Gunnar ed., *Common Security in Northern Europe after the Cold War: The Baltic Sea Region and the Barents Sea Region*. A report from the Olof Palme International Center Seminar, Stockholm 18-20 March 1994. Stockholm: Olof Palme International Center, pp. 25-35.

Joenniemi, Pertti (1996), "Kaliningrad: A region in search for a past and a future". Ostsee-Akademie, Lübeck – Travemunde: *Mare Balticum 96*: 84-108.

Kacowicz, Arie M. (1994), "The Problem of Peaceful Territorial Change", *International Studies Quarterly* 38 (2): 219-254.

Kerr, David (1995), "The New Eurasianism: The Rise of Geopolitics in Russia's Foreign Policy", *Europe-Asia Studies* 47(6): 977.

Lake, David A. (1996), "Democratizing Foreign Policy. Part III: The Perils of Principles". University of California. *Institute on Global Conflict and Cooperation Policy Brief,* September.

Lassinantti, Gunnar (1994), "Common Security – Rethinking Old concepts", in in Bäcklund, Gunnar ed., *Common Security in Northern Europe after the Cold War: The Baltic Sea Region and the Barents Sea Region*. A report from the Olof Palme International Center Seminar, Stockholm 18-20 March 1994. Stockholm: Olof Palme International Center, pp. 12-25.

Linderfalk, Björn (1996), "Lithuanian highways get overhaul: Long-awaited Via Baltica credits finally secured", *The Baltic Times*, 19-25 September.

Linderfalk, Björn (1997), "Baltic business: foreign investment shows the way", *The Baltic Times* (40), 19 December 1996 – 8 January 1997.

Matochkin, Yuri (1995a), "From Survival to Development", *International Affairs* (Moscow), no. 6: 8 – 14.

Matochkin, Yuri (1995b), "The Most Western Region of Russia", *Foreign Trade*, no. 9: 18. Moscow: Ministry of Foreign Economic Relations of the Russian Federation.

Nikitin, V.U. (1995), "Big Distance between SEZ and FEZ", *Kaliningrad Pravda*, 9 September. (In Russian). Translated by Irving J. Kern.

Ohmae, Kenichi (1995), *The End of the Nation State: The Rise of Regional Economies*. New York: The Free Press.

Olshansky, Dmitri V. (1993), *Alternative Scenarios of the Disintegration of the Russian Federation*. McLean, VA: The Potomac Foundation.

Peters, Thomas J. (1992), *Liberation management: Necessary disorganization for the nanosecond nineties*. New York: Alfred A. Knopf.

Pond, Elizabeth (1996), "Letter from Davos, Switzerland: Drawing lines in Europe", *The Washington Quarterly* 19 (3): 23.

Rebas, Hain (1994), "Europe and the Future of the Baltic Republics", *Perspectives* no.4: 39.

Redman, Nicholas H. (1995), "Kaliningrad: Russia's Baltic Exclave". *Briefing Paper*, No. 25, September. London: The Royal Institute of International Affairs.

Rosenau, James (1993), *Turbulence in World Politics: A Theory of Change and Continuity*.

Rosenau, James N. (1996), "The Dynamics of Globalization". Paper presented at the Annual Meeting of the International Studies Association, San Diego CA, 18 April 1996.

Scalapino, Robert A. (1995), "Natural Economic Territories in East Asia – Present Trends and Future Prospects", *Economic Cooperation and Challenges in the Pacific. Joint U.S.-Korea Academic Studies* (5).

Shama, Avraham (1996), "Inside Russia's true economy", *Foreign Policy* 103 (Summer): 111-28.

Singer, Marshall R (with the assistance of Paul Kengor) (1996), "After the Collapse of the Soviet Empire: *Weak States in a World of Powers* Revisited". Paper presented at the International Studies Association conference, San Diego, CA, spring 1996.

Vision and Strategies around the Baltic Sea 2010: Towards a Framework for Spatial Development in the Baltic Sea Area (1994). Final draft report 29 July. Third Conference of Ministers for Spatial Planning and Development, Tallinn 7-8 December 1994.

Wonnacott, Ronald J. (1996), "Trade and Investment in a Hub-and-Spoke System Versus a Free Trade Area", *The World Economy* 19 (3): 250.

"Burying the general", *The Economist*, 20 April, 1996

"Federalizing Russia"s Budget System: A Thorny Path" (1995), *The Current Digest of the Post-Soviet Press* 47 (23).

"Kaliningrad bans imports of liquor" (1997), *The Baltic Times* 9-15 January.

"Leaning on the Balts", *The Economist* 27 August, 1994.

"Mergers and acquisitions", *The Economist* 31 August, 1996.

"Miserable in Minsk", *The Economist* 10 August, 1996.

"Yes, Mr. Lukashenka, if you must", *The Economist* 24 August, 1996

11 Kaliningrad:
A Double Periphery?

PERTTI JOENNIEMI
JAN PRAWITZ

What is the issue?

Kaliningrad has been profoundly touched – as indicated by the contributions in this book – by the changes of 1989-91. A distance of some 400 kilometres opened up between Kaliningrad and mainland Russia. Suddenly, with the Soviet Union falling apart, the rather isolated, protective and strongly defence-related region turned into an entity far more exposed to challenges of European integration than Russia in general. The *oblast* became Russia's westernmost part surrounded, somewhat uncomfortably, by two countries – Poland and Lithuania – engaged in developing a deeper relationship with Europe.

The emerging challenges are formidable indeed. An entity that used to be closed, protective and unyielding to reforms has been compelled to open up and relate to an increasingly integrated environment. A site that used to symbolize heroic conquests as well as resistance against invading foreign forces in defence of the fatherland and that functioned as a fortification guarding against unwarranted external influences, is called upon to spearhead change. It is required to tune in with a cooperative setting that breaks with the previous constellation of rather divisive borders.

Kaliningrad has, under the new circumstances, turned into a case in-between the integrating and the less integrated; the needs of partaking in integration have grown while the grip of the previous era is still strongly felt. The *oblast* is, more generally, labelled by a certain duality; it is composed of two sides displaced in time. It reflects the politics of Russia as a state, with international politics in this context made up of the relations among the states and some internal matters being delegated down by the state, but there are also features of region-building and translocalism that have to be taken into account. The latter features assume a more independent character. They require, in being important factors in their own right and not just derivates of the "real" questions, considerable attention.

This implies, both in terms of analysis and practice, that there has to be an ability to cope with two political 'languages' that do not easily translate into each other. Kaliningrad has to be able to deal with traditional issues of "national interest" but also focus on operating at the watershed between the integrated and the unintegrated. The region has to maintain its openness in both directions if it is to function as a bridge-head linking in to the requirements of an increasingly integrated European environment, and it has to do this without distancing itself too far from the more general developments in Russia. Such challenges are not altogether Kaliningrad-specific, but they do tend to be more aggregated and difficult to solve in view of Kaliningrad's particular background and detachment from mainland Russia.

It may be noted, at a more general level, that one of the relevant 'languages' is in essence fixed on territoriality, while the other is more process-oriented. The problem is that both may contain elements that marginalize entities like Kaliningrad and push them into a remote and isolated position. At worst, Kaliningrad turns into a double periphery. The traditional territorial logic clearly exerts a marginalizing effect: it left Kaliningrad in a position of a periphery within the Soviet system (although the inhabitants of the region did enjoy more or less free travel on the eastern side of the Baltic rim) and continues to have a similar impact under the present conditions. In calling for strict and divisive statist borders, the territorial logic favours the centre and discriminates against border areas. Overlapping cases are not tolerated as they are seen as creating ambiguity – and Kaliningrad with its detached and vulnerable position is seen as an obvious candidate for such a posture.

The process of European integration introduces a different perspective in enabling multiplicity and overlapping forms of governance. Instead of being doomed to the position of a hinterland, border areas such as Kaliningrad may become more central. Given the increasing permeability of borders, they may become part of a continuous economic, social and cultural landscape. A regional system may emerge with close interaction among the participating entities creating integrated spaces that diminish the hindrances caused by distance. The spell of the territorial logic can be broken by the utilization and pooling of different location-specific strengths (cf. Scott 1996; Karppi 1997).

There is, of course, no inherent automatism in this as the processes of integration also contain borders, restrictions and limits. Borders have not lost all their meaning. They are still thought to be of importance, but the emphasis is shifting from one frontier to several, from line to zone, from physical to cultural and from impermeable to permeable (cf. Anderson, 1996: 189-191). These changes may be beneficial to entities like Kaliningrad but also the contrary might be true. Kaliningrad may be discriminated against on grounds of the many asymmetries that prevail or a problematic mixture between the "high politics" of Moscow and the "low politics" pursued locally. The neighbours are more important for Kaliningrad than the other way around. The *oblast's* previously rather isolated position means that none of the neighbours is very dependent on Kaliningrad. They tend to overlook its problems. However, the discriminatory aspects – if they are there – pertain to previous experiences, some specific interests and particular ways of reacting to the changes. The negative effects are not an integral part of the new logic – as is the case with the territorial logic – as the centralizing tendencies and the demands for territorial and other forms of controllability are less pressing with the new and there is far more tolerance for uncertainty, non-causality and complexity.

The core question to pursue, in exploring Kaliningrad's situation and its future prospects, hence consists of surveying the region's position in regard to these two 'languages'. The aim here is to excavate to what extent the traditional statist and territorially geared concerns leave space for the new challenges of integration, i.e. is Kaliningrad so hooked to the old agenda of security, exclusion, borders, territorial disputes and more generally classical power political rivalry that little room is provided for the process-oriented to take root? Another crucial question consists of the abilities of Kaliningrad itself to link in with the new and exploit the opportunities that have emerged. What does the *oblast* have to offer as a European and translocal actor? And finally: is there sufficient willingness among the relevant actors – these consisting above all of Russia itself, Germany, Poland, Lithuania and the European Union – to allow Kaliningrad become part of the networking and a process-oriented Europe?

The approach we have adopted here allows an avoiding of the rigidity reflected in the menu consisting of a bad option to be avoided and a good alternative. This bigurgated approach often informs research on Kaliningrad. Dichotomic choices between further militarization and some cooperative solution are easy to make, they are dramatic and eye-catching, but too simple to provide any durable departures. The framework of two 'languages' offers a broader range of options. It does not lead to constellations of either-or, but brings forward a richer repertoire without categorically stating that one option is better than the other. The analysis also assumes more depth as the various options are viewed against the background of the unfolding of political space in Russia and Europe at large. The conclusion summarizes the analysis and engages in a discussion on the measures needed to avert the option of Kaliningrad being trapped in a dual sense.

The image of liability

During the past few years the debate on Kaliningrad has often reflected a traditional statist agenda. The prevailing state of affairs with geographic discontinuity has been depicted as somehow unnatural, and there has been little confidence in the *oblast*'s ability to stay out of trouble. The views on Kaliningrad – if not seen as *terra incognito* – have shown signs of being part of a more general imagery purporting the Baltic Sea region as deeply imbued in power political rivalry and territorial disputes.

This negativity is also reflected in the use of labels such as "Berlin of the Cold War years" (Fairlie 1997), "Gibraltar" (Shumeiko 1995: 4), a "second Cuba", "another Karabah" (Gross-Jütte 1994: 37), or a "Balkan of the Baltic Sea region" (Gross-Jütte 1994: 41). Particularly the latter epithets indicate that it is seen as consisting of an almost insolvable problem with connotations pertaining to confrontation, negative difference, dependency, backwardness, isolation and an anti-western stance. The prospects for reform have been seen as modest. Jakub Godzimirski (1997), a Norwegian-Polish researcher, views Kaliningrad as "one of the most explosive issues in relations between Russia, former Soviet vassals in the region (Poland and Lithuania) and in the Baltic Sea area in the wider meaning of the word".

It may, however, be noted in hindsight that these negativities seem to be misplaced. They tend to distort what the issue is about. Kaliningrad has not been, to any great extent, at the centre of territorial quarrels in any real sense and as Alexander Sergounin (1997a) has observed, such disputes have in recent years played a marginal role in the Baltic Sea region in general. There have been tensions and some issues still remain to be settled, but in general the seriousness of the disputes has not corresponded to the expectations that prevailed during the first half of the 1990s. It has been possible to cope with the problems and in many cases settle them in a rather satisfactory manner.

The difference between fears and reality has in fact been quite conspicuous. The striking thing is that a number of disputes have not broken out. Intellectually, as Tuomas Forsberg (1997) remarks, the puzzle has not been the existence of certain territorial issues but rather their non-existence. He concludes that despite various possible reasons for making territorial claims, the Baltic Sea region has in recent years been relatively free from territorial conflicts. The specificity of this becomes quite clear if the trends around the Baltic rim are compared with other border areas of the ex-Soviet Union and the Balkans.

The case of Kaliningrad appears to be largely in line with the view put forward by Forsberg: the region has not turned into a bone of contention in the way often imagined during the early 1990s. True, there are still issues to be settled but the region's status has not been contested in any serious manner. The territorial question was catalyzed, along with a number of other issues, by the end of the Cold War as one of the disputes that originated with the new relations of power. The feeling re-emerged that the change of ownership which took place towards the end of World War II in the context of the Yalta and Potsdam conferences was unjustified and it was hoped that Russia, as a new-born actor, would be more prepared to remedy the situation than had been the case with the Soviet Union. Various proposals on Kaliningrad's future position emerged and aroused debate. Ideas were put forward with the aim of achieving what was seen as a more legitimate order (cf. Joenniemi, 1997), many of them anticipating a loosening of the *oblast*'s relations to mainland Russia.

However, the currents of opinion that emerged in Germany, Lithuania and Poland have not been strong enough or persistent enough to insert the issue of territorial changes on the official agendas. With the prevailing of the norm of *status quo*, the states of the region have adhered to their course and pursued rather cautious policies. Despite some internal pressure and normative arguments, they have refrained from advancing territorial claims.

It also appears that the various voices advocating territorial adjustment have been losing ground. Some of the bitterness about the historical record prevails, but it appears that some of the heat has evaporated with the opportunity to air the issue more freely. The provocative statements of the early 1990s have by and large disappeared and there is far less questioning of the *oblast*'s position. The problem lies no longer in the demands for change, but rather in a lack of interest and a low level of awareness concerning the problems that the region is experiencing. It also seems that there is less sensitivity now about some of the symbolics involved: "Re-Germanization" no longer has the same frightening connotations that it did still some years ago, and there is greater preparedness to tackle various contentious historical legacies. The Russian authorities themselves increasingly deal with Kaliningrad as a normal part of the country in spheres such as granting visas, allowing tourism or inviting the presence of foreign firms.

Moreover, with the previously rather divisive border becoming more permeable, pre-war residents have been able to pay visits to the region. In some cases they have chosen to engage themselves in activities such as raising monuments or restoring important historical sites. The appearance of less confrontational options, and ones that are less geared towards the specific location of frontiers, provides more space for both official and non-official postures that aim at tackling the relevant issues by applying predominantly cooperative approaches.

It is also to be observed that the more recent discussion in Kaliningrad itself has been less geared towards foreign threats and dangers, i.e. even there the issue is showing signs of transformation. The anxiety about ideas concerning restitution or demands of "demilitarization" advanced particularly in the Polish and Lithuanian discussion in the early 1990s, has declined drastically. Instead, attention has been devoted, for good reasons, to the many current problems. These do not pertain to territorial control but economic decline, various social ills, issues of poor health, crime such as smuggling or decay of the environment, many of these being worse in Kaliningrad than in Russia in general.

Postures of the relevant governments

It has been of particular importance for the territorial issues to have even a chance of declining in significance and alter meaning that Germany has refrained from presenting claims on Kaliningrad. Despite internal pressures, with many East Prussian expatriates and their descendants having emotional ties to what they regard as their *Heimat*, Germany has maintained a low profile. Consciousness concerning the issues involved has been considerable.

The policies pursued have been in line with the way in which the territorial losses have been viewed in Germany in general. The losses resulting from the war are mainly seen as having been caused by Germany's own actions and are therefore accepted as a fact of life (cf. Aspelagh 1992). This conciliatory approach, reflected more specifically in the commitment to the Oder-Neisse line as well as the withholding of claims on Silesia in Poland, has also been a major stabilizing factor in the case of Kaliningrad. In general, Germany has aspired to make borders more permeable. Instead of fortifying their meaning as barriers and means of exclusion, the aim has been to accept their existence but reduce their impact in territorial terms.

The German-Soviet treaty of 1990 which repeated pledges on the inviolability of borders that had been agreed upon as early as the 1970s between the German Federal Republic and the Soviet Union, rests on such a reasoning. The parties confirmed that they had no territorial claims whatsoever, nor would they assert such claims in the future.

Chancellor Kohl and President Gorbachev deviated from the overall pattern when in 1989 they played with ideas of creating an autonomous German republic in Kaliningrad. The plan indicated that under specific conditions, alternative options might be considered by both Germany and Russia, this generating some fears of a German-Russian condominium among the neighbours. However, the idea coined by the two leaders expired with the fall of the Soviet Union and has not been raised since (Redman 1995: 3). The two powers reverted to their more traditional postures as confirmed more explicitly in the 1990 treaty.

Germany has in general adhered to quite restrictive policies and there are no indications of any "normalization" in this respect. There is no gradual change in sight with Germany transforming into a traditional European power, i.e. one aspiring for territorial gains. Rather it seems that, due to re-unification, Germany's interest, if there ever has been any, in additional territory has declined. The entity that emerged with reunification has its hands full in being forced to deal with what is already there. Moreover, it is recognized that German claims would be detrimental to the claimant itself. The net effect of all this has been a careful avoidance, on

Germany's part, of re-awakening territorial quarrels and keeping a rather low profile on disputed issues.

The policies pursued have also yielded results. For example, Alexander Anisiomov (1995: 28), a Russian Government official, describes Bonn's position on Kaliningrad as "proper, restrained and prudent". There is hence little reason for any reversal which would only endanger the aim of preserving good relations with Russia but also complicate interaction with Lithuania and Poland. All three would easily find each other – if their suspicions were to be aroused – in the common course of pooling resources in order to resist German aspirations, with Germany becoming somewhat isolated in Baltic and European affairs (Hubel 1994: 89).

The legacy of the past is still present to such a degree that not just Germany but also all other relevant actors cannot afford to ignore it for a moment. The very idea that history might repeat itself in one way or another continues to have a certain impact on the situation. The various parties are constantly at risk of locking themselves into positions that may prevent any durable solution from emerging. Given the fears that Germany might aspire for additional ground, the continued presence of the military in Kaliningrad is seen by some people locally, and more generally by Russia, as a source of stability and reassurance. The problem, however, is that the same troops tend to be a major source of concern in the surrounding countries. German prudence is obviously a prime factor in alleviating the situation and in preventing a vicious circle from developing. It allows for more relaxed policies to emerge. Other important actors in the region are offered an opportunity to arrive at the conclusion that in the end they, too, have more to lose than to gain from a return to traditional territorially geared policies. The endeavours should be directed, instead of opening old wounds, towards the issues that flow from the fall of the Soviet Union, the socio-economic problems that Russia has experienced over the recent years as well as taking stock of the opportunities offered by European integration.

Besides refraining from territorial claims, Germany seems to pursue a cautious policy of multilateralization. The indications are weak, but particularly in the European Parliament some German members have been advocating a more active role and involvement for the EU. This might, more generally, be interpreted as an effort to link Kaliningrad to the new European process-oriented policies rather than remaining within the context of the traditional, territorially geared logic. The success has so far been modest, but as such the endeavour is principally rather significant. As Germany has been quite interested and active in pushing the borders of the European Union further east in Central Europe, one may expect that the post-territorial logic will sooner or later also be applied to Kaliningrad in a more active manner.

The burden of the past is also declining in Polish policies, although the conclusions drawn remain less far-reaching than in the case of Germany. Poland has, for historical reasons, been quite sensitive to everything pertaining to German-Russian relations and there has been much fear that the country might again be caught in-between. For this and other reasons, the policy adopted has been rather cautious and oriented towards status quo. In aspiring to do away with open problems, the different Polish post-Cold War governments have recognized Russia's territorial integrity. No claims have been made on Kaliningrad despite various public voices demanding stakes at "Krolewiec", i.e. the historical Polish region. The fact that Poland was to some extent compensated at the Potsdam conference in Eastern Poland, after first having been promised the then *Königsberg* region, may have further strengthened the Polish determination not to press the issue. It is also broadly understood that any claims – whether directed against Russia or Lithuania – could prompt German claims on Poland's western territories (Burant 1996: 319). This vulnerability gives further incentives not to open up the question of Kaliningrad.

In recent years Poland has strongly aspired for inclusion among the western countries. The meaning of the western border has, in this context, been played down, while the barrier-nature of the eastern one has been accentuated. The message that Poland has wanted to get across has been: "we are an important part of Europe, particularly as the borderline *vis-à-vis* the East is located at our eastern border". Aimed at fortifying rather than dissolving the border, this representation also determines the perception of Kaliningrad. It is pushed into non-European otherness and left in the 'dark'. The effect has been one of treating the region as a remote and far off corner. No major efforts have been made to take stock of Kaliningrad's vicinity and use it as a resource in the contest of joining Europe. The idea of Kaliningrad as a bridge between Russia and Europe (read: Germany) does not appeal to Poland at all, as is exemplified by a road project in Kaliningrad directed towards Berlin but coming to an abrupt end at the Polish border, or the obvious reluctance of Polish authorities to make it easier to cross the border into Kaliningrad.

However, some rethinking might be expected as Poland is now entering NATO and listed by the EU's Commission as a candidate eligible for negotiations on membership. Being part of a concentric Europe fading towards the east and having secured a "safe" position might do away with some of the earlier reservations. It is helpful in this regard that the drawing of the Polish-Russian border might have been complicated but it has not been a contested one. The representation of Poland as on its way to joining Europe requires that the border provided the image of something firm, stable and natural. It has hence remained a non-issue, perhaps with the exception of the temporary setback caused by the Russian-Belarus proposal in 1996 concerning a "corridor" that would provide Belarus access to the Baltic Sea via Kaliningrad, which has been demarcated, accepted and confirmed in bilateral as well as international treaties. Territorial claims have been foresworn. Jerzy Bahr (1995), the former first Polish Consul-General to Kaliningrad, stated that Poland's line cannot be but impartial, "neither anti-Russian, nor anti-Lithuanian, nor anti-German".

Security and territoriality have in the Polish case been closely coupled, although in recent years it seems that Poland has been somewhat less constrained by the "logics of geopolitics" (Godzimirski 1997). No doubt the active policies of Germany to integrate Poland into a variety of Western institutions, among them NATO and the EU, has contributed to this change. It is increasingly felt that the choice is no longer joining Germany against Russia, or Russia against Germany, but one of joining a stable Europe.

As a result of some rethinking the policies pursued have become two-fold in the sense that the formal recognition of Russia's territorial integrity has been complemented by an active aspiration to advance local development with the help of cross-border cooperation and opening up for various subregional links through the northeastern provinces of Poland (Pacuk and Palmowski 1997). This has proved to be beneficial for these relatively poor parts of the country. Although the political debate has been largely dominated by geopolitical concerns, there are thus also some signs that Poland may want to – in some particular ways – link Kaliningrad with the new, more process-oriented European agenda. The aim is one of creating a more continuous economic landscape that transcends purely national regulations – with borders as one of their representation.

Lithuania has to some extent followed a similar line, although in its case the exclusion of Kaliningrad from Europe would also entail a form of self-exclusion. Lithuania hence has a need for somewhat different, less exclusive representations. In aspiring for normality, a Russian-Lithuanian agreement was signed as early as 1991, with both parties recognizing the inviolability of the entire length of the Kaliningrad border. The fact that Lithuania is a benefactor of the *status quo* since the Second World War, with Vilnius having previously been part of Poland, explains some of the prudence (Burant 1996: 314). However, in some respects the problem of Kaliningrad has been lingering on. For historical reasons, security concerns and the transit issue on land and in the air, still cause occasional friction. Kaliningrad thus remains, despite the temporary agreement between Lithuania and Russia, an issue in Lithuanian-Russian relations.

In a speech at the UN General Assembly in 1994, President Brazauskas indicated that questions pertaining to the region could be discussed in the context of the Stability Pact, i.e. a forum proposed by France and implemented in the context of the EU and the OSCE (Palazkis, 1994: 120). However, as Russia's role in view of the Pact became relatively marginal and as Russia expressed reservations against bringing up the status of Kaliningrad on international diplomatic fora, this idea failed to yield results (Swerew 1995: 16). It is nevertheless interesting to note that Lithuania aspired for internationalization by proposing that the question of Kaliningrad be linked to a broader European integration-oriented process. In this respect the Polish policy seems to differ from the Lithuanian one.

Although there has been little movement in terms of principles, some progress has been achieved in practice. A Lithuanian consulate was opened in Kaliningrad in 1994 and Kaliningrad has a trade representation in Vilnius. Russian citizens permanently residing in Kaliningrad and Lithuanian citizens may visit each other up to 30 days without visas (Songal 1995: 63). These measures indicate that both Russia and Lithuania are actively applying a process-oriented logic and wish to do away with some obstacles to this logic and to dissolve barriers of distance. The prospects for Lithuania and Russia signing a more permanent agreement on transit are not judged to be altogether dim (Fairlie 1997), despite some internal voices in Lithuania that still are causing friction in the relations between the two countries.

Russia itself has contributed to the non-emergence of territorial claims by refraining from any further fuelling of territorial disputes around the Baltic rim. The policy pursued has been one of adherence to the present borders, despite the fact that large numbers of ethnic Russians now live outside the state of Russia. Tuomas Forsberg (1997b) assumes that despite minor border incidents and some speculations based on threats made by Russian nationalists such as Vladimir Zhirinovski, the emergence of territorial conflicts appears unlikely. The prevailing situation is strengthened by Russia refraining from territorial claims in the Baltic Sea area. Such a stance narrows the option available for others to unsettled territorial issues, including those involving demands for Russia to make concessions.

It seems in general that the governments which for historical, strategic or economic reasons could have been interested in raising territorial claims have abstained from doing so. In contrast to some other cases in the Baltic Sea region (Pytalovo/Abrene and Petserinmaa/Ivangorod), the status of Kaliningrad has not been openly contested.

The fact that Kaliningrad's position has not been challenged in a traditional power-political manner and according to a territorially geared logic is certainly quite important. There are no clear signs of external powers aiming to exploit in a traditional fashion the opportunity that has emerged. They do not seem to want to make use of Kaliningrad's vulnerability in order to extend their own borders. On the contrary, the signals sent convey a determination to stick to the present borders and there are also many signs that the territorial logic is in general losing its impact.

In search for a past and a future

With the power-political rivalry declining in significance and the wrongdoings of the past being openly aired, some more positive images have also entered the debate. It has been recognized that bordering areas, among them Kaliningrad, are not automatically doomed to the periphery. They may – in the best of cases – become significant sites mediating political, economic and cultural contacts. Frontiers are no longer barriers with the hard-edged clarity that they used to have, but junctures conducive to cooperation.

These perspectives give a different complexion to the debate on Kaliningrad. The stressing of closeness and Kaliningrad's access to major European centres generates expressions like a "Luxembourg" (Dörrenbächer 1994) a "Switzerland of the Baltic" (Matochkin 1995: 8) or a regional "Hong Kong" (Galeotti 1993: 58). These visions depict the region as turning, utilizing its location and prospects for linking into

European integration, into a blessing not only for itself but also for the broader politico-economic environment. Instead of remaining a detached "fortress", it might develop into a link with considerable potential for interaction across previous cleavages. Liberated from the constraints of territorial logic, Kaliningrad could achieve connotations of positive difference, openness, cooperation, growth as well as peace and stability. It seems to be increasingly understood among the relevant actors that the problems which are there do not have their background in conflicts between states, but pertain more to the situation locally in Kaliningrad and in Russia more generally. There is a growing conviction that concerted efforts, involving Russia as well as a number of other actors, have to be made if the region is to be provided with a chance of moving towards a more sustainable development.

The basic tenets of a new kind of thinking have been described by Richard Rosecrance (1996: 45) as follows: "Developed states are putting aside military, political and territorial ambitions as they struggle not for a cultural dominance but for a greater share of the world output". He asserts that there is an emancipation from land as a determinant from production and power. The traditional power-political and territorially fixated logic is increasingly surpassed by a different one, a logic that is based on viewing centrality vs. marginality as the core issue.

These changes also have a certain impact on the issue of Kaliningrad. There is less emphasis on territoriality *per se*, and the agenda determining the fate of the region is not seen as given to the same extent as before. The deep split that cut across Europe during the postwar period giving added weight to security-oriented concerns and pushing regional and local issues into the background, has now evaporated. The borderlines and territorial delineations employed have become less strict. They no longer rule out shifting and overlapping patterns of cooperation as categorically as previously. Space is also allowed for configurations other than the clearly statist ones. Kaliningrad stands to gain – at least potentially – from the changes under way, having been distinctly peripheral within the previous setting. It becomes more difficult (although not impossible) to relegate it to a position of an outpost against threatening otherness and to treat the region as being void of any subjectivity of its own.

Steps forward

The decline of security-oriented concerns also applies to Russian politics. Russia's official doctrines, adopted in 1997, are based on the premise that the most probable threats are not external but internal. Russia hence appears to feel – and this has a number of implications for particularly exposed regions like Kaliningrad – reasonably secure against any annexation or take-over with the decline of the traditional power-political agenda. The likelihood of any foreign power engaging itself in altering frontiers in a manner challenging Russia's sovereign ownership is felt to be rather low, thus implying that territorial issues become less pressing. The more relaxed atmosphere, combined with the cautious policies of all the relevant state-actors in Europe and an open discussion, implies that at least elements of mutual confidence has started to appear between Russia and its neighbours.

These trends favour the more cooperative forces in Russian politics and speak for a return to more reformist policies. It appears that the best is made of this opportunity, and there is also more space available for Kaliningrad to be integrated with its environs. Under the prevailing conditions it is possible to carry out reforms and to pursue integrative policies without having constantly to fear for the losing of territorial control. It has become possible for Russia to drop claims for absolute control over the region, among other reasons because the control that is there does not stand challenged. An atmosphere of danger is less imminent, as indicated by moves away from containment and deterrence as well as by Russia's lower military profile.

These moves clearly stand for an increased propensity to live with more permeable borders and less protective policies. There has been some efforts to make use of the opportunities as evidenced by the plans on the Free Economic Zone (FEZ) and more recently the Special Economic Zone (SEZ), these presupposing sound political relations with neighbours, open borders and considerable foreign presence in the region.

The idea of a Free Economic Zone represented an endeavour towards differentiation and, as such, went in the right direction. The idea was also welcomed in the neighbouring states; the opening up towards the non-Russian environment was reflected in the increased economic transactions. There was, in the early 1990s, a clear recognition of the need to empower the local authorities in order to be able to create a commercially competitive and economically viable environment in Kaliningrad and a considerable preparedness to expose the region to market forces. However, there was also a desire to maintain strong ties between the region and Russia and to retain Kaliningrad's nature as a military stronghold.

The failure really to implement the FEZ and the consequent economic decay combined with a somewhat more stable political environment in Russia, has paved the way for another attempt, although it remains to be seen whether the Special Economic Zone has better chances of success than the FEZ. The first signs of breaking the deadlock are encouraging, and the somewhat more top-heavy model of the Special Zone might yield results, provided that there is sufficient political stability in Kaliningrad as well as in Russian politics at large.

But it still remains unclear whether Kaliningrad, and Russia more generally, can take advantage of the new options opening up. The region could be less constrained by a number of factors and interpretations that have previously been conducive to its peripheralization. The core issue is whether Kaliningrad is able to achieve a position on the new agenda or whether it will remain firmly embedded within the old one. To get onto the new, there should be a transcending of the limits of traditional thinking, a linking with the deepening integration, an adaptation to the market principles as well as an enhancing of the democratic structures. Kaliningrad should aspire for the role and identity of a regional actor in a regionalized Europe by joining various networks such as those of the Baltic or European cities, the twinning of cities in Europe, port towns and various groupings of regional actors. It has an EU-representation in Brussels (the premises for this are provided by the Danish city of Aarhus) and Kaliningrad is permitted to sit in on some of the working groups coordinating policies in the Baltic Sea area. There are, in other words, some positive signs, but the measures taken are as yet insufficient in view of the needs.

There is still a long way to go for Kaliningrad to develop into a bridge-head of Russia's Europeanization. The new European integration-centred agenda, with less emphasis on standardization and homogenization and more tolerance for deviating cases, still presents difficulties. No doubt the options are potentially there with the tendency of territorial entities to become less fixed within the current European system. The role and policies of such actors are not as firmly determined by their geographic location as they used to be, and the norms determining the value, meaning and position of various formations are increasingly open to interpretation.

The framing of political space allows for a broader range of alternatives and spurs plurality, but the Russian attitude towards such pluralistic thinking tends to remain cautious. New and previously unexplored ideas pertaining to the new European agenda are easily interpreted as elements of unwelcome ambiguity and thus in conflict with the requirements of 'security'. At least through the beginning of the 1990s, with Russia facing potential disintegration, the idea of cross-border cooperation remained a somewhat daring notion. During the second half of the 1990s the tensions in the relations with the Baltic countries and the issue of NATO enlargement seem to have kept reforms at bay. The military establishment in particular viewed the new process-oriented visions with considerable suspicion, although even its attitudes have become more forthcoming over time.

Kaliningrad itself has displayed limited abilities of manoeuvring in regard to the more process-oriented challenges. The skills needed to utilize the new opportunities have turned out to be modest. In recent years the *oblast* has been unable to keep up with the pace of economic development in Russia, and is certainly falling behind in comparison with the nearby regions in Poland and Lithuania. In the future this discrepancy will in all probability grow unless concerted efforts are made to reverse the trend.

It may be observed that the degree of autonomy granted by the central government remained limited and the favours promised were only implemented in part. These problems in tuning in to the new have been further exarcebated by local struggles for power, clashes between military and civilian actors and the failure of the local administration to make the best of the opportunities that have been there. It also appears that unclear relations and schemes applied in the distribution of gains between the local and the central leaders are a source of considerable friction. This is to say that conflicting interests, rather than any reasons in principle, stand in the way of adapting to the requirements of the new environment. In general, the political, economic and cultural preconditions in the region to grant Kaliningrad a special status have been lacking.

The new plurality is taken to be questionable as undisputed territorial ownership is highly valued and frontiers are still regarded, locally in Kaliningrad and by many in Russia in general, as important instruments for exclusion. Genuine, cross-border regional cooperation is often impossible because it would be interpreted by the central government as an infringement of its exclusive prerogative to conduct foreign relations.

Regional efforts not seriously initiated, sanctioned and supervised by Moscow are viewed with suspicion. There is a frequent uneasiness about changes in frontiers, whether functional or spatial. They are taken to endanger the balance of power and authority, to undermine habits and cultural patterns, to threaten fixed identities and to create general unease and insecurity. Exposure to external political, economic and cultural influences easily triggers a statist and military security discourse and, despite some rethinking, distinct frontiers are still thought of as indispensable instruments for political, military and cultural defence. The bifurcated logic with its sharp divisions into "us" and "they", contrasting Russia with Europe, still informs much of the politics pursued.

These reactions and feelings are not Kaliningrad-specific as such, but the *oblast*'s geographic detachment from the centre seems to make them more outstanding and sharp than in most other parts of Russia. Thus the opening up for foreign investment, which is quite essential for the *oblast*'s development, tend to raise fears of foreign intrusion and/or local dissidence. It is feared that if foreign influence, and German influence in particular, gets too strong, then Kaliningrad could somehow go its own way. Foreign initiatives for further contacts are interpreted, especially among the nationalists and communists, as endeavours to drive a wedge between the mainland and Kaliningrad. It also appears, that because of its exposed situation and the need to open up, Kaliningrad easily becomes a victim of disputes on which way to go that pertain more broadly to Russia as a whole. Hence there is only limited preparedness to encounter the realities of European integration, and to do this without feeling threatened and exposed to intolerable challenges.

However, Kaliningrad is also seen as standing for the idea of bridging Russia to Europe. Located far to the west and surrounded by neighbours increasingly complying with EU norms and modes of cooperation, Kaliningrad would stand to gain from tuning in to these changes. It could, more generally, serve as a test-case and spearhead for Russia as a whole. Recently both President Yeltsin and Prime Minister Chernomyrdin have testified that Russia aspires seriously to become a member of the European Union, although the most immediate aim is to join the World Trade Organization. The more these ambitions influence the policies pursued, the more closely one may expect the debate on Kaliningrad to be linked with a process-oriented logic.

In any case the coining of the idea of the SEZ seems to indicate that Kaliningrad is still looked upon as a kind of gateway and a key indicator of Russia's approach towards the nearby environment and the rest of Europe. The garrison-model has been held in check and there is an endeavour to allow Kaliningrad to take advantage of its vicinity to Western Europe, and thereby to accept some differentiation of political space. The two models of a "gateway" and a "fortress" are not poised against each other to the same extent as previously in the Russian or the international debate, and this opens up for a more relaxed and many-sided discussion on the options available.

Despite the primacy of statist policies, it appears that the central authorities have a relatively positive attitude towards various schemes of trans-local cooperation, this including some early regional endeavours of cross-border cooperation. The use of this dimension might considerably enhance Kaliningrad's position and break with the vicious circle that tends to obstruct efforts aimed beyond any statist delineations. The answers might be provided by micro-regionalism or trans-regionalism, combined perhaps with more general agreements stabilizing the position of Kaliningrad regionally and internationally. Paradoxically enough NATO's enlargement might turn out to be conducive to this with an agreement reached between Russia and the West, but certainly other agreements, and of more civilian character, are also needed for a functioning framework to emerge.

Arms control and confidence-building

As regards the determinants influencing Kaliningrad, a general conditioning framework already seems to be in place. The new European agenda pertaining to integration increasingly has the upper hand. It will, in the contest between the old and new, also set the terms for relations with Russia. If tensions occur between the two agendas, the issue will be settled by the "Eastern" side having to adapt to the "Western" one.

This is to say that Kaliningrad may be expected to lower its borders and to move towards a certain de-territorialization of politics. Many of the previous concerns will in all probability be downgraded. Kaliningrad is provided with an opportunity to liberate itself from a variety of constraints and utilize the increased freedom by linking up and linking in. Security-related arguments no longer detain and arrest integrative developments to the same extent as they did.

However, in the process of adaptation and re-focusing it is also necessary to address the old-style issue of "hard" security, armament and arms control. Although traditional military security is now a less central concern, it is certainly still relevant. In general, security-related worries tend to push regional and local issues into the background. The pre-eminence of security rules out shifting and overlapping patterns of cooperation and favours clear, statist configurations. New ideas, suggesting a more flexible political landscape, are taken to be in conflict with security considerations. Insofar as traditional conceptualizations of security prevail, Kaliningrad will remain peripheral: it will continue to be relegated to a position of an outpost against threatening otherness, void of any subjectivity of its own.

The task is, more precisely, one of getting around the either/or relation between security and regionality by applying a two-track approach. The contradistinction that has been there has to be defused and formulas found for the themes of security and cooperation to work in tandem.

In the context of the Barents Euro-Arctic region the solution has been to side-step security. In a curious way the strategic realities have been deliberately ignored and cross-border cooperation has been initiated despite the fact that the area hosts an abnormal concentration of conventional and nuclear military force. In a similar fashion the Council of Baltic Sea States (CBSS) emerged and grew in strength during a period when many tough military issues remained unresolved between Russia and the Baltic states. The CBSS is also grounded on a certain decoupling of security and regionality, although the separation has been less distinct than in the case of the Barents region.

However, such a dislinking to pave the way for strictly civil regional cooperation seems to be less applicable in the case of Kaliningrad. The *oblast*'s dilemma is that it has been so intimately linked with security that there is little room for "compartmentalized" solutions. The "hard" and the "soft" aspects of security are closely intertwined and the local does not stand out from the more general. Due to the legacy of the Cold War almost everything pertains to security. As was evidenced by the debate on NATO's enlargement, Kaliningrad as a local site has at least a potential role to play within broader nuclear constellations and it is also regarded as indispensable in terms of Russia's conventional defence. This implies that there is little room for any local cooperation sufficiently detached from security concerns that could take off without concerns for security being raised. Once activated, 'security' will in all probability restrict endeavours of cooperation or prevent them altogether.

Kaliningrad hence seems to be short of departures providing solid foundation for regional cooperation; it is blocked in a dual way. The incentives for civilian cooperation across frontiers are weak as the *oblast* is relatively poor in natural resources and offers few advantages in terms of transit. Moreover, the options that are there are heavily controlled and restricted by security concerns, and security as such has not generated any cooperative solutions. It has remained exclusive rather than inclusive and has foreclosed more than opened up contacts with the nearby neighbours.

As the prospects for breakthroughs in civilian cross-border cooperation appear limited and offer little incentive for expansion on their own merits, it becomes logical to work on the security-related side. It seems that in the case of Kaliningrad concerns for security have to be confronted head-on; this is because the *oblast*'s vulnerability to securitization. Instead of side-stepping and turning a blind eye to 'security', as has been done in the Barents region, one has to search for security-related themes that do not just allow for but in fact invite region-specific solutions. Local measures are to be explored – once a more general framework is in place – to remove the danger of Kaliningrad once again turning into a confrontatory issue. Various concerns for security have to be transformed, despite some obvious hindrances, into incentives for cooperation.

This is no doubt a demanding task. Region-specific arms control and confidence-building measures have so far not ranked very high among the priorities of the relevant actors, and there has been little dialogue on improving security by region-specific measures. Russia has either aimed for bilateral talks (with some success, as indicated by the temporary agreement on transit as well as borders with Lithuania) or utilized a broad multilateral context. Until recently there has been some hesitation about participating in anything PfP-related around the Baltic rim due to suspicions that the arrangement works basically as a waiting-room for NATO, although this attitude seems to be changing. Russia is involved in the S-FOR operations in Bosnia where the countries of the Baltic Sea region actually meet, but it is not linked to the Baltic Battalion (BALTBAT), nor does it seem likely that it will join the planned BALTRON or BALTNET. Poland and the Baltic states have for their part not been interested in entering into a dialogue with Russia while they have been searching for security guarantees in the context of NATO, and Finland as well as Sweden have been hesitant to shoulder any regional responsibility, particularly if that could be interpreted in terms of providing security guarantees with a military dimension to the Baltic countries.

However, the prospects for discovering themes pertaining to security yet conducive to regional cooperation are not altogether bleak. The NATO enlargement issue has no doubt heightened tensions and pinpointed Kaliningrad as a particularly sensitive issue, but it has also helped to tune down some controversies. NATO has made it clear that it is not going to accept new members that have open, unsettled issues with their neighbouring countries. This condition, once understood and reflected upon, has in all probability tuned down border disputes and undermined proposals such as renaming or demilitarizing Kaliningrad.

The post-enlargement situation, with Russia integrated into the new arrangements, might turn out to be conducive to negotiations and provide a framework for tackling various issues pertaining to Kaliningrad as a military base. The Partnership Charter signed in Paris in May 1997 legitimizes NATO's enlargement and thereby its increased presence, with the forthcoming membership of Poland, around the Baltic rim. On the other hand the deal also justifies the territorial defence that Russia has in Kaliningrad. There are thus less grounds for complaints that Russia is militarily too strong in the region or proposals for measures of "demilitarization". In case there remain dilemmas along these lines still to tackle, the Charter sets out the basic conditions upon which a settlement could rest.

The agreement between NATO and Russia consists, in one of its parts, of the idea that instead of dealing with issues of arms control and disarmament in the context of the negotiations leading to the Charter, these will be brought up while revising the Treaty on Conventional Forces in Europe (CFE). Talks started among the CFE state parties in Vienna in January 1997. With the block nature of the Treaty abolished and national ceilings agreed upon as a principle for departure, Kaliningrad will appear in a different light than previously. A system of territorial ceilings is being discussed to stop any destabilizing build-up of forces. This is to ensure Russia that NATO's enlargement will not mean a build-up of western forces in the new NATO countries. However, the limitation could equally apply to the Military District of Kaliningrad.

An agreement on sufficiency would be quite important. Instead of an implicit deal there could be a general framework regulating essential security-related issues pertaining to Kaliningrad. Such a deal would provide, in one of its aspects, Russia with guarantees on free and unhindered land, sea and air transit under conditions that measures in defence of Kaliningrad do not infringe upon the security interests of the neighbouring countries.

However, in addition to conventional forces, there are also Kaliningrad-specific nuclear issues that warrant attention. These have to be dealt with for security to be conducive to regionalization. The issues manifested themselves in the context of the debate on enlargement by Russian voices hinting that Kaliningrad's nuclear dimension might have to be upgraded, including a possible forward deployment of tactical nuclear weapons. This upgrading would change very little on the nuclear maps as the threat is not dependent on the specific stationing of such weapons. However, some Western experts have warned that the signals and the symbolic effect of a deployment along these lines would be disastrous: "Regionally we would be back in a Cold War situation, or next thereto" (Huldt 1996: 21). The prospect for some real moves in nuclear policies towards more offensive postures remains remote, but obviously the very signalling that took place highlights Kaliningrad's vulnerability. The argument might also re-occur in the post-enlargement phase due to Russian fears of becoming encircled, and with an emphasis on building defences westwards to counter among other things Poland's membership of NATO.

The overall setting in the sphere of security provides some openings, and one may also observe that the garrison nature of Kaliningrad has become less pronounced due to Russia's financial difficulties, a general decline in military preparedness and the fact that conflicts have been shifting more and more to the south. It appears, more generally, that Kaliningrad has turned into a regional concern around the Baltic rim and is less part of a more general military setting.

In some issue-areas security has already developed into a unifying theme that supports region-specific arrangements around the Baltic rim. The BALTOP sea rescue exercises in 1994 initiated a praxis of annual joint sailings of the region's navies. Such exercises introduce a cooperative dimension into the regional military constellation. When the Russian Navy celebrated its 300th anniversary in July 1996, the navies from Denmark, Germany, Lithuania, Poland, Sweden and the United states took part in the festivities in Kaliningrad. Confidence-building on the basis already established should be continued and provided additional forms.

It may be observed that although "hard" security still works to constrain regionalist schemes, the sphere of the "soft" has expanded inviting for regional cooperation. Proposals on schemes urging the armed forces of the region to work together, for instance of search and rescue, mine clearance, emergency-handling, coastguard or fisheries enforcement operations, including appropriate joint exercises, are under consideration. This preparedness points to an increasing propensity to introduce region-specific measures with the purpose of bridging bilateral or multilateral dividing lines. The moves are relatively modest, but such schemes are nevertheless important in themselves in diminishing the impact of old-style issues and in providing additional space for new ones to unfold.

Nuclear issues are the "hardest" of the hard, and it would be quite unconventional to propose any region-specific restrictions. However, in the case of Kaliningrad it might be possible to break the rule as the issue at stake is primarily one of tuning down the verbal threats and undermining a signal with destabilizing effects. The OSCE could be a useful forum for the negotiation of a deal or the registration of reciprocal unilateral assurances concerning the non-deployment of nuclear weapons and short-range ballistic missiles in Central Europe, including Kaliningrad on the Russian side.

The impact of the European Union

It is quite important for the more general situation around the Baltic rim that the influence of the EU has been growing. The EU is obviously unable to provide security in any "hard" sense, but it can significantly contribute to a diffusion of a number of conflicting issues and, among these, reduce Kaliningrad's vulnerability to securitization. With the stronger presence of the EU, politics is changing its key. A new agenda is emerging and there is a scaling down of the importance of the old one. The Union's nature as a civil power is upgrading various domestic and transnational concerns. Moreover, it is deflating traditional "high policy" issues, including security. In general the presence of the Union fortifies an inclusive, integration-oriented logic and introduces, in this context, a process of de-bordering using instruments such as the TACIS and PHARE programmes. Spurring the formation of regions is part of this process. As an issue pertaining to competition for growth, dynamization and participatory politics, regions tend to be taken off the traditional statist agenda. More room is left for the various local actors to manoeuvre and utilize the process of de-bordering.

In providing "soft" security, the EU helps to remove possible sources of conflict – both international and domestic – and to avert non-military threats to human welfare and survival. The simplest way of doing this is by raising the standard of living and by reducing differences in those standards between nearby actors through more effective economic cooperation. The pursuit of prosperity among states turns more interdependent, thereby raising awareness of common interests mediated through cultural, educational and social exchanges as well as improving of intra-regional and trans-regional transport and communication links. These "socializing" effects, and the evolving habit to move across frontiers, can be particularly helpful in easing tensions pertaining to more traditional conceptualizations of security.

As to frontier disputes, the EU tends to put the contending parties under pressure to reach an accommodation. The message is that frontier disputes are marginal and anachronistic. They are purported as part of the traditional, territorially fixed agenda and are no longer relevant to the same extent as before. Expectations to comply with and live up to the new post-territorial agenda fall on the member states, but the pressure has also been strongly felt by states trying to get closer to the Union. The expectation shouldered on the candidates is: if you want to join Europe, behave and live by the new rules. The effect of this requirement has been quite powerful, as evidenced by changes in the Polish and Lithuanian policies *vis-à-vis* Kaliningrad.

The EU has recently pursued rather active policies in its endeavours to link the Baltic countries and Russia more closely to European integration. The inclusion of Estonia among the six countries regarded as eligible for negotiations on future membership is one sign of this. The EU Commission takes part in both the CBSS and BEAR, i.e. processes that are also important for Kaliningrad in making – if the general logic of the EU policies also apply to Russia and the *oblast* – the border of "Europe" more permeable, strengthening a cooperative framework in northern Europe and making it easier for non-statist actors to link up to the processes in motion. A multi-layered pattern has started to take shape, although the actors of the region are still searching for ways to make sense of this.

The EU's stronger presence certainly ties in with the recent memberships of Finland and Sweden, but it also reflects a growth of the EU's interest towards the north-east and the evolvement of a kind "Northern dimension" in its policies. The accession talks with Poland fortifies the trend (and brings Kaliningrad specifically on the agenda of the EU). Various regionalist arrangements and cross-border cooperation form part of the pattern as measures needed in cushioning, warding off and smoothening the effects of the 'dividing lines' of integration.

In its strategy for future relations with Russia, adopted at the Madrid European Council in 1995, the EU committed itself to establishing a substantial partnership with Russia in order to promote democratic and substantial reforms and the respect of human rights and to consolidate peace, stability and security with the aim of avoiding new dividing lines. The aspiration has been one of integrating Russia fully into the community of democratic nations. The strategy has been followed in 1996 by an Action Plan, which lists practical measures and activities aimed at contributing to Russian democratic reforms, economic development, co-operation in justice and home affairs, a dialogue on security in Europe and co-operation in the field of foreign policy. The Action Plan codifies and registers the bilateral efforts of the members in their co-operation with Russia. There is no special mentioning of the Baltic Sea region, but its objectives are certainly relevant for developments in Russia's north-western areas, including Kaliningrad (cf. Möttölä 1997).

The EU's Baltic Sea Region Initiative, a programme prepared by the Commission and published in May 1996, is another indication of a "soft" approach. Utilizing the magnetism of integration, with the EU as its main anchor, allowed the establishment a Baltic Round Table. The idea, put forward for consideration to the European Council in June 1993 and implemented in 1993-94, forms part of a larger proposal and was introduced in the context of the European Pact of Stability, also known as the Balladur plan. The project at large was addressed to those Central and East European countries which, in some senses, are considered as future members of the EU. The prime participants of the Baltic Round Table have been Estonia, Latvia, Lithuania and Poland. They were asked to provide solutions to a variety of problems regarded as more domestic than foreign, and to tackle the issue by exercising power over themselves rather than putting pressure on any external country.

More specifically, the topics discussed at the Baltic Round Table covered regional transborder cooperation, issues related to minorities, cooperation in economic, cultural and legal questions as well as environmental issues. The participants were expected to pursue a conciliatory line, settle open issues and engage themselves in good neighbourly relations. They were expected to demonstrate competence within a rather concentric setting, with the European Union at the centre of such a configuration. The core issue has not been sovereignty, but one of counteracting marginalization in the form of being pushed into a periphery position in an increasingly cooperative Europe. The OSCE had the task of evaluating the results of the various 'tables', among them the Baltic one, and finally a pact was concluded and signed. In general the Balladur Plan envisaged a list of incentives which the EU might use in favour of states which agreed to observe the principles that the final, evaluating conference adopted.

The process did not touch upon Kaliningrad directly, but it is conceivable that similar arrangements are at some proper juncture extended to cover the region. Ideas to this effect have been recently explored in the context of the OSCE and they might also turn Kaliningrad-specific. The European Union itself might become interested in initiating such a move, particularly as Kaliningrad – with the future membership of Poland – is located at the EU's border. Russia – given its growing interest in getting closer to membership – could accept it as a form of dialogue. Entering talks would no longer be in conflict with the line pursued by Poland (as it did during the period when Poland was merely in the waiting-room to the EU), and the formation of a "table" dealing with the issue of Kaliningrad would probably be acceptable to the other countries around the Baltic rim. In any case, the central question consists of the stance adopted by the EU, and the other actors have to position themselves accordingly.

Increasingly perceived as the EU's "near abroad", Kaliningrad is in need of special attention and multilateral measures in order to be able to cope with the challenges. Both the endeavours of Russia and the EU are needed in developing further overarching cooperative structures and in the creation of a sufficiently stable environment, one that safeguards against further degeneration. The EU needs, for example, assurances that Russia does not object to the EU being engaged in Kaliningrad. Both Moscow and Brussels are concerned that the privileges granted to Kaliningrad are not utilized for smuggling, drawing advantages by circumventing import-export quotas, falsifying certificates of origin or misusing various regulations to advance free trade and integration around the Baltic rim.

Furthermore, to make possible such proposals such as those aimed at turning Kaliningrad into a visa-free region for visitors staying in Kaliningrad but not allowing them to travel to other parts of Russia, to keep the visa-free arrangements with Lithuania in place, and for similar arrangements to be considered with Estonia and Latvia, some over-all talks are needed (cf. Fairlie 1997). Already the perspective of wider implementation of the Schengen regulations around the Baltic rim requires considerable coordination. Otherwise Kaliningrad could suffer severely and become increasingly isolated, i.e. the effect would become one of establishing new, divisive borderlines and hindrances to integration.

Even with the introduction of broader region-wide talks some fundamental differences will of course prevail at least for some time; Russia is in many ways not on level with the increasingly late modern European Union and Kaliningrad will remain a relatively modest actor in the Baltic Sea region. It is also probable that Russian policies *vis-à-vis* the external environment will continue to consist of a mixture of cooperation and conflict. The utilization of notions of danger will not disappear altogether, although such notions will probably be tuned down, and it has to be taken into account that the old-style agenda of security, exclusion, borders, sovereignty and national economies will retain considerable value on the Russian side. Kaliningrad itself has for quite some time been firmly embedded in the old, Soviet-time culture, and many of the structures of that period are still there. A host of rather concrete reasons suggest that Kaliningrad will have severe difficulties in rapidly changing course: its economy remains geared towards military-strategic rather than economic and social considerations, the territorial discontinuity that has emerged implies that the *oblast* has a peripheral position in relation to the domestic Russian market and the transit issues continue to introduce some uncertainty.

Moreover, the new cooperative setting in no way automatically improves the *oblast*'s position as the neighbours, including St. Petersburg, often view Kaliningrad as an economic rival. They endeavour to weaken rather than strengthen the position of the *oblast*. Their success is reflected in Kaliningrad receiving less investments than other ports nearby, and while Klaipeda, Gdansk and most other ports around the Baltic rim are booming, Kaliningrad has been in decline. The region's mission in

Moscow will remain quite small, and it is unlikely – as proposed by the local think-tanks – that Kaliningrad will achieve representation in the Russian Cabinet or be upgraded to a republic (cf. Fairlie 1997). The asymmetries that tend to peripheralize Kaliningrad are hard to tackle and they could, in a broader perspective, considerably restrict Russia's integration with other parts of Europe. In fact, the issues involved are of such a magnitude that they call for broader attention and consideration of ideas, such as the establishment of a Kaliningrad-specific "table" modelled on the experiences with the Stability Pact.

President Yeltsin's statement during the Helsinki summit in March 1997 concerning Russia's interest in joining the European Union, a goal later confirmed by Prime Minister Chernomyrdin, signals a new thinking on the Russian side. The further abandonment of autarchic aspirations and an endeavour to link up to broader European and international developments, implies a loosening of the straight-jacket of centralism (cf. Sergounin, 1997b), accepting diversification and making use of specificities such as Kaliningrad (among the eight "economic associations" established in Russia there is also the North-West regional association encompassing the Republics of Karelia and Komi; the regions of Arkhangelsk, Vologda, Kaliningrad, Kirov, Leningrad, Murmansk, Novgorod and Pskov; the Nenets area; and St. Petersburg City). It calls for an encouragement of the forging of new transnational ties, an enhanced division of labour and greater regional interaction, including a strengthening of schemes for cross-border cooperation.

The Russian aspirations are of considerable significance, but the EU still has an important role in setting the stage. The Partnership and Cooperation Agreement with Russia, signed in June 1994, provides some of the framework, as do the Commission's Baltic Sea Initiative, presented in the context of the Visby Summit in 1996, and the Kalmar Action Programme, which form the basis of the Community's action in the Baltic Sea region. However, some further and more far-reaching steps are needed. The Partnership agreement has to be made more specific and space for deepening integration provided. This is bound to take place once the European Union enters into further talks with Russia in order to develop trade relations, deepen the relationship and integrate Russia into the international economy. This is one of the issues that needs to be tackled in the context of the core decision, that the EU has to take during the process of deepening and enlargement.

The way forward towards such a posture might involve a new agreement that provides the more general framework for cooperation. It is quite probable that special attention is warranted, in that context, to Kaliningrad. Recognized as an inalienable part of Russia, the region could be invited to become part of the Europe economic area, therewith to outface the Federation as a whole. The arrangement could take the form of a special clause inserted into the agreement specifying the relations between Russia and the EU. In being increasingly present around the Baltic rim, the European Union has an interest in preventing the *oblast* from degenerating further and in creating links that would allow the local to benefit from contacts with the region-wide and more broadly the international. The EU might establish a liaison bureau to provide information, assist in the planning and implementation of various projects, especially those pertaining to cross-border cooperation, and to facilitate the incorporation of Kaliningrad into the European transport and telecommunications systems.

The main significance of such a special clause would be to set the rules of the game and provide a horizon needed in furnishing Kaliningrad with a more central, predictable and cooperation-geared position in Russian politics, in relation to its nearby neighbours, the Baltic Sea region and Europe at large. It would, as a move of inclusion, clearly locate Kaliningrad within an EU-ordered Europe and undermine various efforts of exclusion.

Conclusions: Kaliningrad and the figure of Europe

Given the enormity of Russia's legacy and the immensity of the problems left over from the previous period, Kaliningrad's ride towards a linkage and bridge to Europe is hardly going to be a very straight or smooth one. The options available to the *oblast* are rather limited.

It would be overly optimistic to think differently, considering the *oblast*'s location, the burden of history, the asymmetries of the situation, Kaliningrad's dependency on fluent transit, hard currency requirements, visa arrangements and customs procedures due to its separation from the mainland. Kaliningrad has frequently been depicted as an issue that severely hampers – potentially or actually – the more general developments around the Baltic rim. It does not just stand in the way of overcoming the post-Cold War division between East and West and leaving behind the position of a European semi-periphery; it also adds credibility to a more general discourse on danger, conflicts and the necessity to stay behind well-defined and strongly defended territorial borders.

But the chances are definitely there, and they seem to be growing with the emergence of a post-wall Europe. Options are opening up once the territorial determinants of social life and political processes become less strict. It appears that Kaliningrad's main asset consists of giving credibility to Russia being an European polity. The region constitutes, in this perspective, a key site in the discourse on broader issues. It holds out what might be called security at an existential level; the *oblast* forms an arena which allows Russia, if it so wanted, to express its identity in non-adversarial terms and to reconcile its uniqueness with membership of a broader European and international community.

This is to say that it is not just distance *per se*, i.e. borderlines in a geographic and physical sense that are at stake; many political, cultural and mental barriers must also be dealt with in staking out a more favourable place for Kaliningrad in present-day Europe. It constitutes one of the sites where one has to settle whether Russia and Europe stand apart or whether they have a complementary relationship to each other. Policies may be pursued that make it more difficult to push Russia into some eastern otherness in order to achieve a distinct and orderly presentation of Europe, one with clear-cut external borders and a firm understanding of where it ends. The relevant actors are offered, with the emergence of a more pluralistic Europe, the option of capitalizing on the weakening of many of the previous restrictions that have pertained to Kaliningrad and turning the region into a representation that is simultaneously Russian and European.

However, given the lack of a deeply rooted and broadly legitimate past, the future of the region tends to be conceptualized in terms of what is already there. Images of a different, less isolationist future easily generate fears that Russia and the current inhabitants of Kaliningrad would lose what emerged with the outcome of the Second World War. Changes are resisted as there is nothing really of their "own" that they can project into the future. Alternative paths are inevitably seen as backlashes, and there is hence little tolerance for plurality. The reactions become defensive and leave little room for anything creative.

Some of the issues are quite sensitive, like the question of Kaliningrad not having a Russian but a predominantly German past, and the airing of these issues has created uncertainty and bad feelings. However, with the falling of the walls in Europe there is no other option than to face the past. In an atmosphere where 'security' no longer constitutes a label that almost automatically triggers demands for extraordinary and protective countermeasures, even the symbolic and identity-related matters pertaining to the name of the region can be discussed. Ground can be searched for identities and departures that rest on a non-adversarial relationship with the neighbours. Although no immediate and altogether problem-free solutions appear to be at hand, at least the existence of some problems related to the name of Kaliningrad can be recognized, thus legitimizing a search for ways to settle them.

In order to stake out a future that is different from the Soviet period, it is also necessary to face a variety of historical issues. The name of the *oblast* is a case in point. Kaliningrad became a misnomer once the Soviet era and the post-war period has lost its appeal. The issue is not only that Kaliningrad is deeply imbued in Soviet history (Mikhail Kalinin, who died in 1946, was a political leader and President in the Soviet Union; he never visited the region, thus symbolizing the power of the centre to name places without paying attention to anything local). The name of Kaliningrad also tends to signal an atmosphere of danger, threat and a self-understanding adversarial to the neighbours, one that goes against any opening up and becoming part of European integration. Entities such as St.Petersburg can easily link themselves to previous history, distance themselves from the Soviet period and thereby also better link in with current developments in Europe. That option is not as easily at hand for Kaliningrad because of its special history.

Obviously, becoming *Königsberg* once again is not much of an alternative, and for example the proposed name of Kantgrad sounds artificial, although it does contain some of the elements that are needed to signal that the region has a history that goes beyond the post-war years and a Russian presence in the region. Having a past that one can address and look upon as something shared, makes it easier to discuss a future for the *oblast* under considerably changed circumstances. An option that might be worth exploring is capitalizing on the fact that Peter the Great visited the region during his famous journey to Europe.

A representation along these lines would contain something old and as well as new and have both Russian and European connotations. It would weaken the sovereignty-infused inside/outside logic and strengthen the image of a westward-looking Russia, one that is prepared to encounter

European realities by linking in to various cooperative schemes, and to do so without feeling threatened and exposed to intolerable challenges. It would strengthen the culturalization of political space, do away with the bifurcated logic of the previous situation and signs that too easily trigger a statist and military security discourse, including demands of 'demilitarization'. Furthermore, it would articulate a vision of the future by calling upon the past in a way that avoids the minefield of territorial quarrels and wrongdoings in the past in hooking on to something that is distinctly Russian but yet breaks out of the isolationist and sometimes even xenophobic period of past history.

This is more important than it seems at a first glance. For Kaliningrad to achieve some subjectivity of its own and to avoid the danger of double peripheralization, it has to link up with something that has been there prior to the Soviet period. For the post- to have a chance, there has to be something pre-. If it is furnished only with images of being a product of the Soviet era, it will go down the drain along with many other remnants of that period and become part of the new setting on terms that the region is unable to influence. Given the importance of symbols, the policy of naming has considerable significance, and a re-naming of Kaliningrad would signal that there exists a competence and power over oneself needed in dealing with the current challenges.

The very fact that new options can be discussed and looked for indicates that the nature of Kaliningrad, as an issue, is changing. It is not just perceived as a traditional issue pertaining to distance, borders and more generally territoriality, but it has also gained features of an opportunity and a resource with European connotations. Undoubtedly the new thinking that is behind the more positive representations still has to become much stronger in order to yield decisive results. However, some new ideas are there, and they look set to stay. They have gained some standing in the Russian debate, enjoy support in the neighbouring countries and are reflected – although not yet sufficiently – in the policies pursued by the EU to try and come to grips with what soon may become the Union's eastern border and part of an increasingly EU-ordered Europe. Presumably this latter factor will in the future be rather important in the years to come leading, in the best of cases, to de-securitisation in the sense of removing a number of hard security issues from the agenda, and reducing possible threats by increasing the scale of common undertakings.

References

Anderson, Malcolm (1996), *Frontiers: Territory and State Formation in the Modern World.* Oxford: Polity Press.

Anisimov, Alexander (1995), "The Region in the Context of International Relations", *International Affairs* (Moscow), No. 6, pp. 26-32.

Aspelagh, Robert (1992), "Tragic Pages: How the DDR, FRG and Japan Processed their War History – Lessons for Education for Peace", *Peace Education Miniprints*, No. 39. Malmö: School of Education.

Bahr, Jerzy (1995), "There is no Potsdam Problem", *Kaliningradskaya Pravda*, June 10, 1995 (also in *Biuletyn Kaliningradszki*, no. 6, 1995).

Burant, Stephen, R. (1996), "Overcoming the Past: Polish-Lithuanian Relations, 1990-1995", *Journal of Baltic Studies,* vol. XXVII, Nr. 4, pp. 309-330.

Dörrenbächer, Heike (1991), "Sonderwirtschaftszonen: Ein Beitrag zur wirtschaftligen Entwicklung der USSR", *Osteuropa Wirtschaft*, vol. 36, no. 2, pp. 87-103.

Dörrenbächer, Heike (1994), "Die Sonderwirtschaftszone Jantar von Kaliningrad (Königsberg). Bilanz und Perspektiven", *Arbeitspapiere zur Internationalen Politik, 81.* Bonn: Europa Union Verlag.

Fairlie, Lyndelle, D. (1997), *Kaliningrad: Strategies for Non-sovereign Areas in Asymmetrical Relationships.* Paper presented at a Conference on Border Regions in Transition, Sortavala and Joensuu, June 14-18.

Forsberg, Tuomas (ed.), (1995), *Contested Territor: Border Disputes at the Edge of the Former Soviet Empire.* Aldershot: Edward Elgar.

Forsberg, Tuomas (1996), "Explaining Territorial Disputes: From Power Politics to Normative Reasons", *Journal of Peace Research*, vol. 33. no. 4, pp. 433-449.

Forsberg, Tuomas (1997), "Settled and Remaining Border Issues around the Baltic Sea", in: Bjarne Lindström and Lars Hedegaard (eds.), *The Yearbook on North European and Baltic Integration.* Springer Verlag International: Berlin.

Galeotti, Mark (1993), "Kaliningrad: A Fortress Without State", *IBRU Boundary and Security Bulletin.* No. 1, July, pp. 56-59.

Gärtig, Thomas (1994), "Stand und Optionen in der Freien Wirtschaftszone "Jantar"", in: Ernst Müller-Hermann (ed.), *Königsberg/Kaliningrad unter europäischen Perspektiven.* Bremen: H.M. Hauschild, pp. 181-189.

Godzimirski, Jakub, M. (1997), *Soviet Arbitrariness and Baltic Security: The Case of Kaliningrad.* Paper presented at the NUPI Conference on the long-term security prospects for the Baltic Sea Area, Oslo, May 23-24.

Grosse-Jütte, Annemari (1994), "Die Region Kaliningrad/Königsberg: Chance oder Gefahrenherd im Ostseeraum?" *Aus Politik und Zeitgeschichte. Beilage zur Wochenzeitung Das Parlament* B 18-19, pp. 32-45.

Hubel, Helmut (1994), "Nordic and Baltic Security after the East-West Conflict", in: Arne Brundtland, Olav and Don M. Snider (eds.), *Nordic-Baltic Security: An International Perspective.* Washington: The Center for Strategic Studies and the Norwegian Institute for International Affairs, pp. 81-99.

Huldt, Bo (1996), "Kaliningrad as a strategic hub: after the Cold War?" *Forum Kaliningrad 1996. Slutrapport.* Karlskrona: The Baltic Institute.

Joenniemi, Pertti (1997), "Kaliningrad: A Region in Search for A Past and a Future", *Mare Balticum 1996.* Lübeck-Travemünde: Ostsee-Akademie, pp. 84-108.

Karppi, Ilari, J. (1997), *Human Resources Development in Economic Border Regions and Spaces.* Paper presented at a conference on Border Region in Transition, Sortavala/Joensuu, June 14-18.

Matochkin, Yuri (1995), "From Survival to Development", *International Affairs* (Moscow), No. 6, pp. 8-14.

Möttölä, Kari (1997), "Security around the Baltic Rim: Concept, Actors and Processes", in: Bjarne Lindström and Lars Hedegaard (Eds.), *The Yearbook of Baltic and North European Integration.* Berlin: Springer Verlag International *(forthcoming).*

Pacuk, Malgorzata and Tadeusz Palmowski (1997), "Changes and Perspectives for the Economic Development of the Kaliningrad District in the Light of Regional Baltic Co-operation", in: Bjarne Lindström and Lars Hedegaard (eds.), *The Yearbook on North European and Baltic Integration.* Berlin: Springer Verlag.

Palazkis, Justas (1994), "Fast unser Land oder Nachbarland?" In: Ernst Müller-Hermann (ed.), *Köningsberg/Kaliningrad unter Europäischen Perspektiven.* Bremen: Hausschild Verlag, pp. 115-127.

Redman, N.H. (1995), "Kaliningrad: Russia"s Baltic Exclave", *Briefing Paper,* No. 25. London: Royal Institute of International Affairs.

Rosecrance, Richard (1996), "The Virtual State", *Foreign Affairs* vol. 75 July/August, pp. 45-61.

Scott, Allen J. (1996), "Regional Motors of the Global Economy", *Futures,* no. 5, pp. 391-411.

Serguinin, Alexander (1997a), "Post-Communist Security Thinking in Russia: Changing Paradigms", *Working Papers* 1997: 4. Copenhagen: Copenhagen Peace Research Institute.

Serguinin, Alexander (1997b), *Factors of Russia's Regionalization. The Internal Dimension.* A Study produced for the INTAS programme and the Copenhagen Peace Research Institute.

Shumeiko, Valdimir (1995), "The Status of the Kaliningrad *Oblast* under International Law", *Lituanus,* no. 1, pp. 7-52.

Songal, Alexander (1995), "Searching for More Effective Cooperation Mechanisms", *International Affairs* (Moscow), no. 6, pp. 62-66.

Swerew, Jurij, M. (1996), "Russlands Gebiet Kaliningrad im neuen geopolitischen Koordinatenfeld", *Berichte des Bundesinstituts für ostwissenschaftliche und internationle Studien*, no. 6.

Appendix I: Kaliningrad – Enclave or Exclave?

PERTTI JOENNIEMI

Both the notions of an *enclave* and *exclave* are employed in describing Kaliningrad's current geopolitical position. It appears, however, that *exclave* is more common than *enclave*. The SIPRI (Stockholm International Peace Research Institute) Yearbook used to operate with *enclave* but introduced a change in 1993 and Kaliningrad in now depicted as an *exclave*. In the special issue of the Moscow-based journal "International Affairs" (No. 6, 1995) Vladimir Shumeiko, Alexander Anisimov, Magdalene Hoff and Heinz Timmermann viewed Kaliningrad as an *exclave*, whereas Yuri Matockin looks upon it as an *enclave*. Alexander Songal operates with the term *semi-enclave* and this term – indicating perhaps a more relaxed attitude towards encirclement – was also used by Governor Matochkin in presenting Kaliningrad at a seminar arranged in 1996 by the Baltic Institute in Karlskrona.

The editors of "International Affairs" remark that in describing Kaliningrad two notions are used: *"enclave*, part of a country enclosed within a foreign territory, and *exclave*, a portion of a country which is separated from the main part and surrounded by foreign territory" (p.9). They do not go beyond that observation by taking a stand of their own, and in this sense the editors accept the use of two different notions regarding one and the same region.[1]

One might conclude, however, that the term *enclave* departs from the region itself and is used in elevating the insular nature of Kaliningrad and in pinpointing the fact that the surrounding territory is "foreign" (although Kaliningrad is not entirely encircled by Poland or Lithuania) while *exclave* emphasizes the distance and the break between the centre and its more peripheral part. The underlying norm seems to be that various pieces of territory "naturally" belong together, despite the distance. *Exclave* refers to exclusion while *enclave* has connotations of inclusion.[2] In both cases the message is that the entity in question is part of a whole in the context of an uncontested sovereignty. It seems that those looking upon Kaliningrad from a distance prefer the term *exclave*, i.e. they employ the perspective of the centre while those coming from the region itself are inclined to stress the foreignness of the immediate environment and the element that introduces the break in territorial continuity. They operate with an understanding that corresponds to the Oxford Dictionary definition, one defining an *enclave* as a "portion of territory entirely surrounded by foreign dominations". (In the context of the UN General Assembly practice this concept is enlarged so as to mean a small sized territory entirely surrounded by a foreign country except for those parts where it is limited by sea.)

Basically the two concepts describe the very same state of affairs and have a complementary relationship. Both deal with territorial discontinuity in the context of recognized sovereignty within certain spatial coordinates, but focus on different aspects and have deviating points of departure.

For a more systematic enquiry I am using a figure in the following that originates from a study on divided states carried out by Bjørn Møller at the Copenhagen Peace Research Institute.[3]

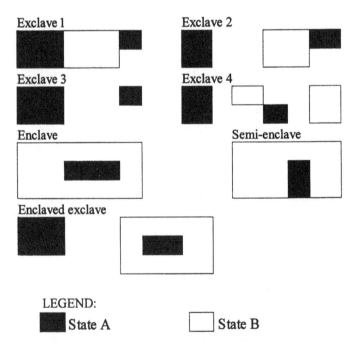

Figure I.1 Territorial Anomalies: Enclaves and Exclaves

In the context of the figure an *exclave* (1) is a part of a state that is physically separated from the rest by (part) of another country. An example thereof is Alaska which is separated from the rest of the USA by Canada. Kaliningrad corresponds to the same pattern, although it is separated from the rest of Russia by two countries: Poland and Lithuania. There is a long-distance sea-link to St. Petersburg, and by land all the main lines of communication with mainland Russia pass the territory of at least two sovereign states (Poland and Belarus or Ukraine; Lithuania and Belarus or Latvia).

An *exclave* (2) is a variation of the former, where the exclave forms part of an island, the rest of which is a separate state. Examples consist of Malaysia and the UK (with Northern Ireland).

An *exclave* (3) is something as common as an island belonging to a mother country (however, usually the requirement is that enclaves have to be surrounded by foreign land and not isolated by sea). An example is Sicily, or if one wants to stress the distance one might refer to some of the French islands in the Pacific. Taiwan – as China sees it – might correspond to this pattern.

Exclaves of type (4) are, likewise, islands, yet with the added twist that one state's island exclaves are intermingled with those of another state (or other states). An example consists of the Greek or Turkish islands in the Aegean Sea – or the competing or intermingling claims to the Spratley Islands in the South China Sea.

An *enclave* is a whole country/region that is completely surrounded by another state. Examples include Lesotho (surrounded by South Africa), the Holy Seat (surrounded by Italy), or San Marino. A semi-enclave is a country that is surrounded by on the three sides by another state, i.e. whose outlet is to the sea as used to be the case of Ifny located on the Atlantic coast of Africa prior to its reversion to Morocco and also Gambia constitutes such a case. An *enclaved exclave* (the term being an indication of the complementary nature of these two concepts) is an *exclave* belonging to one country, but completely surrounded by another (i.e. Kaliningrad does not fit this pattern). An example consisted of West Berlin during the Cold War.

Some of the above mentioned cases are "divided areas or states" in the sense of being physically disunited, and in some cases (USA-Alaska for example) this is obviously no problem in any political sense. In other cases, however, it may be a serious problem. It may, for instance, be so for the future state of Palestine which will, at best, be divided into two halves (Gaza and all or part of the West Bank). Alternatively, it would be a problem for Israel to be intersected by a 'Palestinian corridor' that might unite the two parts of Palestine. It may also be a problem for Republika Srpska, an entity that emerged from the Dayton Agreement, to be separated from its 'mother country' (Serbia) as well as a rather peculiar shape.

Solutions to such problems have – as pointed out by Bjørn Møller – involved the breaking up of the 'oddly shaped' states, as happened to Pakistan with the secession of (which is now) Bangladesh; or the forming of a larger political entity including all three (or more) pieces of the puzzle (as is the case with German unification); or the absorption of the exclave by the surrounding state. In some cases, however, the states involved have learned to live with the prevailing conditions. Whereas odd shapes, sizes and territorial discontinuity do not by any necessity represent 'divided states', they may in some cases do so. It only presupposes that one of the odd formations, or some party concerned and unhappy with the state of affairs, raises the issue and problematizes the situation.

This, however, is a profoundly political matter, i.e. a matter of choice depending on the underlying norms and the way one looks at sovereignty and links it up with territorial continuity. There are thus neither any objective criteria of dividedness, nor any law of nature requiring that there has to be spatial and territorial continuity, and thus a certain "wholeness". During the modern period there has undoubtedly been an aspiration towards clarity and continuity present, but currently the development seems to head towards increasing "messiness" as indicated by arrangements such as "no fly zones", internationally protected areas etc. It does not make much sense to view Kaliningrad as an *enclave* encircled by the EU, or EU's *exclave*. The terminology does not fit the emerging post-sovereign political landscape. Deviations are hence increasingly part of the pattern, and terms such as *enclave* and *exclave* do not signal the existence of anything extraordinary and profoundly exceptional. Those aspiring for order and the application of uniform criteria in the delineation of political space do not share this view, but it seems that they have the tide increasingly against them.

Kaliningrad is obviously an *exclave* as seen from Moscow and the rest of Russia, but it is also possible to use the term *semi-enclave* if one wants to underline its insular nature as a region detached from its own centre and being surrounded by foreign countries except for the access to sea.

Employing a perspective that stresses access by land appears to underline the exceptionality of Kaliningrad while there is nothing particular in its nature of an "island" for those accustomed to a sea-based way of looking upon regions at a distance from the centre. From this latter perspective semi-enclave is clearly preferable to exclave, although the best solution is to abstain from conceptualizations such as enclave and exclave altogether and to revert to more general terms such as "region" in order not to add to the problematique by the use of the concepts applied.

Notes

1 Jakub M. Godzimirski lists Kabinda and Walvis Bay in Africa, Kaliningrad in Europe as well as Nakhichevan (separated from Azerbaijan by the Armenian territory) in Transcaucasus as 'classical exclaves'. He also brings up Gibraltar, Macau and Nagorno-Karabakh among the 'quasi-exclaves' of present-day international relations. See Jakub M. Godzimirski, *Soviet Arbitrariness and Baltic Security: The Case of Kaliningrad*. Presentation at the NUPI Conference on Long-Term Security Prospects for the Baltic Sea Area, Oslo, May 23-24, 1997.

2 Christian Wellmann thinks that enclave is more ideological. It indirectly questions, he argues, the legitimacy and normality of the Russian sovereignty over the territory of Kaliningrad. See Christian Wellmann, *The Kaliningrad Oblast in the Context of Baltic Sea Region Security*. To be published in a book edited by T. Jundzis (forthcoming).

3 The treatment is part of an endeavour to systematize territorial anomalies. See Bjørn Møller, The Unification of Divided States and Defence Restructuring. China-Taiwan in a Comparative Perspective. *Working Papers,* No. 9, 1996, Copenhagen Peace Research Institute.

Appendix II: Relevant Legal and Political Frame

JAN PRAWITZ

Introduction[1]

Today's Europe is very dynamic as compared to the Cold War period. A number of new states have emerged. Some states were split up. The two Germanies merged into one state. One consequence of the dissolution of the Soviet Union was the geographical isolation of the Kaliningrad *oblast* from the rest of the Russian Federation, forming an exclave of Russia located between Lithuania and Poland, and bordering on the Baltic Sea.

But there are a number of basic principles, norms, and provisions of international law agreed in the past and intended to be in force for long time, which do not change easily and which would thus provide a long term basis and frame for the security and the development of states in the European region and in many cases globally as well.

Such basic principles are included in the Charter of the United Nations, the various principle documents adopted by the Conference on Security and Cooperation in Europe, relevant arms control regimes, and the international law of the sea. While many norms were agreed to have a general application, they may be relevant also for discussing Kaliningrad-related issues and provide imperative procedures for the international solution of problems and for the designing of legitimate solutions to such problems.

The supreme of all norms is of course the Charter of the United Nations, adopted in 1945, applying globally and to all 185 UN member states.[2] The UN Charter includes a number of provisions that disputes and conflicts must be settled with peaceful means, although individual or collective self-defence by military means would be permitted. The UN Charter also prescribes procedures in case there is a threat to world peace and security.

266

The establishment of the Kaliningrad *oblast*

The current geographical entity of Kaliningrad *oblast* was defined at the Potsdam summit conference 17 July to 2 August 1945 between the UK, the USA, and the USSR following the surrender of Germany in World War II. Today's city of Kaliningrad was then under the name of *Königsberg* the capital of the German province of *Ostpreussen*, before the war an exclave of Germany between Poland and Lithuania. The idea that *Königsberg* and a surrounding area should be transferred to the USSR after the war was raised by Josef Stalin already at the Teheran conference (1 December 1943) and later followed up at Yalta (8 February 1945).

By decision at the Potsdam conference (23 July 1945), the German province of *Ostpreussen* was withdrawn from the allied occupation administration of Germany and divided in a southern part that was incorporated into Poland and a northern part with the capital *Königsberg* that was incorporated into the Soviet Union.³ Most of the latter area was constituted as a special administrative district while the smaller Memel area was added to the Lithuanian SSR. In 1946, the city was renamed Kaliningrad and the surrounding area was named Kaliningrad *oblast* and became part of the Russian Soviet Federated Socialist Republics (RSFSR).

This revision of pre-war borders and the establishment of the Kaliningrad *oblast* as part of the Soviet Union and later the Russian Federation have repeatedly been confirmed. The dissolution of the Warzaw Pact and the Soviet Union has not challenged this outcome of the war. When ideas are raised today that Kaliningrad should be granted this or that special status, the future is in the focus and the area's pre-World-War II status is considered past history.

OSCE and related documents

The regional Conference on Security and Co-operation in Europe (CSCE)⁴ adopted at its first summit meeting, 1 August 1975, its basic document, *The Final Act*⁵, including a security chapter with ten fundamental principles ("commandments") agreed to govern future security issues in Europe. The ten CSCE principles are:

- Sovereign equality, respect for the rights inherent in sovereignty

- Refraining from the threat or use of force
- Inviolability of frontiers[6]
- Territorial integrity of states
- Peaceful settlement of disputes
- Non-intervention in internal affairs
- Respect for human rights and fundamental freedoms, including the freedom of thought, conscience, religion or belief
- Equal rights and self-determination of peoples
- Co-operation among states
- Fulfilment in good faith of obligations under international law

This "decalogue" of principles, rigid in terminology as it is, was elaborated and interpreted already in the Final Act itself and has been the subject of further development and interpretation over the years that followed, especially after the end of the Cold War. In particular, the principles were reaffirmed, further elaborated, and complemented at the CSCE Summit meetings in Paris 19-21 November 1990[7] and in Helsinki 10 July 1992,[8] and at a number of other instances. The development of the commandments have been analysed by Adam Daniel Rotfelt.[9]

Following the adoption of the CSCE commandments, a number of elaborate agreements on confidence- and security-building measures (CSBMs) regarding military activities were negotiated and agreed upon, first in the Final Act itself, and later in subsequent CSCE documents, i. e. the Document of the Stockholm Conference on Confidence- and Security-Building Measures and Disarmament in Europe (1986); the Vienna Document 1990 of the Negotiations on Confidence- and Security-Building Measures; the Vienna Document 1992 of the Negotiations on Confidence- and Security-Building Measures; and the Vienna Document 1994 on Confidence- and Security-Building Measures. These provide transparency and predictability in military matters in Europe.

In addition, the legally binding Treaty on Open Skies on mutual airborne inspection was agreed in 1992.[10]

The CSCE follow-up conference in Madrid in 1983 adopted a mandate for designing CSBMs.[11] Such measures should i.a. apply equally to all parts of Europe including its adjacent ocean and sea areas and be militarily relevant subject to verification. Agreed CSBMs should apply only to such military activities at sea which constitute a part of activities on land, but not to independent naval activities. Agreed measures should not diminish the security of any state. No provisions specifically addressing weapons of mass destruction were foreseen.

The principle that agreed CSBMs should apply equally to all parts of Europe means that it was not possible to tailor special measures and procedures for limited "sub-regional" areas, as was done in the past. The régime of the Åland Islands is an example of such a subregional regime.[12] Any new provision applying to the Kaliningrad *oblast* alone must therefore be designed as an exception to the general Madrid mandate.

An important milestone in the history of the CSCE was the agreement on the "*Charter of Paris for a New Europe*" signed at the Summit meeting on 21 November 1990. The Charter outlined a programme for "a new era of Democracy, Peace and Unity" specifying on Human Rights, Democracy, Rule of Law, Economic Liberty and Responsibility, Friendly Relations among Participating States, Security, Unity, and the relations between the CSCE and the World.

The Charter also created a new political machinery for political negotiation and conflict resolution, including a permanent *Conflict Prevention Centre* (CPC) for assisting in reducing the risk of conflict.

In addition, a permanent *Forum for Security Co-operation* was set up, following the 1992 Helsinki follow-up meeting. The mandate of the Forum was to start new negotiations on arms control, disarmament, and confidence- and security-building; to enhance regular consultation and to intensify co-operation on matters related to security; and to further the process of reducing the risk of conflict.[13]

Before the Charter of Paris, arms control and confidence- and security-building measures (CSBM) in Europe were generally considered instruments for indirect promotion of policies leading to security, stability, and détente. After the Charter of Paris, fora and institutions are available in Europe where political agreement on issues and conflicts can be worked out by means of routine political negotiations, based on its new programme of principles. Today, the role of arms control and confidence- and security-building measures would thus rather be instruments for direct implementation of politically agreed solutions.

Arms control

In addition to CSBMs, more solid arms control measures have also been agreed and codified inside and outside the CSCE, now OSCE, applying both globally and regionally in Europe.

Since 1987, dramatic reductions of all categories of nuclear weapons have been agreed regarding both strategic and sub-strategic (tactical) weapons. The first major result was the INF agreement[14] in December 1987 between the USA and the Soviet Union eliminating all intermediate- and short-range land based missiles. This agreement covering all so called eurostrategic weapons is now fully implemented and all landbased intermediate range nuclear weapons eliminated. The heavily militarized Kaliningrad *oblast* is thus no longer targeted by such missiles.

Second in the strategic domain but of little relevance to a discussion on Kaliningrad was the 1991 START agreement and the 1993 START II agreement on reductions of strategic nuclear weapons over a time period ending in 2003.[15]

Third and very relevant were the unilateral declarations in the fall of 1991 on withdrawals of all sub-strategic nuclear weapons from theatres of deployment and from general purpose naval ships to be dismantled or kept in centrally located storages. The unilateral declarations were made by the US President George Bush on 27 September 1991 and by the Soviet President Mikhail Gorbachev on 5 October 1991 later confirmed by Russian President Boris Yeltsin on 29 January 1992.[16]

These commitments are now implemented. In particular, all tactical nuclear weapons of the former USSR have been transferred to the territory of the Russian Federation for dismantlement or storage. Many tactical nuclear weapons have been dismantled, particularly in the USA, but many remain in central storages ready for redeployment if needed.

Fundamentally important for the security in Europe as these declarations are, legally their status is weak. Their non-legal form makes them more vulnerable to spontaneous changes of mind than a legally binding treaty would do. And still, Russia would be legally free to station or stockpile nuclear weapons in the Kaliningrad region.

About that time, nuclear weapons also lost most of their doctrinal role in Europe as instruments of warfighting and flexible deterrence, and are now considered "weapons of last resort".

The corner stone of all nuclear arms control, Non-Proliferation Treaty,[17] has today 187 parties, including all five established nuclear weapon states and all European states. It should be noted that while Lithuania and Poland are non-nuclear-weapon states parties to the NPT, the Kaliningrad *oblast* is part of a nuclear-weapon power. The treaty prohibits all non-nuclear-weapon states from possessing and "controlling" nuclear weapons but does not prohibit them from hosting on their territories such weapons of nuclear-weapon allies. But the latter fact would be redundant as regards Kaliningrad and its neighbourhood as long as the unilateral declarations on tactical nuclear weapons are scrupously implemented and as long as Lithuania and Poland are not members of a defence alliance with a nuclear-weapon state.

Related to the NPT are the nuclear security assurances to non-nuclear-weapon states parties to the NPT, including positive guarantees adopted by the UN Security Council taking note of both existing negative nuclear assurances[18] and the positive assurances where the five nuclear-weapon states undertake to provide *"immediate assistance, in accordance with the UN Charter, to any non-nuclear-weapon state party to the NPT that is a victim of an act of, or an object of a threat of, aggression in which nuclear weapons are used"* (Op. 7).[19]

The net result of the NPT regime would imply, therefore, that there would be no adversary nuclear weapons stationed in the immediate neighbourhood of Kaliningrad. Should Poland and/or Lithuania later be admitted as members of NATO under its current statute, that might theoretically change, but seems not do so in the foreseeable future.[20] The unilateral declarations on tactical nuclear weapons, the weapons-of-last-resort doctrine, and the guarantees would further contribute to the downgrading of any possible nuclear threat in the area making the military situation a mostly conventional one.

The elimination of all chemical weapons was finally agreed and signed in Paris on 13 January 1993.[21] The treaty will enter into force on 29 April 1997. Preparations for destruction of existing chemical weapons are well under way, although neither USA nor Russia have as yet (1 April 1997) ratified the treaty. Already on 1 June 1990, the USA and the USSR agreed to an early beginning of the destruction of their chemical weapons. Thus, the threat from attack by such weapons and by biological weapons prohibited already in 1974[22] could be considered remote.

The Sea-Bed Treaty[23] of 1970 prohibiting emplacement of weapons of mass destruction on the sea-bed applies to the Baltic Sea-Bed, but the regime is somewhat unclear in the Baltic. Among states with a coast in the Baltic Sea, Estonia and Lithuania are not parties to the treaty, and among the nuclear weapon states, France is not a party to the treaty. There would thus be a legal loophole permitting emplacement of nuclear weapons in the Baltic, but the real risk that this will be done seems remote.

In the conventional military field, major reductions of conventional armaments in Europe, the CFE Treaty,[24] was agreed before the reorganization of the Soviet Union and the emergence of the many new states in Central and Eastern Europe.

This agreement in the conventional field refers to maximum permitted levels of arms and forces in various regions of Europe. The real levels would in many states be lower for financial or other reasons. The agreements do not include measures regarding weapons of mass destruction and naval forces being outside these regulations. The CFE agreement was intended to achieve a reasonable balance between the two blocs existing at the time, NATO and the Warsaw Pact. After the dissolution of the latter, the rationale for the treaty did also change in several respects. One development was that the Kaliningrad *oblast*, since 1994 a military district by itself, became the only remaining part of the former Baltic Military District of the Soviet Union. As the Baltic republics did not accede to the CFE Treaty upon becoming independent in 1991, relatively large military ground forces could thus legally be concentrated in Kaliningrad.

At the review conference of the CFE parties in May 1996, some adjustments in the geographical definitions in the treaty were agreed, but without consequences for the status of the Kaliningrad Military District. Further negotiations on adjusting the treaty terms to new circumstances started in January 1997 and might influence also force levels in the Kaliningrad area. At the time of writing, the NATO states have proposed for consideration a new CFE system of national, territorial, and zonal ceilings rather than the bloc-to-bloc approach of 1990. The proposal explicitly mentions the Kaliningrad region as a territory to be addressed separately.[25] These negotiations will probably take some time.

The law of the sea

At long last, the 1982 Convention on the Law of the Sea (UNCLOS)[26] entered into force in November 1994. At that time, many of its security related provisions have since long been respected as customary law. UNCLOS can be considered the "constitution" of the sea areas and regulates e.g. the rights of coastal states to establish territorial waters and exclusive economic zones at sea, the rights of flag states regarding transit and freedom of navigation and overflight, and rules for delimiting sea areas between neighbouring states.

The Kaliningrad *oblast* has inherited some maritime sovereignty rights and agreed delimitations from the former Soviet Union. For instance a 12 nautical miles wide territorial sea and an economic zone, the delimitation of which was in the Kaliningrad area, was agreed with Poland and Sweden. Delimitation of its territorial waters and exclusive economic zone towards the "new" neighbour of Lithuania remains to be defined and agreed, however.

It should also be noted that the Baltic Sea is an enclosed sea area, the entrance to which is considered historical straits according to UNCLOS (Art. 35c) where transit is based on long-standing international treaties.[27] Other inlets to the Baltic Sea are two canals between the German city of Kiel and the North Sea, and between the Russian city of St Petersburg and the White Sea. The latter has limited capacity and is frozen in winter.

Cooperation and protection of the environment

There are several multilateral treaties on the protection of the environment and the preservation of natural resources that specifically focus on the Baltic Sea.[28] In addition there are also number of bilateral agreements applying in the Baltic area.

Fundamental is the United Nations Convention on the Law of the Sea (UNCLOS) prescribing norms for the protection of the marine environment and conservation of living resources. Coastal states have the over all responsibility in their exclusive economic zones and the internationally recognized right (with exceptions) to enforce its legislation for this purpose. This is an important provision as regards the Baltic Sea where geography does not permit any true high sea areas outside of the economic zones.[29] In addition, states with coast in an enclosed sea are prescribed to cooperate for the purpose of protecting their common sea. While UNCLOS entered into force in 1994, many industrial states have not yet become parties. This time delay is partly due to the complicated nature of UNCLOS, i.a. requiring elaborate national legislation to be adopted by the parties. Eventually, though, all states around the Baltic Sea are foreseen to ratify the convention.

"The Convention on Fishing and Conservation of the Living Resources in the Baltic Sea and the Belts" was agreed in 1973, a decade before the agreement of generally applicable UNCLOS, and entered into force a year later. All Baltic coastal states and the European Union are parties to the Convention. It commits the parties to *"cooperate closely with a view to preserving and increasing the living resources of the Baltic Sea and the Belts and obtaining the optimum yield"*. It also established the International Baltic Sea Fishery Commission (Warsaw) to fulfil the obligations prescribed.

"The Convention on the Protection of the Marine Environment of the Baltic Sea Area" was agreed in 1974 and entered into force in 1980. Under the Convention, the Baltic Marine Environment Protection Commission (Helsinki) was established to coordinate the execution of the prescribed obligations. The parties are prescribed to individually or jointly take all appropriate measures to protect and enhance the marine environment of the Baltic region. The Convention does not apply to the military sector.

In addition to the treaties mentioned above, the Convention on the Conservation of European Wildlife and Natural Habitats of 1979, and the Convention on Long-range Transboundary Air Pollution of 1979 should be mentioned as very relevant.

Notes

1 This review was produced in January 1997.
2 The few non-member states are insignificant for the discussion in this project.
3 Communique of the Potsdam Summit Conference, Part VI, 2 August 1945.
4 At the CSCE Summit meeting in Budapest 5–6 December 1994, the CSCE was renamed the Organization for Security and Cooperation in Europe (OSCE).
5 Many CSCE agreed documents including the *Final Act* are not ratified treaties

and are by the signatories considered as "politically" rather than legally binding. Others as the CFE and Open Skies treaties are legally binding, however.

6 This most important norm did permit changing of borders by agreement. The unification of Germany, the dissolution of the Soviet Union, the establishment of former Soviet republics as independent states, and expanding territorial waters into the high seas, would be in accordance with this norm.

7 Compare *Joint Declaration of Twenty-Two States* (the original parties to the CFE Treaty), 19 November 1990, and *The Charter of Paris for a New Europe*, 21 November 1990.

8 *The Helsinki Document 1992: The Challenges of Change*, 10 July 1992.

9 A. D. Rotfelt, "European security structures in transition", in *SIPRI Yearbook 1992*. Oxford: Oxford University Press, 1992, pp. 563-582; "The CSCE: towards a security organization", in *SIPRI Yearbook 1993*, pp. 171-189; "Europe: towards a new regional security régime", in *SIPRI Yearbook 1994*, pp. 205-237; "Europe: the multilateral security process", in *SIPRI Yearbook 1995*, pp. 265-301; and "Europe: towards new security arrangements", in *SIPRI Yearbook 1996*, pp. 279-308.

10 *The Treaty on Open Skies* was agreed on 24 March 1992 and has not yet entered into force.

11 Concluding Document of the Conference on Security and Cooperation in Europe, 9 September 1983.

12 An account and analysis of demilitarized zones in Europe established since the 17th century has recently been published by C. Ahlström, "Demilitariserade och neutraliserade områden i Europa" [*Demilitarized and Neutralized Areas in Europe*] (in Swedish), *Meddelanden från Ålands Högskola* Nr 7, Mariehamn, 1995.

13 CSCE Helsinki Document 1992.

14 *The Treaty between the USA and the USSR on the Elimination of their Intermediate-Range and Shorter-Range Missiles* (INF Treaty) was signed by Presidents Reagan and Gorbachev in Washington, D.C., on 8 December 1987. The treaty entered into force on 1 June 1988.

15 *Treaty between the USA and the USSR on the Reduction and Limitation of Strategic Offensive Arms* (START) signed in 1991 and entered into force in December 1994; and *Treaty between the USA and the Russian Federation on Further Reduction and Limitation of Strategic Offencive Arms* (START II) signed in January 1993 and not yet in force. At the US-Russian Summit meeting in Helsinki, 20-21 March 1997, an extention of the implementation period to 2007 was agreed together with a decision in principle on further

reductions (START III) to be implemented at the same time (*Joint Statement on Parameters of Future Reductions in Nuclear Forces*, Helsinki, 21 March 1997).

16 For the full text of the Bush, Gorbachev, and Yeltsin-statements, see e.g. *SIPRI Yearbook 1992*, 1992, pp. 85-92. In the fall of 1991, after the failed 19 August coup in Moscow, with the dissolution of the Soviet Union imminent, and a dangerous possibility that 14 Soviet republics seeking their independence could also become *de facto* nuclear-weapon states by taking over the control of tactical nuclear weapons that happened to be stationed on their soil, it became clear that substantial measures to guarantee the central control of tactical nuclear weapons would be immediately necessary. The urgency of the situation provided no time to negotiate an elaborate treaty on tactical nuclear weapons together with adequate verification machinery. Instead, the necessary measures were defined by means of coordinated unilateral declarations.

17 *The Treaty on the Non-Proliferation of Nuclear Weapons* (published in UN *Treaty Series*, Vol. 729, No. 10485) was opened for signature on 1 July 1968 and entered into force on 5 March 1970.

18 The content of the unilaterally declared negative nuclear security assurances are summarized in *Compilation of Basic Documents relating to the Question of Effective International Arrangements to Assure Non-Nuclear-Weapon States against the Use of Nuclear Weapons* (UN document CD/SA/WP.15, 16 March 1993) and in *Developments with regard to effective arrangements to assure non-nuclear-weapon states against the use or threat of use of nuclear weapons* (Document NPT/CONF.1995/PC.III/6, 12 July 1994).

19 UN Document Res S 984 (1995), unaminously adopted on 11 April 1995, Op. 7. Basic declarations were made on 5 and 6 April 1995 by the Russian Federation (UN Document S/1995/261), the UK (S/1995/262), the USA (S/1995/263), France (S/1995/264), and China (S/1995/265). The value of this guarantee is limited as the nuclear-weapon states are also permanent members of the Security Council with a right of veto. The "threshold states" are not, however.

20 The Ministerial Meeting of the North Atlantic Council, 10 December 1996, states in its Final Communique (para 5) that "enlarging the Alliance will not require a change in NATO's current nuclear posture and therefore, NATO countries have *no* intention, *no* plan, and *no* reason to deploy nuclear weapons on the territory of new members nor any need to change any aspect of NATO's nuclear posture or nuclear policy — and we do not foresee any future need to do so".

21 Convention on the Prohibition of the Development, Production, Stockpiling

and Use of Chemical Weapons and on their Destruction.

22 *Convention on the Prohibition of the Development, Production, and Stockpiling of Bacteriological (Biological) and Toxin Weapons and on their Destruction* (UN Document A/RES/2826 (XXVI), Annex) was opened for signature on 10 April 1972 and entered into force on 26 March 1975.

23 *Treaty on the Prohibition on the Emplacement of Nuclear Weapons and Other Weapons of Mass Destruction on the Sea-Bed and the Ocean Floor and in the Subsoil Thereof* (The Sea-Bed Treaty; UN Document A/RES/2660 (XXV), Annex) was opened for signature on 11 February 1971 and entered into force on 18 May 1972.

24 *The Treaty on Conventional Armed Forces in Europe* was signed on the 19 November 1990 at the same CSCE Summit meeting in Paris adopting the Charter of Paris. The CFE Treaty entered into force on 9 November 1992. The régime was later complemented by the Final Document of the Extraordinary Conference of the States Parties to the CFE Treaty (Oslo Document) as well as the Concluding Act of the Negotiation on Personel Strength on Conventional Armed Forces in Europe (CFE-1A), both adopted in 1992; and the Final Document of the First Conference to Review the Operation of the Treaty on Conventional Armed Forces in Europe and the Concluding Act of the Negotiation on Personnel Strength of 31 May 1996.

25 Atlantic News No. 2895, 22 February 1997.

26 *United Nations Convention on the Law of the Sea.* (UN Sales No.E.83.V.5).

27 Transit in the straits leading into the Baltic Sea is regulated by the *Traité pour l'abolition des droits du Sund et des Belts* agreed on 14 March 1857 between Denmark, Sweden-Norway, Austria-Hungary, Belgium, France, Great Britain, the Netherlands, Russia, and the states of Germany.

28 For an introduction, see A. H. Westing (Ed.), *Comprehensive Security for the Baltic: An Environmental Approach*, PRIO and UNEP, Sage, London, 1989; especially the article by B. Broms, *Multilateral Agreements in the Baltic Region*, pp. 62-71.

29 According to UNCLOS, coastal states have the right to establish Exclusive Economic Zones 200 nautical miles wide from the coastal baselines. Nowhere in the Baltic Sea, is there a coast to coast distance exceeding 400 nautical miles.

Index

For Product Safety Concerns and Information please contact our EU
representative GPSR@taylorandfrancis.com Taylor & Francis Verlag GmbH,
Kaufingerstraße 24, 80331 München, Germany

Printed and bound by CPI Group (UK) Ltd, Croydon, CR0 4YY
08/05/2025
01864362-0006